BEST LITTLE STORIES
FROM THE CIVIL WAR

C. Brian Kelly

with

VARINA:
FORGOTTEN FIRST LADY

Ingrid Smyer

BEST LITTLE STORIES FROM THE CIVIL WAR

More than 101 vignettes drawn from the annals of the American Civil War—soldiers, sailors, slaves, the politicians, the women, and many other "faces in the crowd." Drummer boys, generals, spies, heroes and victims. Presented with profile of Mrs. Jefferson Davis, under the title *Varina: Forgotten First Lady*, by Ingrid Smyer. Illus., with bibliography. ISBN 0-9624875-7-0. $14.50 retail.

© 1994 by C. Brian Kelly and Ingrid Smyer-Kelly

MONTPELIER PUBLISHING
POB 3384, University Station
Charlottesville, VA 22903-0384
(804) 980-3745

First printing   December 1994
Second printing   November 1995

Typesetting & Page Design
Lani Aikin Boaz, Papercraft Printing & Design Co.
Charlottesville, Virginia, U.S.A.

For our children,
Beth, Charlie, Fran, Hal, Jimmy, Katheryn, Sid

Cover based upon design by Stephen S. Vann

TABLE OF CONTENTS

SELECT GUIDE

PORTENTS

BEGINNINGS

MIDDLES

Ends

VARINA: FORGOTTEN FIRST LADY SHORT CHRONOLOGY

ACKNOWLEDGEMENTS AND BIBLIOGRAPHY

Select Guide To Battles & Personalities Herein

—Battles—

—Major Personalities—

Boyd, Belle, see Parallel Spies.

Breckinridge, John C., see Jaws of Death.

Chesnut, Mary Boykin (and husband James, Jr.), see Hello, Richmond; Unnecessary Tragedies; What Does a Slave?; Varina: Forgotten First Lady.

Custer, George Armstrong, see Swinging His Arms (and for Tom Custer, see So Very Personal).

Davis, Jefferson, see Portents; Fresh Start Sought; Who the South Was; Social Notice Taken; Hello, Richmond; Davises Everywhere; Close Connections; War's Sting Delayed; Varina: Forgotten First Lady.

Davis, Varina, see Portents; Social Notice Taken; Hello, Richmond; What Does a Slave?; Close Connections; Varina: Forgotten First Lady.

Douglass, Frederick, see Portents.

Farragut, David, see They Also Served.

Forrest, Nathan Bedford, see Injury Added to Insult; Brave Men Spared.

Frémont, John C., see They Also Served.

Garfield, James A., see Hello Washington; Miss Kate's Brief Run; Surviving to Serve Again.

Gordon, John Brown, see "Shot for You", Coincidences at Gettysburg.

Grant, Ulysses S., see Heart in the Throat; Complete Conquest Required; Sidling Down to Richmond; Longest Siege; Embarrassing Outing; Close Connections; Julia Reads a Note; Always a Clear Course.

Hayes, Rutherford B.; McKinley, William; Harrison, Benjamin, Cleveland, Grover, and Arthur, Chester A., see Surviving to Serve Again.

Portents

Portents

1809

On a bed of cornhusks, inside a house with one door and one window, a cabin, really, with a dirt floor, a young frontier woman bore down hard one February morning and squeezed out from her body, her womb, a baby . . . a boy.

A little later that Sunday, a nine-year-old cousin asked the mother what she was going to name the newborn child. "Abraham," she said, "after his grandfather."

The next morning, the same boy held his new cousin for the first time. But the baby cried, and young Dennis Hanks quickly gave him up. "Take him," he said. "He'll never come to much."

1810

Another family . . . a father, imprisoned for owing money, released in the spring of the year. Mother and father consider their situation and decide they cannot afford to remain at the grand family estate in Westmoreland County, Virginia. They travel by carriage to take up residence in a small house in Alexandria to the north, across the Potomac from the newly established and still abuilding Federal capital.

Young Robert was three years old as his parents passed into "genteel poverty". But not into a gentle life. Two years later, his military-hero father, Henry "Lighthorse Harry" Lee, once Governor of Virginia, and a Congressman, was beaten and mutilated by a mob in Baltimore. Recovering with difficulty, left disfigured, broken in spirit, he made his farewells in 1813 to family,

1

commonwealth and country . . . all for a new life in Barbados. He meant to return soon, and finally, after a few years, he indeed was on his way back. But he fell ill aboard ship, went ashore at Cumberland Island, Georgia, and died there March 25, 1818. Son Robert E. by then was just eleven years old.

1832

For the second time in four years, South Carolina acted to *nullify* tariffs imposed by the Federal government in Washington. Andrew Jackson, President at the time, was on one side—the Federal side—of the issue, while his Vice President, South Carolina's own John C. Calhoun, was on the other side. So much so that he resigned the vice presidency to carry on the fight in the U.S. Senate. For months, too, the air was full of impassioned, dangerous words for the still-young Republic: nullification, states rights . . . *secession*.

After winning re-election in 1832, with Martin Van Buren of New York as his ticket mate, Tennessee's "Old Hickory" still had to deal with the South Carolina thorn in his side. By now, the disgruntled state had canceled its earlier nullification actions, only to try another—this time to nullify Congressional action authorizing the use of Federal force against the state.

Here was a most difficult and delicate dilemma for President Jackson, and in the midst of deliberations with Cabinet members, Senators and others from on high, he called for a faithful comrade-in-arms from old wars against the Creek Indians in Alabama and the British at New Orleans. Closeted in the White House, they shared a decanter of whiskey, and talked of old times . . . and new times, new issues. Like the thorny nullification issue.

To Sam Dale, Jackson said, "They are trying me here; you will witness it; but by the God in heaven, I will uphold the laws."

And Dale said he hoped things would go right. Whereupon, Jackson slammed his hand down on a table, so hard he broke a pipe, as he said, "They SHALL go right, sir!"

It wasn't long after Dale's visit that Andrew Jackson sent

fighting ships to Charleston harbor, denounced any state's pretension to rights of nullification or secession and, on December 10, 1832, issued his Proclamation on Nullification, after which the storm died down for the time being.

In Illinois, meanwhile, a country lawyer named Abraham Lincoln read Jackson's Proclamation most carefully. He would read it again when composing his inaugural address of 1861.

1833

Nearly 15, Fred was hired out to a farmer and "pious" church-goer named Edward Covey. This was in Maryland. "I had been at my new home but one week before Mr. Covey gave me a very severe whipping, cutting my back, causing the blood to run, and raising ridges on my flesh as large as my little finger." Fred was whipped about once a week for the next six months or so. Until he fought back, actually. Even then, he remained a slave and it would be years before he found freedom, his means of escape to the North still a secret when he published his autobiography in 1845.

Beyond his own experiences, his book presented quite an indictment. As a young child, he saw a black woman, "Aunt Hester", beaten with hands tied above her head and the rope looped over a joist above. He told of an overseer named Austin Gore who shot a slave named Demby in the face for refusing to stand still for a whipping. Another white man, Thomas Lanham, also of Talbot County, killed two slaves, "one of whom he killed with a hatchet, by knocking his brains out." A Mrs. Giles Hicks, angered at a slave teenager who fell asleep while babysitting, hit the girl with a stick and injured her fatally. An old black man oystering on the Chesapeake Bay strayed over a neighbor's property line . . . and was shot by the neighbor.

And so on. Mere whippings are hardly worth mention, there were so many. The Reverend Rigby Hopkins, for instance, "always managed to have one or more of his slaves to whip every Monday morning." There was always some reason, some excuse.

"It would astonish one, unaccustomed to a slave-holding life, to see with what wonderful ease a slaveholder can find things, of which to make occasion to whip a slave. A mere look, word or motion—a mistake, accident or want of power—are all matters for which a slave may be whipped at any time. Does a slave look dissatisfied? It is said, he has the devil in him, and it must be whipped out. Does he speak loudly when spoken to by his master? Then he is getting high-minded, and should be taken down a buttonhole lower. Does he forget to pull off his hat at the approach of a white person? Then he is wanting in reverence, and should be whipped for it. Does he ever venture to vindicate his conduct, when censured for it? Then he is guilty of impudence—one of the greatest crimes of which a slave can be guilty. Does he ever venture to suggest a different mode of doing things from that pointed out by his master? He is indeed presumptuous and getting above himself, and nothing less than a flogging will do for him. Does he, while plowing, break a plow? or while hoeing break a hoe? It is owing to his carelessness, and for it a slave must always be whipped. Mr. Hopkins could always find something of this sort to justify the use of the lash, and he seldom failed to embrace such opportunities."

Fortunately, Fred found his way out of slavery. On his personal journey leading to freedom, he secretly learned to read and write. He learned so well, in fact, that he later became a famous orator, abolitionist, and diplomat. A leader among blacks, he was known by his later name, Frederick Douglass.

1843

Near Christmastime, and the 17-year-old planter's daughter was on her way for a festive visit at the plantation of one Joseph Davis. His niece came for her, "accompanied by a servant-man leading a horse with a lady's side-saddle." The young visitor's "*impedimenta*" would go along in a carriage, and in short order they rode over "rustling leaves" and through "thick trees" to the Davis home, known as "The Hurricane".

There she soon became acquainted with the owner's younger brother, then 36 . . . and the real object of the visit.

Her impression was that he looked closer to 30 than 36, that he was "erect, well-proportioned, and active as a boy". Moreover: "He rode with more grace than any man I have ever seen and gave one the impression of being incapable of either being unseated or fatigued."

That very day, the impressionable but sophisticated young woman wrote to her mother that she couldn't tell if he were "young or old". She added: "He looks both at times; but I believe he is old, for from what I hear he is only two years younger than you are."

Even so, he impressed his brother's guest "as a remarkable kind of man, but of uncertain temper, and [he] has a way of taking for granted that everybody agrees with him when he expresses an opinion, which offends me . . . " To his credit again, he had a winning manner of expressing himself and a "peculiarly sweet voice."

She went on to write that he was the "kind of person I should expect to rescue one from a mad dog at any risk, but to insist upon a stoical indifference to the fright afterward."

But then again, "I do not think I shall ever like him as I do his brother Joe." And, a real shocker—"Would you believe it, he is refined and cultivated and yet he is a Democrat!"

So wrote the little miss from a staunch Whig household of Joe's young (but oh, so old!) brother. Even so, the next month Varina Howell was engaged to her host's graceful sibling. The next year, February of 1845, they were married—Mr. and Mrs. Jefferson Davis.

1858
In the House of Representatives, Washington, D.C., Galusha Grow of Pennsylvania uttered a few anti-slaver remarks, then wandered over to the Democratic side of the aisle to talk to a colleague. From there he responded to still another member's re-

marks, even though he was not at his seat . . . or even among his fellow Republicans.

None of this was lost upon South Carolina's Democratic Representative Laurence M. Keitt, who told the Pennsylvanian to "go back to your own side of the hall".

Grow replied: "This is a free hall and every man has a right to be where he pleases. I will object when and where I please."

Whereupon, Keitt said, "Sir, I will let you know that you are a black Republican puppy."

Grow then said the hall belonged to the American people, he could stay where he pleased, "and no slave driver shall crack his whip over my head".

Seconds later, the fists flew, right in the House chamber. Keitt went down, knocked out cold by Grow's punch to the jaw. But the fight didn't end there . . . or with them.

It wasn't as shocking as the time, in 1856, that South Carolina's Representative Preston Smith Brooks strode into the Senate chamber and broke his gutta-percha cane beating the stridently abolitionist Senator Charles Sumner of Massachusetts, but it was a bona fide fight on the House floor, all right. Others immediately plunged into the melee. It is said that knives and even pistols were in evidence. Someone hurled a large spittoon, and Representative William Barksdale of Mississippi lost his wig to a Wisconsin member. When Barksdale got it back, he put it on backwards. The levity that resulted helped to restore order to the House.

In 1863, Barksdale was killed at Gettysburg, Pennsylvania. In 1864, Keitt was killed at Cold Harbor, Virginia.

1859

FOR SALE, headlined the advertisement in major Southern newspapers, LONG COTTON AND RICE NEGROES.

Followed by:

"A gang of 460 Negroes, accustomed to the culture of Rice and Provisions, among whom are a number of good mechanics and house servants. Will be sold on the 2nd and 3rd of March next, at Savannah, by

"JOSEPH BRYAN

"TERMS OF SALE—One third cash; remainder by bond, bearing interest from day of sale, payable in two equal installments, to be secured by mortgage on the Negroes, and approved personal security, or for approved city acceptance on Savannah or Charleston. Purchasers paying for papers.

"The Negroes will be sold in families, and can be seen on the premises of Joseph Bryan, in Savannah, three days prior to the day of sale, when catalogues will be furnished."

How much for a good strong Negro male in 1859, on the eve of the U.S. Civil War? According to a story appearing March 9, 1859, in the *New York Tribune,* that figure was $1,600.

The slave, himself—or herself—though, did not wish to be at top price. Not at all. He or she would rather be, or at least appear to be, less than physical perfection itself, since at top price the slave had little hope of earning, and saving, the money needed to purchase freedom. Said the *Tribune* account of Bryan's sale: "But let him [the slave] have a rupture, or lose a limb, or sustain any other injury that renders him of much less service to his owner, and reduces his value to $300 or $400, and he may hope to accumulate that sum, and eventually to purchase his liberty."

The advertised sale, the largest slave sale in the South for several years, "went on for two long days, during which time there were sold 429 men, women and children." They generated a total take of $303,850, it seems.

They were sold by an absentee owner, a recently divorced man from Philadelphia—a Northerner, who afterwards, the *Trib* said, was seen "solacing the wounded hearts of the people he had sold from their firesides and their homes by doling out to them small change at the rate of a dollar a head."

1860

It was no accident, that blue cockade seen on the men's hats outside a meeting hall in Charleston, South Carolina, this 20th day of December. The blue cockade deliberately recalled the nullification controversy that had upset President Andrew Jackson three decades earlier. Only now, the word, the movement that was in the air, a mood become avalanche, was *secession*!

The hall was the gathering place for the South Carolina Convention, which by a vote of 169 to 0 adopted an ordinance cutting the state's ties with the Union. The reaction in Charleston was jubilation—parades, bonfires, church bells pealing, even cannons speaking their piece. After the fateful document was signed that evening, wrote elderly Virginia agronomist (and avid secessionist) Edmund Ruffin, "Every man waved or threw up his hat & every lady waved her handkerchief."

Another onlooker was Samuel Wylie Crawford, a U.S. Army doctor recently assigned to duty in Charleston. Outside the hall, he wrote, "the whole city was wild with excitement as the news spread like wildfire through its streets." Indeed, "old men ran shouting down the streets."

To be sure, not everyone in Charleston looked with favor upon the action making South Carolina the first state to quit the Union. Judge James L. Petigru better understood the trials ahead than most of his fellow citizens. "I tell you there is a fire," he warned; "they have this day set a blazing torch to the temple of constitutional liberty, and, please God, we shall have no more peace forever."

In far-off Washington, by chance it was South Carolina's fiery Representative Laurence Keitt who carried the news to a wedding reception attended by President James Buchanan. Hearing the commotion behind him as Keitt arrived, Buchanan asked Virginia Congressman Roger A. Pryor's wife what was going on. She found Keitt "leaping in the air, shaking a paper over his head, exclaiming, 'Thank God! Oh, thank God! South Carolina has seceded!'"

She returned to Buchanan's side, bent over and told him, "It appears, Mr. President, that South Carolina has seceded from the Union." Stunned, Buchanan fell back into his chair, clutching its arms. He asked her to call his carriage—he would be leaving right away. "There was no more thought of bride, bridegroom, wedding cake or wedding breakfast," wrote Mrs. Pryor.

1860

Future President of the United States to future Vice President of the Confederate States of America: The USA would not—that is, NOT—attempt to dictate policy on slavery within the CSA. So wrote Abraham Lincoln to Georgia Representative Alexander H. Stephens on December 22. "The South would be in no more danger in this respect," wrote President-elect Lincoln to his one-time colleague in the U.S. House, "than it was in the days of Washington. I suppose, however, this does not meet the case. You think slavery is a *right* and ought to be extended; while we think it is *wrong* and ought to be restricted. That I suppose is the rub."

1860

If President Buchanan was stunned by the secession of South Carolina (no real surprise to most political onlookers), South Carolina in turn was about to be outraged by the audacity, the effrontery, of the U.S. Army officer commanding a few troops at Fort Moultrie in Charleston Harbor.

How dare he? But . . . on the night after Christmas, he did. Without notice or any other kind of warning, he moved his entire garrison from the exposed, unprotected spit of land also known as Sullivan's Island to the real island out in the harbor, more isolated, more difficult to get at—Fort Sumter.

Moultrie, as Abner Doubleday noted, to South Carolinians "was almost a sacred spot, endeared by many precious historical associations, for the ancestors of most of the principal families had fought there in the Revolutionary War."

Doubleday, later famous for his dubious claims to be a baseball pioneer, was a young Federal officer taking part in the nighttime move on December 26. His commander at Fort Sumter, the man who decided his men would be safer, his delicate position in a sea of hostility stronger, was Major Robert Anderson. And never mind that Anderson's own father had fought the British at the same Fort Moultrie and had been kept prisoner in Charleston! All that aside, Charleston was outraged.

When Anderson's small command of 61 enlisted men, 7 officers and 13 musicians began to discharge from their boats on the wharf at Sumter, local workers engaged in improvements at the island fort "rushed out to meet us," recalled Doubleday. Most of them were angry and called out, "What are these soldiers doing here?" A "demonstration" with bayonets forced them back, "and the disloyal workmen were shipped off to the mainland."

On that mainland, meanwhile, Charleston was agog over Major Anderson's surprise move. Diarist Mary Boykin Chesnut, wife of a former U.S. Senator from South Carolina, wrote that Anderson had "united the Cotton States." Reflecting the mood of those around her, she also noted: "Those who want a row are in high glee. Those who dread it are glum and thoughtful."

The talk in Charleston the next day, December 27, was, "Fort Sumter must be taken," even though Sumter was one of the strongest Federal bastions in the South. With obvious trepidation, she had to wonder: "How in the name of sense are they to manage it? I shudder to think of rash moves."

1861

The trouble with Fort Sumter was that it really was an island situated in hostile waters, and as the year began it was, by order of South Carolina's authority, cut off from the mainland—no communication, no supplies for Major Anderson and his garrison of 80 souls.

In far off Washington, the policymakers of the Federal capital were awaiting a change in Presidents at the very moment of the young Republic's worst crisis ever. Winfield Scott, General in Chief of the U.S. Army, had obtained permission to send Major Anderson help in the form of supplies, ammunition and additional troops.

The supplies and 250 reinforcements did set sail, but in an ordinary, civilian merchant ship called *Star of the West*.

At Fort Sumter, Anderson was expecting his re-supply and reinforcement to be accomplished by U.S. Navy warships.

Star arrived off the harbor entrance at 1:30 in the morning of January 9, then hove to in the main shipping channel to wait for daylight before proceeding farther.

As daylight began to reveal her outlines, she was moving again. Artillery hidden in nearby sandhills opened fire. The first shot was traditional—across the bow. When *Star* kept moving, the cannon fire continued, rapid if a bit wild. Two rounds struck the merchant ship, which ran a flag up and down a forward mast as if a plea for Anderson to tell her what to do. Now, too, Fort Moultrie lay in the *Star's* path, manned by hot-eyed South Carolina secessionists. And Moultrie's guns, while not yet in range, did open fire.

At Fort Sumter, all was confusion and disarray at the unexpectedness of the ship's appearance. Army surgeon Samuel Crawford, one of Major Anderson's seven officers at the island outpost, later wrote that Anderson didn't know what to do, since he had anticipated a warship rather than a merchant vessel. And further, snarled halyards prevented his men from replying quickly to the *Star's* signals.

The *Star of the West* was not about to present her vulnerable broadside for a raking by the batteries at Fort Moultrie, and so the rescue ship turned and pointed toward the open sea. Major Anderson was about to order Fort Sumter's own guns into action—against Fort Moultrie. But he saw the *Star* turn away. "Hold on," he told his men. "Do not fire."

It was all over in just a few minutes. "The flag of the country had been fired on under our very guns, and no helping hand had been extended," wrote Dr. Crawford, who soon would be giving up his medical bag to become an active combat commander—and eventually a major general in the Union Army.

1861

After a flutter of messages back and forth between Major Anderson at Fort Sumter and various authorities representing the newly formed Confederate States of America, there came a final, most formal notice to the U.S. Army officer at 3:30 a.m. April 12.

"Sir: By authority of Brigadier General Beauregard, commanding the provisional forces of the Confederate States, we have the honor to notify you that he will open fire of his batteries at Fort Sumter in one hour from this time."

Beginnings

First Time Out

What was it like, that first time under fire? In real battle, U.S. Civil War? Brothers of the native soil against brothers of the same good earth?

Said (or wrote) an officer from Maine sometime after: "The behavior of those who were hit appeared to be singular; and, as there were so many of them, it looked as if we had a crowd of howling dervishes dancing and kicking around in our ranks."

Said (or wrote) a Confederate cavalry colonel: "Barely in position, I heard a distant cannon, and at the same instant saw the ball high in the air. As near as I could calculate, it was going to strike about where I stood, and I dismounted with remarkable agility, only to see the missile of war pass 60 feet overhead."

An unnamed soldier added: "For the first time in your life you listen to the whizzing of iron. Grape and canister fly into the ranks, bomb-shells burst overhead, and the fragments fly all around you."

Officer from Maine again: "A bullet often knocks over the man it hits, and rarely fails by its force alone to disturb his equilibrium. Then the shock, whether painful or not, causes a sudden jump or shudder."

Rebel colonel: "I felt rather foolish as I looked at my men, but a good deal relieved when I saw that they, too, had all squatted to the ground, and were none of them looking up at me. I quickly mounted and ordered them to 'stand up.'"

Unnamed soldier: "A friend falls; perhaps a dozen or 20 of your comrades lie wounded or dying at your feet; a strange, involuntary shrinking steals over you, which it is impossible to resist."

Maine officer: "Now, as every man, with hardly an exception, was either killed, wounded, hit in the clothes, hit by spent balls or stones, or jostled by his wounded comrades, it follows that we had a wonderful exhibition. Some reeled round and round, others threw up their arms and fell over backwards, others went plunging backward trying to regain their balance; a few fell to the front, but generally the force of the bullet prevented this, except where it struck low and apparently knocked the soldier's feet from under him. Many dropped the musket and seized the wounded part with both hands, and a very few fell dead."

Rebel colonel: "We were soon ordered to charge, and drove the enemy through the tall prairie grass, till they came to a creek and escaped. We passed some of the dead and wounded, the first sad results of real war that I had ever seen."

Unnamed soldier: "You feel inclined neither to advance nor recede, but are spell-bound by the contending emotions of the moral and physical man. The cheek blanches, the lip quivers, and the eye almost hesitates to look upon the scene."

Maine: "The enemy were armed with every kind of rifle and musket, and as their front was three times ours, we were under a crossfire almost from the first. The various tunes sung by the bullets we shall never forget . . . . The fierce *zip* of the Minié bullets was not prominent by comparison at that particular moment, though there were enough of them certainly. The main body of sound was produced by the singing of slow, round balls and buckshot fired from a smooth-bore, which do not cut or tear the air as the creased ball does.

"Each bullet, according to its kind, size, rate of speed, and nearness to the ear, made a different sound. They seemed to be going past in sheets, all around and above us."

Colonel: "At night the heavens opened wide, the rain fell in torrents; not even a campfire could be kept to light up the impenetrable gloom, and I sought a comfortable mud-hole to sleep as best I could.

"The pale rigid faces that I had seen turned up for the evening sun appeared before me as I tried in vain to shield my own [face] from the driving rain, and as the big foot of a comrade, blundering round in the darkness, splashed my eyes full of mud, I closed them to sleep, muttering to myself, 'And this is war.'"

Soldier: "In this [frozen] attitude you may, perhaps, be ordered to stand an hour, inactive, havoc meanwhile marking its footsteps with blood on every side. Finally the order is given to advance, to fire, or to charge. And now, what a change! With your first shot you become a new man. Personal safety is your least concern. Fear has no existence in your bosom. Hesitation gives way to an uncontrollable desire to rush into the thickest part of the fight. The dead and dying around you, if they receive a passing thought, only serve to stimulate you to revenge."

Further: "You become cool and deliberate, and watch the effect of the bullets, the shower of bursting shells, the passage of cannon-balls as they rake their murderous channels through your ranks, the plunging of wounded horses, the agonies of the dying and the clash of contending arms, which follows the charge, with a feeling so calloused by surrounding circumstances that your soul seems dead to every sympathising [sic] and selfish thought."

So it was for the newcomer to battle, it seems. But when it's all over, what then?

Walking the battleground, among the dead and groaning wounded, said the unknown soldier, "[you] begin to realize the horrors of war, and experience a reaction of nature." Wondrously, "the heart opens its floodgates, humanity reasserts herself again, and you begin to feel."

You now help the wounded, friend or foe. *Foe, too? Yes.* "The enemy, whom, but a short time before, full of hate, you were doing all in your power to kill, you now endeavor to save."

You provide water, food, whatever he needs. "All that is human and charitable in your nature now rises to the surface." In sum, amazing. And oh, so true: "A battlefield is eminently a place that tries men's souls."

FRESH START SOUGHT

How to start an "instant" government? That was the challenge for a mere 38 men representing the "secesh" states early in 1861, and the solution they came up with—in amazingly short time—was a mirror image of the very government they were so avowed to leave behind.

They wished for a president, and for a congress, naturally, and of course a constitution, all very much like the democratic system they had known so well and so long. All in all, it would seem, their creation wasn't all that different in its framework from the government seated in Washington, D. C.

In framework, yes, but in substance, a few major, *major* differences! One, the very issue that affected all differences between the two governments, the two nations now, was slavery.

The Union—that is, the Federal government of the United States—had not yet banned slavery. That was yet to come. Lincoln had not yet written his Emancipation Proclamation. Fort Sumter, in fact, had not yet been fired upon.

No matter. The secession leaders gathering in Montgomery, Alabama, to form a new union chose to have a constitution very similar to the familiar U. S. Constitution, to have a president and congress all their own (but *their* president to be limited to one six-year term only).

The delegates assembled of course made no bones about their view of slavery. It would stay! Their constitution ruling all matters of law within their nation (just like the U.S. Constitution) expressly sought out and addressed this most acerbic issue. No law, the new charter said, would be allowed if it had the effect of "denying or impairing the right of property in Negro slaves." In short, the institution of slavery would be protected—indeed, it would be frozen in place—by constitutional mandate. (Although the African slave trade, in the same breath, was banned outright.)

They had gathered on February 4, 1861, *weeks* before the firing on Fort Sumter, mind you, the 38 various delegates of six seceding states, (with Texas soon expected, as well). Howell Cobb of Georgia had been elected president of the convention of *secesh* states that convened in Montgomery at the noon hour, and he lost no time in stating their common cause. "The separation is perfect, complete, and perpetual," he said. "The great duty is now imposed upon us of providing for these States a government for their future security and protection."

In Washington the same day, a Virginia-sponsored Peace Convention also convened, 131 delegates from 21 states searching for a way to mend the national rift. Former President John Tyler, himself a Virginian, presided over this convention.

Congress, too, was meeting—the U.S. Congress, that is. And it was now official—the Electoral College vote for Abraham Lincoln as President. To wit: Lincoln, 180 votes; John C. Breckinridge of Kentucky (a future Confederate general), 72; John Bell of Tennessee (the Constitutional Union's presidential candidate), 39; and Stephen Douglas, Democrat and Senator from Illinois, Lincoln's famous debate rival, only 12.

Also on February 4 in Washington, Louisiana's two U.S. Senators, Judah Benjamin and John Slidell, left their Federal seats to join Louisiana in the secession. Benjamin would serve as Attorney General for the new nation, then as Secretary of State.

The next day, February 5, John Tyler told *his* convention that "the eyes of the whole country are turned to this assembly, in expectation and hope." Unfortunately, not *all*, for in Montgomery, at that *other* convention, the Confederacy's future Vice President, Alexander Stephens of Georgia, pushed through a slate of rules for the *secesh* convention's business. Then, South Carolina's Christopher Memminger submitted a fateful resolution urging the creation of "a Confederacy of the States which have seceded from the Federal Union." A committee would study on it and present a plan for forming the new nation's government.

Events clearly were moving beyond redemption.

On February 6, Abraham and Mary Todd Lincoln were hosts at a farewell reception for friends, neighbors, and politicians at the Lincoln home in Springfield, Illinois—like Montgomery, a state capital. He would be leaving February 11, the day before his birthday, for the journey to Washington, never to return.

February 7 dawned, and before that day's end, Christopher Memminger's Committee of Twelve brought forward its plan of government. The entire convention now met in secret to debate the content of the report. Details of the South's fresh start, it seems, would be argued *in camera*.

The big day for the nation aborning was February 8, and the vote taken that evening was without a single dissent—adopted was a provisional constitution. *Provisional*, that is, because the document still had to go before the several seceding states for their ratification.

That, too, would be accomplished with surprising speed for such a weighty matter. And why all the rush? Why, to have all in place and functioning by the time that Lincoln would be sworn in—March 4—as the *unacceptable* new President of the Federal Union. Amazingly, the Southern secessionists had their provisional by-laws and governmental framework in operation within a week of their first meeting on February 4. And it only took a month for the various states to ratify a permanent constitution just slightly different from the provisional one, and both hardly at odds with the original U.S. Constitution—*except for the slavery clause*.

Such similarity was no accident, really. As one of the *secesh* delegates later wrote, " . . . there was a marked and purposed agreement with the Constitution of the United States." It wasn't that the South left the U.S. Constitution behind, but rather that it withdrew from "wicked and injurious perversions of the compact."

A name for the new nation of course was needed, and what should it be? The "Republic of Washington"? Or another "United States of America," and fie to those who might think that name already secured by the Union *perversion* of the old order? But no, none of the above. In the end, the new nation's name simply reflected the Memminger resolution's language calling for a "Confederacy of the States" seceding from the Union. And so it was, *the Confederate States of America (CSA)*.

All this, in its record-setting time, took place at the hands of the 38 delegates who had repaired for their work to a still barren-looking new city, a state capital, to be sure, situated on the bluffs of the Alabama River and marked by a handsome Greek-revival capitol building. The town of 40 years' duration thus far offered only two hotels of any size, the Montgomery and the Exchange House.

At this new news center, the famous British journalist William Howard Russell of *The Times* of London found slave pens and slave auctions quite active. The visiting Englishman—whose own government had banned slavery throughout the British Empire in 1834—compared hapless Montgomery to some woebegone town in central Russia. Not too complimentary for what today is one of the most striking assemblages of government structures in the world—a modern Athens, really.

Who, meanwhile, were the men—indeed, all delegates were white and male—who devised convention, constitution, congress, executive branch and, in such short time also, electoral machinery designed to give the new republic a chief executive?

Said Alexander Stephens afterwards: "They were men of substance as well as of solid character—men of education, of reading, or refinement, and well versed in the principles of government." Stephens and others wrote that the secret deliberations—press and public barred—were orderly, calm, even dignified in tone. And brief, with little fire-eating oratory. (But still *secret*. No public allowed. Some people did object to that.)

Indeed, still another reason for all the haste, aside from presenting the hated Lincoln with a government-in-being, was to be in place before the more wild-eyed rebels could let loose their guns on stubborn Major Robert Anderson and his Federal troops quartered on an isolated island in Charleston Harbor—Fort Sumter, of course. Further, future allies among the wavering border states—and the onlooking outside world, too—must be convinced, posthaste, as to the legitimacy of the new American Revolution, the new Montgomery declaration of independence from tyranny, the grave proclamation of states' rights.

By February 9, then, all were ready to move a step farther and elect a president and a vice president, and in the politicking that went on the night of February 8 and all day February 9, a Saturday, the name of a moderate from Mississippi gradually rose to the fore as more extreme candidates were cast aside, along with a few favorite sons offering no compelling appeal overall. And that man, no raging secessionist himself, a West Point graduate, a Mexican War veteran, a son-in-law at one time to the late President Zachary Taylor, a former U.S. Senator and Secretary of War under a thoroughly "Yankee" President (Franklin Pierce of New Hampshire) . . . that man was at his Mississippi plantation, called Brierfield, peacefully pruning rosebushes with his wife Varina when the word came, the morning after the Saturday evening session in Montgomery officially nominating and electing him *President.*

So it was that a still fairly young United States of America was presented with a mirror image of itself, small in leadership numbers, weak in resources but vast in territory. So alike were the two nations that even their day-to-day, more mundane laws would be the same—since the delegates assembled in Montgomery had made no bones about this aspect, either. All laws of the Federal Union, they had decided, would be the laws of the Confederacy as well. Except, of course, when they were in conflict with the new Confederate Constitution.

Eerily, we might now say, too, so many years later, the two mirror-image nations had two incoming Presidents in the late winter of 1861 who were both born in Kentucky, a border state that itself would be torn asunder and see its people play mirror-opposite roles in the war to come. Moreover, Abe Lincoln and his counterpart from the South, one Jefferson Davis, both left their homes on the same day, Monday, February 11, for their respective trips to their respective capitals, for their respective inaugurations as President.

Who the South Was

If you think about it, the South that formed the Confederacy was a far cry from the aristocratic Southland that provided one U.S. President after another following the Revolutionary War, that during the Revolutionary period itself had produced a George Washington, Thomas Jefferson, George Mason, James Madison, James Monroe, George Wythe, and a host of other striking leaders. It was the old Southland, too, that gave the New World its model legislative body—the Virginia Assembly—and that provided the Supreme Court its first historical "superstar", John Marshall.

Consider, too, that the same region produced the author of the Declaration of Independence and led in the framing of the U.S. Constitution. And yet, you could say it failed in its statesmanship during the Civil War.

The fact is, the Southland that produced the Confederacy was NOT the same Southland that contributed so much to the nation earlier. It was now, in 1861, a region with shifted center of gravity; it was now a land of rugged, rough-and-tumble frontier types, a land of *nouveau riche* rather than aristocratic gentry, as noted by Burton J. Hendrick in his 1939 work, *Statesmen of the Lost Cause*.

Its leaders, wrote Hendrick also, bore little resemblance to the traditional Southern aristocrats. "Really, the Confederate States of America rose in a region as recently frontier in character as the West that produced Abraham Lincoln. Of the seven states that formed the Montgomery government, only two—South Carolina and Georgia—existed before 1787."

Indeed, four of the Confederacy states—Florida, Louisiana, Arkansas, and Texas—plus a good part of Mississippi, were Spanish-owned, Spanish-ruled at the time of the Union's birth in the 18th century. Conspicuously absent at the Confederacy's formation in mid-19th century (but joining in later) was that font of early American leadership, Virginia, to say nothing of Tennessee and North Carolina.

The fact is, argued Hendrick with persuasive merit, traditional "Southern aristocrats" were hard to find in the Confederacy's ranks of civic leadership.

Jefferson Davis, like Lincoln a mere 120 miles away, was born in a log cabin in Kentucky. Davis and his fellow leaders of the first Confederate states "hardly resembled" the leaders produced in the tobacco lands of old Virginia and the Carolinas. The Confederacy of 1861 was a South moved westward, "a land of newly acquired wealth, not particularly well-mannered or cultured, but pushing, self-assertive and arrogant."

It wasn't even *all-Southern*, come to think, "for the hordes that had rushed into the cotton El Dorado of the Southwest were composed not only of quick fortune-hunting sons of Dixie, but of adventurers from the North and New England." Here were the breeders of the new South's civilian leadership. "Merely to catalogue the most important of these [Confederate] chieftains shows how the insurgent South, in its social and economic aspects, differed from the land of Washington and Jefferson."

Not only had President Davis been swaddled in a log cabin like his counterpart Lincoln, but Vice President Alexander Stephens had been a "corn dropper" on his father's "slaveless farm and chore boy in tasks usually assigned to Negroes." Further: "The Secretary of State . . . was the son of the keeper of a dried fish shop in London. The Secretary of the Treasury, born in Germany, spent his childhood in a Charleston orphanage. The Secretary of the Navy, son of a Connecticut Yankee, started life as assistant to his widowed mother in running a sailor's boarding house in Key West, Florida. The Postmaster General, a son of a tanner, had for a time engaged in an occupation that made any man an outcast in the South—that of plantation overseer." And so on.

That they were somewhat more plebeian in background than their Revolutionary forebears becomes obvious under such examination. But if the South failed to produce great civil leaders, what about the military side of things?

Here, it cannot be denied, the South excelled in the commanders it found. And look, noted Hendrick again, where *they* came from—the superstars at any rate. "Of the five Confederate generals who won worldwide fame—Lee, Jackson, Stuart, Joseph E. Johnston, Longstreet—four most suggestively were from Virginia; Longstreet came from Georgia, also a state of the old South. That is to say the leaders who gave the Confederacy prestige were mostly Virginians of superior breed, while the cotton belt was the region that provided the politicians who failed."

Whether of "superior breed," or not, however, those distinctly superior military men in the end couldn't do the trick, either—new or old, the South that went to war against the North in 1861 simply didn't have the resources to prevail.

FATE MAKES A CHOICE

It was a pretty little speech, and a sensible one . . . but with war afoot, every man's fate was all atangle. The place, oddly you might think, was Alcatraz Island in San Francisco Bay, future site of the notorious Federal prison. The principals were two U.S. Army officers—Lieutenants James B. McPherson and Edward Porter Alexander. The time was *ante-bellum* by just days, since it was fateful April of 1861.

Young Alexander, a West Point graduate and native of Georgia, had learned of his home state's secession from the Union and he was determined to do the same—resign and join the newly formed Confederacy. He had orders to transfer back east from his posting with the Army Corps of Engineers in Washington State, and his thought was to *boat* homeward with wife Bettie via the Panama Isthmus before taking the ultimate step. Arriving at San Francisco, however, he found two complications—their ship for Panama already had left and, further, he had new orders directing him to McPherson's small command on Alcatraz Island.

The fresh orders meant that Alexander must resign on the spot, and still find some way to convey himself and his wife across the continent, on their own. Looking back now, it seems so incongruous, but Alexander evidently felt no hesitation in explaining his predicament to fellow Union officer McPherson, even though Alexander very shortly could be (and indeed *would* be!) at war against the Federals, McPherson among them. The two young men obviously liked one another and had no problem in discussing Alexander's request to submit his resignation to McPherson for forwarding to higher command. Alexander would take a leave of absence to travel on home to Georgia and be in place when the acceptance would come through the chain of command. *All so very proper!*

McPherson promptly agreed to place no impediment in Alexander's way, *if he must go*. He, in fact, would do all in his power to facilitate Alexander's plans. But that was not all McPherson had to say, it turns out. Don't go, he pleaded. "Those urgent orders to stop you here [at Alcatraz] are meant to say that, if you are willing to keep out of the war on either side, you can do so. . ."

It was a real siren's song that McPherson delivered for his young companion's benefit. Don't go. Stay and avoid fighting against your own people. Stay, he said, and spend the war on the West Coast on fortification duty. The pending war would be no 90-day affair, as some were predicting, but would be fought to the bitter end. "If you go, as an educated soldier, you will be put in the front rank. Only God knows what may happen to you individually, but for your cause, there can be but one result. It must be lost."

And why so? "Your whole population is only about eight millions, while the North has twenty millions. Of your eight millions, three millions are slaves who may become an element of danger. You have no army, no navy, no treasury and practically none of the manufactures and machine shops necessary for the support of armies and for war on a large scale. You are but scattered agricultural communities, and you will be cut off from the rest of the world by blockade. Your cause must end in defeat, and the individual risks to you must be great."

McPherson of course was correct in every particular, and to his baleful outlook for Southern fortune he added the postscript that Alexander could stay safely on the West Coast, advancing rapidly in rank while senior officers went east and were consumed by the war; he could make wise investments from a knowledge of local land values to be gained as an Army engineer in the San Francisco Bay area—in four years' time, he would be a rich man. "Briefly, remaining here you have every opportunity for professional reputation, for promotion and for wealth. Going home, you have every personal risk to run, and in a cause fore-doomed to failure."

Alexander of course was impressed by his comrade's earnest warning. Indeed, "it made me realize, as I had never done before, the gravity of the decision which I had to make."

Even so, the young Georgian was unswayed. When all was said and done, his choice came down to one thought—"I must go with my people." His people were those of Georgia, not the United States.

He conceded McPherson's dire warnings probably would prove true, but explained that his people believed their cause was liberty, and that was that. "If I don't come and bear my part, they will believe me to be a coward. And I shall not know whether I am or not. I have just *got* to go and stand my chances."

As fate would have it, future Confederate general Alexander would introduce wigwag signalling to the Confederate cause, would be the Confederacy's first aerial balloonist for reconnais-sance purposes and, most important, would emerge from the Civil War as one of its leading artillerists.

His signals warning of a Union flank attack at First Bull Run [First Manassas] contributed to the Southern victory there; his artillery was most instrumental in turning back Ambrose Burnside at Fredericksburg, and, more anecdotal, it was one of his guns that sent a brick caroming off the head of "Fighting Joe" Hooker at Chancellorsville, after which the stunned Hooker remained un-characteristically timid and ineffective in his command position, then to be relieved by Lincoln shortly before the Battle of Gettys-burg. Alexander's artillery also served admirably at Gettysburg, Spotsylvania, Cold Harbor and during the siege of Petersburg. He was with Robert E. Lee at the surrender at Appomattox (which he advised against). After the war, he became a railroad president—and author of a widely hailed memoir of his Civil War days. In short, he emerged a Southern hero, a ranking figure of the Civil War . . . his reputation of course far greater than any he would have built by remaining safe and out of the way on the West Coast, as his would-be mentor McPherson had urged.

As for that officer, also outstanding and widely admired, fate was not so kind. Also reaching the rank of general, McPherson served through U.S. Grant's Tennessee campaign of 1862, in the siege of Vicksburg and in William Tecumseh Sherman's Atlanta campaign of 1864 . . . until cut down and killed by desultory Confederate gunfire outside Atlanta.

They say that his commander Sherman cried when he heard of McPherson's death.

Alexander never saw his fellow West Pointer again after their parting at San Francisco in early 1861. "Our sad parting," Alexander called it in his post-Civil War *Military Memoirs of a Confederate*.

Racing to War

The events after South Carolina's secession vote on December 20, 1860, came in sporadic bursts. And Fort Sumter was not always the focus, although, true, on December 27, South Carolina did seize the nearby Federal facilities Fort Moultrie and Castle Pinckney, and South Carolina did send a delegation to Washington with the demand, delivered before New Year's, that Federal troops leave Charleston and environs. To which President James Buchanan, surprisingly stern in this instance, said no, Fort Sumter would be defended "against all hostile attacks, from whatever quarter." By New Year's also, South Carolina had taken over the Federal arsenal at Charleston.

Fast forward from there—*January 3, 1861*, Georgia seizes Fort Pulaski at Savannah. *January 9*, Mississippi secedes and South Carolina fires upon the Fort Sumter relief ship, *Star of the West*. *January 10*, Florida secedes. *January 11*, Alabama secedes. *January 19*, Georgia secedes. *January 26*, Louisiana secedes. *January 29*, Kansas becomes a state—slave free. *February 4*, provisional Confederate government taking shape in Montgomery, Alabama. Virginia-sponsored Peace Convention meeting in Washington. *February 9*, Jefferson Davis selected as Confederate President. *February 13*, Electoral College count: Lincoln officially new

President. *February 18*, Jefferson Davis inaugurated as President, CSA, and stirring tune *Dixie* breaks out in Montgomery. *February 23*, Lincoln secretly trains into Washington, any and all assassination plots foiled for the moment. And now Texas secedes. *February 26*, Federals abandon Camp Colorado, Texas. February 27, Jefferson Davis names three would-be peace commissioners to negotiate with Washington. The Peace Convention in the capital city sends its recommendations to Congress after much internal argument . . . no salvation for the Nation here. *February 28*, North Carolina says "no" to secession, will stay in the Union . . . for a while. *March 1*, military control of the Charleston area officially passes from state control to that of the Confederate government. President Davis names Brigadier General Pierre G.T. Beauregard overall commander. *March 2*, The Confederacy welcomes its first convert, Texas. And Texas, for her part, seizes the Federal revenue cutter *Henry Dodge* at Galveston. *March 3*, today is Sunday. In Washington, a busy Abe Lincoln hosts his Cabinet appointees at dinner, visits the Senate. Next day will be an even bigger one. In Charleston, Beauregard takes command of his troops. *March 4*, Lincoln's inauguration as 16th President. In time of unprecedented national crisis, he will be a new President, his administration from Cabinet on down will be new; indeed, even his political party, Republican, is new to the seat of power. How will it all end?

BETTER ANGELS INVOKED

At the inauguration on March 4—Lincoln doffed his hat, tall, black and made of silk, preparatory to delivering his inaugural address and . . . hesitated. Where to put it? Two men reached for it. One, a young reporter named Henry Watterson, who in just a few weeks would be a Confederate soldier; later, he would resume his journalistic career . . . for Southern newspapers, and often on the run from Mr. Abe Lincoln's Yankee troops. The other reaching for the hat, and more successfully at that, was the Senator from Illinois, Mr. Stephen Douglas, Lincoln's own rival and debating opponent of considerable fame, the very man, a Democrat, defeated by Lincoln in the presidential race of 1860 (although, true, the rebellious *Southern* Democrats had been represented in the same hustings by Vice President John C. Breckinridge of Kentucky).

Lincoln, not yet sworn in, said in his inaugural speech that while he had no intention of interfering with "the institution of slavery," he also felt, "No state, on its own mere action, can get out of the Union." He waxed a bit poetic and obviously was appealing for good will on all sides when he said, to a nation not yet one century old, the American Revolution only about 80 years behind: "The mystic chords of memory, stretching from every battlefield, and patriot grave, to every living heart and hearthstone, all over this broad land, will yet swell the chorus of the Union, when again touched, as surely they will be, by the better angels of our nature." More bluntly, he also did warn: "In *your* hands, my dissatisfied fellow countrymen, and not in *mine*, is the momentous issue of civil war. The government will not assail *you*. You can have no conflict without being yourselves the aggressors. *You* have no oath registered in Heaven to destroy the government, while *I* have the most solemn one to 'preserve, protect and defend' it." And so, the immediate issue was not slavery, but secession. Or, as Lincoln saw it, the Union, the Union, the Union. He was sworn in *after* his speech, incidentally, by Chief Justice Roger B. Taney, the jurist famous for his majority opinion in the Dred Scott case declaring a slave was not a citizen with the right to sue in a Federal court; the jurist from Maryland who was a Democrat and former slave-owner himself.

It was a partly cloudy day in Washington, mild in temperature—in the fifties.

Lincoln had spent the night at Willard's Hotel, and he rode to the Capitol in an open carriage, accompanied by outgoing President James Buchanan, Democrat. Security was tight, and almost everybody knew that war was both likely and imminent Buchanan just that morning had received word saying Major Robert Anderson, commander of the garrison trapped on the island of Fort Sumter in Charleston harbor, could not hold out against the forces arrayed against him unless he was reinforced by 20,000 men. That word was passed along to Lincoln even before he rose to speak on the wooden platform erected for his inauguration at the East Portico of the Capitol. Begun about 1 o'clock, the inaugural speech took about 30 minutes, during which time, it is reported, Senator Douglas held Lincoln's hat for him.

SOCIAL NOTICE TAKEN

Social notes from all over . . . At the recent inaugural festivities for His Excellency Mr. Davis in Montgomery, the noted hostess Aurelia Blassingame Fitzpatrick, wife of the former U.S. Senator, raised more than a few eyebrows when she boldly poked the Confederacy's newly installed leader in the back with her parasol, merely to gain his attention so that she might have a word with him.

Tis said also that she was not hesitant, whether then or on other occasions, to urge her own husband upon Mr. Davis as a candidate for his Cabinet. The audacious Aurelia shocked some of the other ladies yet again upon telling Mr. Davis his reference to a possibly long war was "too gloomy" a remark to make.

Far from gloomy were the bright balls and dinner parties attended by fabulous Southern belles whose encouragement would mean so much to their men at war. One young lady, Ida Rice, was so popular that her countrymen named a cannon in Charleston harbor for her.

Returning to the inaugural ceremonies themselves, wasn't it a sight when all those pretty young ladies on a balcony above the swearing-in let loose a cascade of flowers upon Mr. Davis!

Quite a flutter of attention has been stirred also by adoption of the official Confederate flag—a handsome and eye-catching standard of red, white, and blue (like the Yankee flag in colors only!). How fitting that the flag should be hoisted at the new capital for the first time by Letitia Tyler, granddaughter of the former President and Virginia Governor John Tyler . . . namesake also of his first wife, Letitia, who bore him seven children before her passing during his presidency.

Speaking of Washington, and things *Union*, one true Southern lady who would prefer to put true embarrassment behind her is Elodie Todd of Selma, Alabama, half-sister to Mary Todd Lincoln, who sits in the Union White House presently as wife of Abraham. It may be fact that Miss Elodie is engaged to her handsome Captain Nathaniel H.R. Dawson, but that perfectly proper liaison has not protected her from hearing the most ugly sentiments expressed within her hearing about the husband of her sister. Said the future Mrs. Dawson in a letter to her beloved, "People constantly wish he may be hung and all such evils may attend his footsteps."

Doing her utmost to bear up, Miss Elodie donated the Captain's "Magnolia Cadets" of Selma a silken banner to take into battle with them—battle against her sister's Union, quite naturally.

All over Alabama in these exciting and turbulent days, the ladies have been making many a wondrous contribution to the cause. Nor have they shirked at patriotically offering their men to the gods of war!

For instance, Maria Ellington of Russell Country recently marched into the field where her own two sons were busy at their work and told them to join the army and serve until whenever the war against the Union should end. Further, an anonymous letter-writer not only told readers of a Montgomery newspaper that mothers should offer their sons to battle, but also advised those same sons "they must die" facing the enemy and entrust themselves "in His care Who is the God of war."

In Selma, meanwhile, at least one lady took it upon herself to avoid stepping out with any man who was *not* in uniform. Another Selma lass broke off an engagement to a young man who had not yet enlisted. Adding deepest sort of insult to injury, she sent him a skirt and ladies' undergarments, together with her tart advice, "Wear these or volunteer."

With activities and sentiments like these, can there be any doubt as to the future prospect of the Confederate cause!

Indeed, if the ladies could only join their menfolk at the front lines, there would be no lingering doubts whatsoever. For example, word has been received of the confrontation off Appalachicola, Florida, where a Yankee ship had the audacity to stop and board a Confederate blockade-running ship. As the Confederate flag sadly fluttered down from its proud perch, Mrs. F. Holland of Greenville snatched it up before any onlooker, Yankee or Rebel, could move. Wrapping the proud flag about her own body, she told the startled onlookers that she would die rather than surrender the "holy banner." Even her husband was aghast, but the Yankee officer in charge honored her stand (perhaps somewhat sardonically, true) with a single-gun salute. With heroes, or heroines, like Mrs. Holland, how can the South lose? Truly now?

LINCOLN WINS REBEL DEBATE

Abe Lincoln saw weeks before the firing on Fort Sumter that war was inevitable. He did not wish it, but he was girded for it. It would be a calamity for the Nation, but it must be. After all that had passed by the time of his inauguration March 4, 1861, there seemed no other way to preserve and protect the Union. Secession had frozen in place, a new Confederate government had sprung into being in Montgomery, and at Charleston, the guns were aimed at Major Robert Anderson's Fort Sumter. The fire-eaters were dancing in impatience.

Lincoln had only to say the word, to touch fire to fuse, and it would begin. *War, war, war!*

But Lincoln was wiser than that. And in the South, it took a fire-eater to see "Old Abe's" strategy and to warn against falling into his trap.

The fire-eater was Georgia's former U.S. Senator Robert Toombs, who only weeks before had risen in the august Senate chamber at Washington to castigate the Republicans as "black" and "perfidious," to say that the newly elected Lincoln "is an enemy of the human race and deserves the execration of all mankind." The same Georgian dared the North to make the Southerners stay in. Like a schoolboy thumbing his nose at a potential adversary, he cried: "Come and do it!" Georgia, he declared, was on the war path. "We are as ready to fight now as we will ever be! Treason? Bah!"

Those hot words in fact, marked his swan song as a Senator, for minutes later, in January 1861, Toombs was gone, resigned to join his state in secession (but not before visiting the U.S. Treasury to collect the remainder of his Federal salary and funds that would compensate for the mileage he must travel returning home in such high dudgeon).

Oddly, oddly, it was the same Toombs just a few weeks later, the same newly-installed *Confederate* Secretary of State, who in lonely isolation begged Jefferson Davis and his Cabinet to forbear rather than allow the guns to open fire in Charleston harbor.

The Cabinet meeting that witnessed such surprisingly mild but astute reaction from Toombs took place April 9 (an auspicious date for any Civil War calendar, it turns out!). Word had been received of President Lincoln's message to Governor F. W. Pickens of South Carolina that he, Lincoln, felt constrained to supply the isolated garrison at Fort Sumter, a courteous message but with implications of *come what may*.

It indeed was a gauntlet, even though Lincoln must give succor to his men in their moment of duress; even if they must have supplies to sustain themselves. A gauntlet because Lincoln knew the South must act . . . or back down. And if it be war, he must have the South strike the first blow, to have a unified Union behind him. If only war, at this point, could resolve the crisis . . . it must be war initiated by the other party. Who, indeed, already had fired upon a supply ship once before, back in December of 1860. Who, indeed, had cut off and trapped the garrison of men on the island that was Fort Sumter.

It was Toombs, then, who saw what Lincoln was about. All the Rebel Cabinet was ready to back Jefferson Davis, the new Confederate President, in giving the order to allow force against Fort Sumter—all but Toombs, who came into the meeting room late April 9, but not too late to warn that "firing on Fort Sumter would inaugurate a civil war greater than any the world has ever seen."

He stalked about the room, then suddenly faced Davis.

If the South attacked, Toombs declared, "it is suicide, it is murder, and it will lose us every friend at the North." Further: "You will wantonly strike a hornet's nest which extends from the mountains to the ocean; and legions, now quiet, will swarm out to sting us to death." And an epitaph that also was true: "It is unnecessary, it puts us in the wrong. It is fatal."

Despite the Georgian's entreaty for caution, Lincoln "won" the debate in the Confederate Cabinet meeting. For the word that went out by a messenger boy to a telegraph office across the street suited Lincoln's sad purpose very well. Pierre G.T. Beauregard's forces at Charleston were authorized to go ahead with the seizure of Fort Sumter. And the firing began three days later.

SUMTER'S SILENCE

Both Doubleday and Beauregard later would agree that the first shot fired at Fort Sumter came from a Confederate mortar battery at Rebel-held Fort Johnson.

Here are their running accounts, as later published, but spliced together for these pages. Doubleday, of course, was the Union captain of artillery Abner Doubleday; Beauregard was the colorful Confederate General Pierre G.T. Beauregard, commander of Rebel forces gathered at Charleston.

In their words:

Doubleday: The first shot came from the mortar battery at Fort Johnson. Almost immediately afterward a ball from Cummings Point lodged in the magazine wall.

Beauregard: The peaceful stillness of the night was broken just before dawn. Fort Johnson's mortar battery, at 4:30 a.m., April 12, 1861, issued the first—and, as many thought, the too-long-deferred signal shell of the war. It sped aloft, describing its peculiar arc of fire and, bursting over Fort Sumter, fell, with crashing noise, in the very center of the parade.

Doubleday: In a moment the firing burst forth in one continuous roar, and large patches of both the exterior and interior masonry began to crumble and fall in all directions.

Beauregard: Thus was "reveille" sounded in Charleston and its harbor on this eventful morning.

Doubleday: Nineteen batteries were now hammering at us, and the balls and shells from the 10-inch Columbiads, accompanied by shells from the 13-inch mortars which constantly bombarded us, made us feel that the war had commenced in earnest.

Beauregard: In an instant all was bustle and activity. Not an absentee was reported at roll call. The citizens poured down to the battery and the wharves, and women and children crowded each window of the houses overlooking the sea— rapt spectators of the scene.

Doubleday: When it was broad daylight I went down to breakfast. I found the officers already assembled at one of the long tables in the mess hall. Our party was calm and even somewhat merry.

Beauregard: At ten minutes before five o'clock all the batteries and mortars which encircled the grim fortress were in full play against it.

(At Fort Sumter, meanwhile, an unfortunate waiter in the mess hall was visibly terrified, Doubleday noted. The meal itself was "not very sumptuous." Then came time to respond to the Rebel fire. Doubleday had a historic role at this point.)

Doubleday: In aiming the first gun fired against the Rebellion, I had no feeling of self reproach, for I fully believed that the conflict had been inevitable. My first shot bounded off from the sloping roof of the battery opposite without producing any apparent effect. It seemed useless to attempt to silence the guns there, for our metal was not heavy enough to batter the work down.

(Ashore in the meantime, Beauregard and his compatriots had been surprised by Sumter's absolute silence for two hours or more. But, as noted by Doubleday, and now, by Beauregard, the silence didn't last.)

Beauregard: At last, however, near seven o'clock, the United States flag having previously been raised, the sound of a gun, not ours, was distinctly heard. Sumter had taken up the gage of battle, and Cummings Point had first attracted attention.

(Beauregard and his fellow Rebels were almost happy to see Sumter astir and shooting back.)

Beauregard: It was almost a relief to our troops—for gallantry ever admires gallantry, and a worthy foe disdains one who makes no resistance.

Stomach Pumping Questioned

There was nothing pro forma about the firing on Fort Sumter—in 34 hours, the little island fortress in Charleston Harbor was shelled into submission. A few words from its commander, Major Robert Anderson, effectively give the picture. He described quarters "entirely burned, the main gates destroyed by fire, the gorge walls seriously impaired, the [powder] magazine surrounded by flames and its door closed from the effects of the heat."

By then, April 13, 1861, the Federal garrison had only pork left as provisions and only "four barrels and three cartridges of powder" accessible because of the jammed door to the fort's magazine.

Outside the bar, meanwhile, Federal resupply ships—whose deployment had finally triggered the war's start—merely stood by as Sumter was under bombardment, their commanders unwilling to sacrifice ships or men to a now-hopeless rescue mission.

It was in the evening of April 13 that Anderson agreed to surrender. "The fort was a scene of ruin and destruction," wrote its U.S. Army surgeon Samuel Crawford later. "For 34 hours it had sustained a bombardment from seventeen 10-inch mortars and heavy guns, well placed and well served."

The moment of the inevitable at last had come, he noted. Pierre G.T. Beauregard, to be hailed as the hero of Charleston, wrote of the end in calm, simple terms: "The flag over Fort Sumter at last was lowered, and a white flag substituted for it. The contest was over. Major Anderson had acknowledged his defeat."

While no one on either side was killed in this first real exchange of gunfire of the Civil War, former U.S. Representative Roger A. Pryor of Virginia—now a Confederate colonel—*almost* became a casualty.

Sent to Sumter as one of Beauregard's surrender negotiators, Pryor took a seat at a table in the dark dispensary and, feeling quite thirsty, poured himself a drink from a black bottle on the table without thinking much about what he was doing. Mechanically, you know.

As it turned out, he had gulped down a poisonous compound, iodide of potassium, rather than water. Doctor Crawford quickly pumped his stomach and probably saved Pryor's life—but not without a few questions being raised.

"Some of us," wrote Union Captain Abner Doubleday, "questioned the doctor's right to interpose himself in a case of this kind." The thought was, "If any Rebel leader chose to come over to Fort Sumter and poison himself, the Medical Department had no business to interfere."

Crawford, though, had a well-nigh unassailable response, according to Doubleday. Since the good doctor was responsible for all his medicine as Federal government property, "he could not permit Pryor to carry any of it away."

Robert and Mary

They lived in a columned mansion on a hillside overlooking Washington from the south banks of the Potomac, 1,100 gorgeous acres with an unparalleled view of the Federal city. Unparalleled, too, were their historical ties to the generation that fought and won the American Revolution, the very event creating the city spread out before their eyes at every dawn's light.

Off and on over the years it had been a household bustling with visiting children, kissing cousins and other such relatives, friends, and associates, for here was an abode known for warm, gracious living—a wondrous stopping place for the visitor to Washington, for the traveler to South or North.

But time had taken its usual toll. People died, children grew up and went their ways, other events intervened . . . and soon, managing her late father's grand estate—plantation, really—was an aging woman crippled by arthritis and often left alone by her career Army officer's duty assignments elsewhere.

That was when Robert E. Lee decided he had better take leave and stay home to help his wife, Mary Custis Lee, manage their inherited Arlington estate—her childhood home, the home built by her late father, George Washington Parke Custis, the grandson of Martha Washington who had been adopted by the widowed Martha's second husband, George Washington. With the death of Custis in 1857, the mantle of ownership passed to only child Mary. The Lee children by then were scattered, with two sons serving in the Army like their father, and Robert E. Lee, himself, stationed far away at San Antonio, Texas.

Once he heard of his father-in-law's death, Lee—son of the famous Revolutionary War figure Henry "Light-Horse Harry" Lee—was able to take official leave and hurry home.

There, he would be shocked at the state of his wife's health. As she herself had written to a friend, "I almost dread his seeing my crippled state." She meant her difficulty walking by herself; the pain that kept her sleepless at night; her useless right arm and hand.

Lee, a former superintendent of West Point, was able to extend his leave indefinitely—to become, in essence, a farmer.

39

As he took over the reins at Arlington four years before the Civil War began, however, he still was able to accept spot duty with the Army headquartered in the city below the grand brow of Arlington's hillside. He usually crossed the river between, the Potomac, via the low-lying wooden span known as the "Long Bridge".

Usually, Lee's temporary duties involved dull service such as a seat on a court-martial, but a startling exception to that rule was the tumultuous and historic moment he spent in October of 1859 quelling John Brown's bloody raid at Harpers Ferry, upstream on the same Potomac that flowed so lazily below Arlington.

For a time during this period, too, with Lee at home, the great columned house was busy once again with visitors of all kinds—relatives and friends. In the Federal city below, of course, the final debates over slavery and states' rights, union versus disunion, were taking place among the solons of Congress and in the salons and saloons of the politically charged capital city.

After three years at home, Lee finally had to return to Army duty, again posted to Texas. On the Arlington hillside above, alone again, Mary Custis Lee was not unaware of what was transpiring in the city below and in the country at large. With husband Robert gone, she was managing Arlington again . . . but also maintaining a wary vigil as the momentous events unfolded. And among them came the day, Monday, January 21, 1861, when five Southern Senate members, Mississippi's Jefferson Davis among them, announced before a packed audience in the Senate galleries that their respective states had seceded. And with that, each gathered his papers from the schoolhouse desks on the chamber's floor and departed.

Not long after, in February, Mary Custis Lee wrote to daughter Mildred: "The papers are now filled with Mr. Lincoln's arrival in Washington & this week will, I presume, decide our fate as a nation." She could be slightly distracted from such momentous national events by the arrival of a son, wife and grandson for a visit—son William Fitzhugh "Rooney" Lee, wife Charlotte and "the Boy".

In the meantime, Texas at last seceded, too, and Lee was ordered home to Washington, to report to the Army's ranking officer, General Winfield Scott. Lee arrived at Arlington on March 1, and he very shortly faced a momentous personal decision.

"When my husband was summoned to Washington," his wife later wrote, "where every motive and argument was used to induce him to accept command of the Army destined to invade the South, he was enabled to resist them all, even the sad parting voice of his old Commander [Winfield Scott]."

It was almost a week after the fall of Fort Sumter that, by authority of President Lincoln, Lee so famously was offered command of a Federal army charged with subduing the rebellious South. He said no, that "though opposed to secession and deprecating war, I could take no part in an invasion of the Southern States."

After the firing on Fort Sumter, Lee had been distraught in any case, quite unlike the excited, enthused crowds in Richmond. Came the Union Army offer, then Virginia's subsequent vote to secede, and the heartfelt sadness at Arlington only deepened.

The Colonel had gone into nearby Alexandria on business the morning of April 19. He returned with a copy of the *Alexandria Gazette* reporting Virginia's secession vote and handed it to his wife. He still held out faint hope—perhaps the report was in error. On second thought, though, obviously not, and after their supper together he went, alone, to his upstairs bedroom. Below, Mary Custis Lee listened as he paced the floor above, then heard a mild thump as he fell to his knees—in prayer. Below, she also prayed.

Hours later, about midnight, he rejoined her. He showed her two letters he had written. In one, he resigned his commission in the United States Army. In the other, he expressed personal thoughts to General Scott. Later, his wife would write: "My husband has wept tears of blood over this terrible war, but as a man of honor and a Virginian, he must follow the destiny of his State."

Later still, she also would write: "It was the severest struggle of his life, to resign a commission he had held for 30 years."

More immediately, though, to daughter Mildred again, Mary Custis Lee wrote of her "sad heavy heart," and said: "As I think both parties are wrong in this fratricidal war, there is nothing comforting even in the hope that God may prosper the right, for I see no *right* in the matter."

The following Sunday, April 21, was the last day and night that Robert E. Lee would spend at Arlington . . . for the rest of his life. Summoned to Richmond by Governor John Letcher of Virginia, he left by train out of Alexandria Monday morning . . . not to see his own wife, even, for another 15 months.

They both knew at parting that their beloved Arlington estate would fall into Union hands as soon as the Washington-area defenses were organized. How quickly that would come, what might be the final outcome, neither could remotely guess—but certainly neither had any idea that the grand old Custis home would be turned, in the upheaval of war, into a Union cemetery and later into a hallowed, national burial ground, still crowned by those stately columns overlooking the Federal city.

Spy with a Future

The band played "Dixie", and the students were busy hauling their window shades up and down as a homemade semaphore system sending messages to eager Confederate onlookers across the river—the Potomac River. And what did their headmaster think of such nefarious goings-on, right in the middle of the Nation's—the Union's—capital? Why, heck, he's the one who put them up to it in the first place!

No matter, indeed, to Thomas N. Conrad, headmaster of a boys' school in town. No matter at all, safe to say, since he also allowed inflammatory, anti-Union speeches on that memorable school-graduation day in June of 1861 . . . the day also when he was arrested as prelude to being booted out of town, deported across the Potomac to the rebellious Southland beyond.

Not a great beginning, true, to a budding career as a spy—

a Confederate spy operating in the same Federal city of Washington. But Conrad was not a man easily discouraged, even if he could be a bit too flamboyant at times for his own good. Typically, he didn't stay away from Washington for long. After a brief sojourn as a chaplain with "Jeb" Stuart's cavalry troopers, Conrad made his arrangements with officials in Richmond and headed back for Washington. He made contact with foreign diplomats and escorted them to Richmond—a job that was somewhat risky but none too complicated.

Conrad had changed his appearance by now. He boasted a re-shaped beard, a new hair style and machine-made Northern boots instead of Southern hand-mades. He also chewed his tobacco Northern style rather than Southern, and it wasn't long before he was engaged in real espionage.

As anyone watching would have noticed, he developed a habit of visiting the War Department around lunchtime. It seems he had cultivated a coterie of Southern sympathizers among the Department clerks. His habit was to drop by their desks . . . and if they had gone to lunch and left important papers out on their desks, all the better.

No surprise, then, that Headmaster and occasional-Reverend Thomas Conrad was able to warn Richmond of Union General George McClellan's Peninsula Campaign of spring 1862 and of General Ambrose Burnside's pending attack on Fredericksburg later the same year.

But Conrad would suffer his minor setbacks—and barely elude capture. Fortunately for him, he had "developed" a double agent on the staff of the Union counter-espionage agency, and this man, one Edward Norton, warned Conrad in 1863 that he was under suspicion and about to be arrested again. After again unceremoniously leaving Washington—little time to pack—he spent the next few months maintaining a Confederate courier station at Boyd's Landing, Virginia, about 35 miles south of Washington. Apparently working for the Confederate Secret Service, "he built a hut there and named it 'Eagle's Nest'," reports Donald E. Markle in his book, *Spies & Spymasters of the Civil War*. " . . . [At] this location he received communiques from agents in the North and with the assistance of two mounted couriers was able to have the information in Richmond within 24 hours."

Conrad did not always see things eye to eye with his superiors in Richmond. They once had to reject his proposal to assassinate the U.S. Army's presiding general, the aging Winfield Scott. Another Conrad plot, unfulfilled, was to kidnap Abraham Lincoln on one of his trips from the White House to his summer quarters at the Soldiers' Home on the outskirts of Washington. Oddly enough, just days after Lincoln's assassination in April 1865, Conrad was arrested because he looked so much like John Wilkes Booth, Lincoln's assassin. The head of the Union's counter-espionage service, Lafayette Baker, not only ordered Conrad released, but, with the Civil War over, shook his hand.

And what does a successful Confederate spy find to do after the war is over? In Conrad's case, it was a choice in keeping with his *ante-bellum* career—he eventually became a college president. And he married. Oddity of oddities, though . . . when he married, it was to a woman named Minnie Ball (yes, as in the famous bullet of the Civil War, the so-called "Minié ball," after its creator, Frenchman Claude Etienne Minié.)

SWINGING HIS ARMS

"Trifling in ranks," read the first citation calling for demerits against the young West Point cadet. That was in 1857. So was, "Highly unmilitary & trifling conduct throwing stones on post." And 1858 was hardly any better. February 1: "Unauthorized articles in ventilator." March 8: "Cooking utensils in chimney." April 3: "Hair out of uniform . . ." *Mark that one*!

May 14: "Gazing about in ranks . . ." And so on, until his graduation from the Military Academy in June of 1861. . . after the Civil War had begun with the firing on Fort Sumter and a few other minor clashes.

As the demerits and that behavior pattern might suggest, he

graduated 34th in a class of . . . well, 34—dead last. And highest of all in total demerits earned.

And for what further activities had he been cited in those years, beyond gazing about in ranks on May 14 of 1858? Well, they found rubbish behind his tent one time. He had a bad four days in January of 1859: late to parade one day, to company formation for dinner another day, to supper itself that same day and to breakfast still another January day.

In February, a few days later, he was officially chastised for laughing and talking at the wrong time and place; for throwing snowballs, again wrong time and place, and, in March, for throwing bread in Mess Hall!

Over the next few months they got him again and again—for boisterous noise in sink (yes, sink); for idle laughing and talking; for defacing a wall with his pencil; for a room "grossly out of order, bed down & floor not swept."

Nor did his demeanor ever really improve, as appeared more and more clues to his future pattern in life. He liked to do things his own way. He did not buckle easily before authority. He had bread, butter, potatoes, even plates, knives and forks in his quarters one day in March of 1860. The same day, in fact, that his room was cited for being such a mess.

On July 4 that year, not yet abashed, he was spotted swinging arms while marching from dinner. He now gave strong clues to the future man and soldier. February 3, 1861: "Long beard at inspection," and March 10, 1861: "Long hair at insp."

He finished out his career at the Point once more throwing snowballs (in a rare April snowstorm, it seems), sitting at a window in shirtsleeves "with feet on sill, wearing an unofficial ornament on his coat", packing too much "furniture" in his tent and, finally, twice more swinging his arms while on march.

Upon his graduation from West Point, the Civil War interceded just in time for him to avoid a court-martial for a minor offense. He was able to report for duty one July morning and fight the Battle of Bull Run later the same day. A lieutenant to start with, he was a brigadier general of volunteers two years later—at age 23!

He finished the war at U.S. Grant's side at Appomattox with temporary rank of major general—and a name that already was legend, at least in the North.

Phil Sheridan presented this bright young officer with the small pine table that was at Grant's side for the historic surrender ceremony in the Wilmer McLean home at Appomattox.

An old West Point chum was at Appomattox, too—the Confederate Fitzhugh Lee. They embraced, then fell on the ground and 'rassled. Just like the old days.

Earlier in the war, things weren't quite so amicable between the two sides. Daring, flamboyance and something more—a real cruel streak—all contributed to the meteoric reputation.

Daring? At Bull Run, cited for bravery. In the Peninsula campaign not quite a year later, "Little Mac" McClellan was looking for a place to ford the Chickahominy River east of Richmond. With the Rebels thick on the far side, anyone testing the river's depth would be a tempting target. No matter, our West Pointer plunged into the water and pushed slowly across. McClellan was so impressed he promoted the young man to captain and made him a staff aide.

That summer came a battle at White Oak swamp in which the young man killed an enemy officer . . . by chasing him down on horseback, shouting for him to surrender, then shooting him in the back when the Reb continued riding on instead. The West Pointer later came across the victim's riderless horse. He decided to keep it and the saddle—"a splendid one, covered with black morocco and ornamented with silver nails." He also garnered a handsome double-edged sword from his unknown Confederate victim.

Possibly it was his first "kill," says biographer Evan S. Connell, and possibly he didn't even think of the horse, sword, and handsome saddle at the outset. But George Armstrong Custer did write his sister Lydia Ann, "I selected him as my game."

A "Bear" Installed

For an interval after the firing on Fort Sumter, a vast, as-yet-uncommitted never-never-land stood between the two nations of North and South. More populous than any state in the newly-formed Confederacy, and indeed more heavily populated than all but four states in the Union, she was Virginia.

Extending westward as far as Wheeling in today's West Virginia, 425 miles from Atlantic beaches to western mountains, Virginia would be a latecomer to Confederate ranks. She didn't secede until late April of 1861, months after the core states of the Confederacy had formed their new government. And even then Virginia did not rush, pell-mell, into Confederate arms. The sentiment was there, but there were all kinds of arrangements to make, wrinkles to iron smooth.

Two men arriving in Richmond in civilian dress were key figures in the scenario to be played out. Traveling from the north by train, hiring a room at the Spotswood Hotel and then taking his supper before visiting Governor John Letcher on Monday, April 22, one was Robert E. Lee, late of the U.S. Army. Would he accept the Virginia Convention's offer to command the commonwealth's naval and land forces?, the governor asked.

Yes, he would, and on the morning of April 23 he began his new military career in a temporary office not even staffed by a clerk. His General Order No. 1 announced his assuming the Virginia command as a major general.

The second man to appear at the State Capitol in mufti, with fateful impact to follow, was the new Confederacy's Vice President, Alexander H. Stephens, come to seek—and negotiate—Virginia's alliance with the rebellious South. In that event, Virginia's military fortunes, of course, would be determined by a higher command—the Confederacy's.

Secession fever had certainly gripped eastern and central Virginia since Sumter—and especially since Abraham Lincoln's subsequent call for 75,000 volunteer troops from loyal states to help stamp out the *rebellion*. Virginia not only did join the Confederacy after a short interval but soon invited the Jefferson Davis government to sit in Richmond rather than Montgomery, Alabama—an invitation promptly accepted, although this meant the capital of the new nation would be that much closer to Washington. Closer and more vulnerable to possible invasion from the North.

It was Robert E. Lee's job to organize his beloved Virginia's defenses against possible assault from almost any point on the compass. To the east, as likely invasion routes for the Union, were the Chesapeake Bay and major river highways inland, such as the James, the York, the Rappahannock. To the north, were the Potomac and Union territory contiguous with Virginia's borderline; and to the west was a vast mountainous land peopled largely by Union loyalists. Only the vista south from Richmond posed no worry for the new commander.

He began his new work with largely untrained, inexperienced militia at his disposal, few arms, a mere handful of veteran officers available and virtually no navy. In just eight weeks, however, Lee had organized a Virginia army of 40,000 or so, found 46,000 small arms for his men, and brought in cadets from the Virginia Military Institute (VMI) to drill and train many of the new recruits.

He did not accomplish his feat with consistently cheerful mien, it seems. "It was an open secret," wrote one confidant later, "that when he was organizing Virginia's forces at the beginning of the war he was regarded by the militia and other colonels who brought their regiments to Richmond as a sort of 'bear' that when aroused should be avoided by wise people."

A good soldier, an honorable man, and soon to be recognized as the South's great, good, kindly and symbolic leader of leaders, Robert E. Lee did not yet *look* like the legendary figure we all know today. He as yet had no grandfatherly white beard flowing down from chin and cheeks . . . only a dark mustache adorned his face in early 1861.

Certainly, he had much on his mind that might excuse an occasional show of temper. The Union military apparatus, after all, sprawled out from Washington, held the Potomac and the Chesapeake Bay, and was entrenched (even after losing Norfolk) at Fort Monroe in a key corner of the Hampton Roads harbor complex, while also crowding Virginia at every foot of its northern and western borderlines. "The war may last 10 years," Lee wrote to his wife before April was out.

He faced a deadline of sorts at first. When Lincoln issued his call for 75,000 new troops on April 15, he had given the Southern forces seizing Fort Sumter and other Federal properties (Norforlk's naval shipyard soon among them) just 20 days to "disperse and return peacefully to their respective abodes." Quite possibly, that meant Lee only had, from his first day of business as Virginia's military chief, just 12 days to get ready for whatever the North would do next—from his start on April 23 until May 5, the expiration of Lincoln's 20-day ultimatum.

Lee was quite aware, too, that his wife's beloved Arlington estate across the Potomac from the enemy camp was at risk for easy seizure almost any day. Mrs. Lee *must not* tarry there too long.

In the meantime, Lee had begun to assemble a core group of capable officers—many to become historic figures themselves. They included Joseph E. Johnston, John Bankhead Magruder, Richard S. Ewell, J.C. Pemberton, Henry Heth.

The prize catch, though, was the major from VMI who appeared at Lee's office one day to discuss the use of the military academy's cadets. Quickly seized upon as colonel of infantry and sent to hold the newly captured Federal arsenal at Harpers Ferry as long as possible, he was Thomas J. Jackson—later to be known as "Stonewall" Jackson.

It was a state convention that had voted to secede, a decision to be submitted to the voters for ratification on May 23. The same state convention on April 25, three days after Lee took the reins of military command, voted to join the Confederacy. But . . . where would that place Lee, a major general in his own Virginia hierarchy, in respect to the Confederate military apparatus, where the highest ranks issued thus far were those of mere brigadier generals? Would he have a problem dealing with higher authority in overall command, but with lesser-ranking chieftains issuing him its commands?

According to Confederate Vice President Stephens, Lee told him he would be "perfectly satisfied" with the alliance. Further,

Lee said "that he did not wish anything connected with himself individually, or his official rank or *personal* position, to interfere in the slightest degree."

In practical terms, the alliance not only meant the arrival in Virginia of military units from the various Confederate states to the south, but some preliminary confusion as to the validity of the Virginia officer commissions. With the confusion came minor friction, too. "Conflict was in the air," wrote Lee's biographer Douglas Southall Freeman, "and the personal representative of the [Confederate] Secretary of War began to crowd the wire with suspicions of Lee and Letcher, intimating that Lee was 'troubled about rank'".

But Lee assured President Jefferson Davis he was happy with his role as commander of Virginia forces—he and Davis were destined to respect one another and to get on well, in any case. Further, Lee on May 10 was authorized by the Confederacy itself to assume command of all Confederate forces in Virginia, and that pretty much removed the potential of any further divisive conflict. He also was given *Confederate* rank of brigadier general. Thereafter, Lee for a time served both his new nation and his commonwealth.

Early in May, too, he and his colleagues were becoming painfully aware of the wide state of disaffection in the western provinces of *ante-bellum* Virginia. They worried also over the possibility of a Union movement south from Washington—the reason for Lee's build-up of forces at Manassas Junction on the Manassas Gap Railroad below Washington.

Lincoln's apparent deadline of May 4 had come and gone with no major change in the North-South stand-off following Fort Sumter. On May 23, however, Virginia voters *did* ratify their state convention's call for secession. The very next day, Federal troops moved out of their Washington area encampments and occupied the Virginia shoreline on the Potomac. As Lee had feared, Arlington then fell into Federal hands . . . forever, at that. His invalid wife, though, had left the grand estate ten days earlier. Fortunate in this case, but in the days ahead she would find herself in "Yankee" hands, at the mercy of Federal authority after all . . .

DEATH OF A CONGRESSMAN

He helped to form the new Confederacy as a member of the Provisional Confederate Congress that originally met in Montgomery, Alabama, but it wasn't long before he set out to make his mark on the battlefield as well. The "Provisional's" second session, removed to the new capital city of Richmond, had just adjourned when Captain Francis S. Bartow and his Company B, 8th Georgia, marched off—for the duration, it was vowed.

Bartow, an attorney and politician back home in Georgia, had led his Oglethorpe Light Infantry at the seizure of Federal Fort McAllister close on the heels of Georgia's decision to secede in late 1860. Now, leaving Richmond in the spring of 1861, he bravely told his wife *not* to expect him back. If he must die, he hoped to die fighting for Southern liberty on the battlefield. He did—as Georgia's first martyr to the war cause.

Future Confederate Congressman Warren Akin, also from Georgia, was in Richmond and listening when Bartow's death was announced in the House chamber, with appropriate eulogies by several members of the body. A colonel by mid-summer of 1861, Bartow had commanded the 8th Georgia and then the 2nd Brigade of the Army of the Shenandoah in the Shenandoah Valley. He and part of his brigade rushed to the aid of General Pierre G.T. Beauregard at the First Battle of Bull Run [Manassas] on July 21. There, Bartow's command joined other Rebel forces in trying to hold off Yankee pressure against the Confederate left flank.

North of the Warrenton Turnpike and at Henry House Hill, the fighting was difficult. At one point, a Union battery manned by Regular Army men proved especially troublesome for the Southern volunteers. A greatly moved Warren Akins told the essentials of Bartow's story in a letter to Mrs. Akins, penned on the same day that the eulogies were expressed: "After Bartow's 8th G. Regt. was much cut to pieces late in the day, he rode to General Beauregard and said: 'What is now to be done? Direct me and it shall be done if within human power.' Beauregard replied, 'That battery must be taken.' Bartow immediately rallied the remnants of the 8th & ordered the 7th Georgia and one Va. Regt. with the

8th to take it. The charge was made & soon Bartow's horse was shot under him & he was wounded in the leg."

But Bartow was not yet stopped nor even slowed down all that much, it seems. "He then went from company to company, cheering the men & officers onward, telling them 'the day is ours; onward and take the battery!'"

And the Rebels did go onwards, but 40 yards out from the U. S. line the Rebel standard-bearer was cut down.

Far from being left behind, the wounded Bartow was right there still. "Bartow seized the colors, waved it over his head, with his cap in hand, waving it also and bidding his men to follow him—his men falling at every discharge from the battery, almost like wheat stalks before the scythe . . . "

And just then . . .

"Just then a bullet pierced his breast."

But Francis Bartow, Georgia's first hero of the Civil War, wasn't quite to be counted out as yet! For he told the men who gathered 'round him in a sorrowful knot: "They have killed me, but the day is ours. Never give up the field."

And minutes later his fired-up volunteers overran the battery manned by Yankee Regulars, who "were routed and fled from the field."

Bartow died in the arms of another prominent Georgia politician, former U. S. Congressman and future Confederate Congressman Lucius Jeremiah Gartell, present at Bull Run as a colonel with the 7th Georgia. In the same battle Gartell lost a son, and Bartow, wrote Warren Akin to Mrs. Akin, "had an adopted son who was badly if not fatally wounded in the same fight." Already the bitter toll was being felt.

Most Famous Shooter

"Old Ruffin" they called him. Born in ninety-four—1794, that is—he really *was* old, by comparison with the combatants of the Civil War. *Other* combatants, one should keep in mind, since he himself did take part in the fighting—and indeed fired two famous and significant artillery rounds still noted in many histories of the Civil War.

Virginia-born Edmund Ruffin, in fact, remains at the center of an old, old dispute—who fired the first shot of the war?

For years—decades even—many have said it was the fire-breathing secessionist Ruffin himself. Others said no. In any case, it apparently is true that he fired *one* of the very first rounds at hapless Fort Sumter in Charleston harbor.

A gentleman of Virginia's plantation society, Ruffin studied for a time at the College of William and Mary and, in his prime as a serious farmer, was a progressive agronomist, an advocate of crop rotation and president of the *Farmer's Register*. Also a veteran of the War of 1812, he eventually became consumed by the issue of slavery versus abolition. He attended the hanging of abolitionist John Brown and made it his business to present every Southern governor with one of the pikes that Brown would have used to arm revolting Virginia slaves. Ruffin traveled throughout the South years before the Civil War, urging secession, calling for creation of a new country and writing articles in the same vein. One of his publications was *Slavery and Free Labor Described and Compared*.

No surprise, then, that he should have been very much present when South Carolina led the secession way with its defiant vote of December 20, 1860, happily noting the wild cheers of the onlookers at the signing of the secession ordinance that evening.

Then, too, early on the morning of April 12, he was at Charleston's Cummings Point at the tip of Morris Island and there, as an honorary member of the Palmetto Guards, the 67-year-old was accorded the privilege of firing the first round from Columbiad No. 1 at Fort Sumter out in the harbor.

Confederate General Pierre G. T. Beauregard later said, however, the historic Ruffin shot was *not* really the first one of the entire Civil War, as often was alleged ever after. "The peaceful stillness of the night was broken just before dawn," wrote Beauregard. "From Fort Johnson's mortar battery, at 4:30 a.m., April 12, 1861, issued the first—and, as many thought, the too-long deferred—

signal shell of the war. It was fired, not by Mr. Edmund Ruffin of Virginia, as has been erroneously believed, but by George S. James, of South Carolina, to whom Captain Stephen D. Lee issued the order."

Even if Ruffin's gun came into action shortly *after* the signal shell that, quite literally, signalled the start of the Civil War, the fanatical long-haired oldster cut quite a figure in his uniform of South Carolina's Palmetto Guards. After the younger men of the same outfit were sent to Virginia, Ruffin still was much in evidence. "Old Ruffin has honored our company with a visit," wrote Palmetto member Charles M. Furman in May 1861. "The old gentleman intended presenting us with a flag, but finding us well supplied in that particular, he made a donation of one hundred dollars. The old man is a real patriot, his purse, his pen & his aged frame are all in turn called upon to contribute to the great cause upon which his heart is fixed."

Nor was this elderly legend-in-being as yet through with his activity as an amateur artillerist. His next famous shot would come in July—it also is alleged—during the fighting associated with First Bull Run. The hated Yankees were in retreat on the Warrenton Turnpike in the direction of Washington. The roadway crossed two bridges, and Honorary Private Ruffin was nearby, watching the Union flight with members of a Virginia artillery battery. The younger sharpshooters of Delaware Kemper's Battery asked the famous "first-shooter" if he would like to fire an honorary round with a gun aimed at one of the turnpike bridges—the Cub Run span.

He was more than happy to oblige, and, wonder of wonders, it allegedly was Ruffin's own shot that squarely hit the bridge and upended a wagon across its roadway, blocking it.

"Wagons waiting to cross the bridge were now abandoned by their terrified drivers, who chose to wade the creek," wrote Glenn Dedmondt in his book *Southern Bronze*. "A great quantity of wagons and equipment would be later captured by the South as a result of this single artillery round."

All was to no avail, of course, and in the end the South had to bow to the superior manpower and resources of the Union. That was too much for Edmund Ruffin, who in June of 1865—

two months after Lee's surrender at Appomattox—died a still untimely death . . . as a suicide who refused to live in the restored United States.

PERFECT STORM OF BULLETS

It started out as a "revolving door" battle, this first great clash of the Civil War. Each of the two opposing generals—classmates at West Point some years earlier—planned a feint to his battle line's left and a real lunge forward to the right. Had their strategy prevailed without deviation or the confusion of combat, Beauregard might well have marched on into Washington and McDowell into Richmond.

There had been skirmishes along the small creek line below Washington for two days, but it was on July 21 that the real fight ensued—and with it, some famous names and amazing events emerged.

Pierre G.T. Beauregard, for instance, had his headquarters at the McLean House, home of a civilian whose farm bordered Bull Run, Wilmer McLean. As Beauregard himself later wrote, he and his staff were interrupted in a meal by a Union shell that landed in the fireplace. Such events, both during First Bull Run and again a year later at Second Bull Run were more than enough for McLean. In 1863, he moved his family out of the war's path, so he thought. In fact, the second Wilmer McLean House would be the site of Robert E. Lee's surrender to U.S. Grant . . . at Appomattox.

It was at Bull Run also that one Thomas Jackson, Southern general, acquired a well known, even revered, nickname. He and his men had arrived as badly needed, eleventh-hour reinforcements for Beauregard. An excited fellow Reb, General Barnard Bee, sought to inspire his own troops by pointing out Jackson and his brigade: "Look. There stands Jackson like a stone wall! Rally behind the Virginians." Another version has Bee saying after the "Stonewall" reference, "Let us determine to die here, and we will conquer. Follow me."

Bee, unfortunately, was fatally wounded minutes later and soon forgotten, but the name Stonewall has endured.

Also killed in the fighting for Henry House Hill was the battle's only civilian casualty, the home's elderly owner, Judith Carter Henry, a widow.

Returning to the battle scenario, meanwhile, Confederate Colonel Nathan Evans of South Carolina had seen through Union commander Irvin McDowell's diversionary feint to his own left that morning. As explained later by Beauregard, "Evans, seeing that the Federal attack at the [Stone] bridge did not increase in vigor, and observing a lengthening line of dust to the left of the Warrenton Turnpike [the Confederate left, the Union right, that is], became satisfied that the attack at his front was a feint, and that a column of enemy was moving around through the woods to fall on his left flank from the direction of Sudley Ford."

Indeed, that was the case, with then-Colonel Ambrose E. Burnside's brigade at the head of the 18,000-man Union column. In the fight that followed, Bee, Evans, Jackson and others did their best to contain the Union wave, which also included a brigade led by William Tecumseh Sherman.

The fortunes of battle ebbed and flowed through the day. A Richmond journalist watched at mid-morning as both Beauregard and newly arrived General Joseph E. Johnston, senior to the hero of Charleston, dashed "at a headlong gallop" to a threatened sector of their line—the very moment, in fact, that Bee and Evans fell back, and Jackson's brigade planted itself as a stone wall in the path of the enemy.

And what a "thrilling moment!" wrote the onlooking journalist. "General Johnston seized the colors of the 4th Alabama, and offered to lead the attack. General Beauregard leaped from his horse, and turning to his troops, exclaimed, 'I have come here to die with you!'"

More ebb and flow followed, with the Rebs barely holding out while awaiting still more reinforcements. And finally, from left and right, here, to the rescue, came both E. Kirby Smith and Richard Ewell with their respective commands. And not a moment too soon, since there had been, true, bad moments that day for the

Rebs. A Confederate private was with a Maryland regiment rushing from the rail depot at Manassas to Beauregard's aid . . . and encountering a dismaying retreat on the way. "Wagons in great numbers were coming to the rear at headlong speed," wrote Private W.W. Goldsborough of the 1st Maryland Infantry, "and demoralized fugitives by the hundreds from the battlefield were rushing frantically by, crying out, 'All is lost, all is lost, go back, or you'll be cut to pieces! The army is in full retreat.'"

That, of course, was not entirely true, nor a lasting situation, since shortly after, Goldsborough and his fellows took part in a charge that was highly successful. "At the command, with one wild, deafening yell, and amidst a perfect storm of bullets, we drove the enemy pell-mell from their strong position into the thicket in their rear."

And lo, minutes later, Johnston, Beauregard and Confederate President Jefferson Davis himself rode up to congratulate the 1st Maryland's commander, Colonel Arnold Elzey, Davis "beaming with excitement and enthusiasm".

While Elzey did not, himself, win the Battle of First Bull Run, he earned promotion on the spot to brigadier general and effusive praise offered by Jefferson Davis. The battle *was* won, though, by their side—the Confederacy. It *was* the first real battle of any size in the Civil War. It *was* an uplifting victory for the South, but it at the same time spelled ultimate disaster for the South. While it created euphoria in Dixie, it showed a shocked Union that the war was serious business; that the enemy was real, was capable . . . and would fight. The Union response, while often inept, would be serious, no-holds-barred warfare until the issue was settled.

AT EVERY SHOT A CONVULSION

Newspaperman Henry Villard found Union Colonel Ambrose E. Burnside, future general and commander of the Army of the Potomac, riding hatless and swordless, in apparent pursuit of the rear during the Federal retreat at First Bull Run. "I am hurrying ahead to get rations for my command," was Burnside's entirely transparent explanation.

Another newsman, William Howard Russell of the London *Times*, later called home for displaying a *pro-Union* bias in his reportage of the American Civil War, certainly was unsparing in his description of the Union rout at First Bull Run—" 'Turn back! Retreat!' shouted the men from the front. 'We're whipped, we're whipped!' They cursed and tugged at the horses' heads and struggled with frenzy to get past." A veteran war correspondent, Russell had never seen anything like this "cowardly rout—a miserable, causeless panic." Not even as "alarms among camp followers" had he seen the like. "Negro servants on led horses dashed frantically past; men in uniform, whom it were a disgrace to the profession of arms to call 'soldiers' swarmed by on mules, chargers and even draft horses, which had been cut out of carts or wagons, and went on with harness clinging to their heels, as frightened as their riders. Men literally screamed with rage and fright when their way was blocked."

And all they would say when Russell asked what had happened, was the refrain, "We're whipped" or "We're repulsed."

The Englishman, a witness to the Crimean War and other British conflicts, said the road from Centreville to the rear, toward Washington, presented the scene of a totally demoralized army. "Drivers flogged, lashed, spurred, and beat their horses, or leaped down and abandoned their teams and ran by the side of the road; mounted men, servants and men in uniform, vehicles of all sorts, commissariat wagons thronged the narrow ways. At every shot a convulsion, as it were, seized upon the morbid mass of bones, sinew, wood, and iron, and thrilled through it, giving new energy and action to its desperate efforts to get free from itself."

This was the battle, of course, that had attracted innocent—ignorant, too—sightseers from the Nation's capital, gone over the Potomac with picnic baskets to see the Rebs chased away with a whiff of Union grapeshot.

Among the onlookers, Republican Representative Albert G. Riddle of Ohio and two other House members, plus a constituent from Cleveland, went forth early that Sunday morning with "a strong carriage, a pair of stout horses, a good driver, a hamper of lunch, and four of the largest navy revolvers," Riddle later wrote. They traveled beyond Centreville, site of Irwin McDowell's headquarters. They passed William Tecumseh Sherman's troops, and at first the Union soldiers they encountered said the enemy—the Rebs—were in retreat. But later in the day, that tide turned . . . more and more of the men they saw seemed to be drifting, then hurrying, back toward Centreville.

Riddle's own party, unsuccessful in finding defined front lines, was now headed back, too, but at fairly leisurely pace. From his seat in the right hand front of the carriage, the Congressman was surprised to see "a small body of cavalry turn the angle of . . . [a distant] wood, and head toward us at full speed."

It was a puzzle. "Of course I supposed they were our men, or why were they there? but why were they in such a hurry? The whole army I thought was between them and the enemy."

The explanation dawned when Riddle saw the Union stragglers around his carriage spring to life and run to a nearby fence with their weapons "in position to fire." Riddle leaped from the carriage with his revolver after shouting to his companions, "These are Rebs! Jump out and be ready for them."

They were Rebs at that, but they halted 50 or 60 yards away, their charge discouraged by the "stout Virginia fence" between the Congressmen and the cavalrymen. They fired their carbines, however, and killed at least one Union man, David McCook, "a private and a hospital guard."

Riddle's fellow Yankees returned the fire, and as a result, "two or three horses" ran off riderless with the Confederate cavalry troop.

It was right after this event that Riddle and his companions saw what had begun as an orderly Union retreat turn into absolute, mindless panic. Nothing, no plea nor threat, could stop the terrified Union soldiers or their wagon drivers (teamsters)— "Off they went, one and all, off down the highway, over across their fields towards the woods, anywhere, everywhere, to escape."

The Riddle carriage itself was swept up in the surge, he reported. It could be upset or broken up at any moment, but the driver's skill and the strength of the two horses kept the carriage intact and stable even though it was caught up in the mob. But another danger also loomed—"The poor, demented, exhausted wretches, who could not climb into the high, closed baggage wagons, made frantic efforts to get onto and into our carriage."

As Riddle's "wretches" grabbed at every handhold offered by his tossing vehicle, their sheer weight slowed it down to a standstill. "We had to be rough with them," Riddle explained in an account that later propelled him into controversy back home in Ohio, "and thrust them out and off." He and one companion guarded the doors with their pistols.

But then, "one poor devil did get in, and we lugged the pitiful coward a mile or two. He wore major's straps, was hatless, and had thrown away his sword; finally I opened the door, and he tumbled—or was tumbled out."

Minutes later, Riddle and party came across a "poor drummer boy struggling under the horses' feet." Riddle rescued the boy "with much difficulty" and took him in the carriage. They also took aboard an exhausted New York soldier who had somehow lost hat, coat and even shoes. They dropped both off at Centreville and resumed their journey back to Washington. On the way, however, they halted, and joined forces with two U.S. Senators and a visiting Michigan officer to form a line across the road to stop the headlong retreat toward Washington, Riddle said. The seven of them "with loud cries . . . confronted the on-sweeping multitude filling the broad road . . . and with our weapons we commanded an immediate halt then and there, on pain of instant loss of brains, which none of them would miss."

It was a dangerous moment. An angry teamster who had cut his horse loose from a wagon for the flight from the battlefields shot the visiting Michigan officer in the wrist with a revolver, then dashed on down the road. Still, the others held their thin line, if Riddle's story is to be entirely believed. "As the multitude, thus damned up, swelled and raged, the pressure upon us became very great. Loud cries and threats reached us in the deepening twilight."

Just when Riddle's small Congressional line was about to be burst asunder by the swelling mob, a colonel with the 2nd New

York turned out his men from their encampment at nearby Fairfax Courthouse and "took the tumultuous mass of fugitives off our hands."

As Riddle said, it was getting dark by this time—he didn't reach his boardinghouse quarters in town until 2 a.m., and he was too keyed up after the day's events to sleep even then.

Washington the next day, of course, was full of "the wildest rumors" and a good many fears, too. Wouldn't the Rebs now take advantage of their good fortune and march on into Washington?

First Post Mortem

Not many of the participants at ground level, limited to a worm's-eye view of the battle, quite realized at first what had happened . . . or why. Only later, after the smoke had cleared, did the many facets of the clash become evident. For starters, Irwin McDowell had marched southwest from Alexandria, Virginia, opposite Washington, D.C., on the Potomac, to Centreville in northern Virginia, nearly 30 miles. He had with him a veritable host of 35,000 troops, but many were raw militia with short-term enlistments . . . and precious little training.

McDowell at first faced Pierre G.T. Beauregard's 20,000 Confederates, based at Manassas, a strategic rail depot. McDowell moved out on July 18, 1861, and took two entire days to reach the creek called Bull Run, just beyond Centreville. In the meantime, the Confederates were using the time to rush reinforcements, commanded by Joseph E. Johnston, from the upper Shenandoah Valley near Harpers Ferry—they came by train to Manassas, a feat considered the first strategic use of rails in the history of warfare. Johnston brought 9,000 troops, and they enabled Beauregard to hold the line and even to counterattack after McDowell finally mounted his main assault on Sunday, July 21.

Following the feint to his left, McDowell drove against his foe's left with three divisions that crossed Bull Run at Sudley Springs. The left Rebel flank was pushed back to Henry House

Hill, where Thomas Jackson and his brigade so famously held like a "stone wall."

This was in the morning, and the front stretched for 14 miles. Meanwhile, both sides rushed more men to the west, in the direction of McDowell's main attack. It was about 4 o'clock in the afternoon when the tide changed direction, and instead of the Union attacking, it suddenly was the Confederacy. At first the retreat of the Federal right toward Centreville was orderly, but then the famous panic set in, and retreat became rout. The South had won the first major battle of the Civil War, with casualties for both sides that were a shock . . . and yet were as nothing by comparison with what was yet to come. They were on this day: Federals, 2,896 men killed, wounded, captured, and Confederates, 1,982.

And why did *not* the victorious Confederate forces pursue the foe all the way into the Nation's capital, possibly to end the Civil War then and there?

General Johnston once explained—

"My failure to capture Washington received general condemnation. Many erroneously attributed it to the President's prohibition; but Mr. Davis expressed neither wish nor opinion on the subject.

"The conditions forbade an attempt on Washington. The Confederate army was more disorganized by victory than that of the United States by defeat.

"Besides, the reasons for our course were unfitness of raw troops for assailing entrenchments; the fortifications upon which skillful engineers had been engaged since April; the Potomac, a mile wide, bearing the United States vessels of war, which commanded the bridges and the southern shores.

"The Confederate army would have been two days in marching from Bull Run to the Federal entrenchments, with less than two days' rations, or not more. It is asserted that the country could have furnished food and forage in abundance. Those who make this assertion forget that a large Federal army had passed *twice* over the route in question. As we had none of the means of besieging, an immediate assault upon the forts would have been unavoidable; it would have been repelled, inevitably, and our half supply of ammunition exhausted; and the enemy, increased by the army from Harpers Ferry, could have resumed their march to Richmond without opposition.

"And, if we had miraculously been successful in an assault, the Potomac still would have protected Washington and rendered our further progress impossible."

As for McDowell, he had explanations, too—

"It was now about 3 o'clock in the afternoon. Three times had the enemy been repulsed and driven back from the Henry House plateau. The third time it was supposed by us all that the repulse was final, for he was driven entirely from the hill, so far beyond it as not to be in sight, and all were certain the day was ours.

"The enemy was evidently disheartened and broken. But we had then been fighting since 10:30 o'clock in the morning, the men had been up since 2 o'clock and had made what to those unused to such things seemed a long march, though the longest distance gone over was not more than nine and a half miles; and although they had had three days' provisions served out to them the day before, many, no doubt, either had not gotten them or had thrown them away, and were therefore without food. They had done much severe fighting.

"It was at this time that the enemy's reinforcements came to his aid from the railroad train. They threw themselves in the woods on our right and opened fire on our men, which caused them to break and retire down the hillside. This soon degenerated into disorder, for which there was no remedy. Every effort was made to rally them, even beyond the reach of the enemy's fire, but in vain. The battalion of regular infantry alone maintained itself until our men could get back to the position we had occupied in the morning.

"The retreating current passed slowly through Centreville to the rear. The enemy followed us and, owing to the rear becoming blocked, caused us much damage, for the artillery could not pass, and several pieces and caissons had to be abandoned. In the panic the horses hauling caissons and ammunition were cut from their traces and used for escape, and in this way much confusion was caused, the panic aggravated and the road encumbered.

"By sundown it became a question whether we should endeavor to make a stand at Centreville. The condition of our artillery and its ammunition, the want of food for the men, and the utter disorganization and demoralization of the mass of the army seemed to admit of no alternative but to fall back. Our decision had been anticipated by the troops, most of them being already on the road to the rear . . . "

Sherman's Threat Appealed

At First Bull Run, the Union side was noted in some quarters for its 90-day wonders, men whose three-month enlistments were up just about the time of the great battle. The *New York Herald*'s Henry Villard, for instance, rushing to file his story on its outcome, encountered an entire regiment of Pennsylvania 90-dayers leaving the scene because, they said, their enlistments had expired.

Villard could only report the fact, but William Tecumseh Sherman, encountering one such 90-day wonder in his own command, resorted to sterner measures. Then-Colonel Sherman, a Union brigade leader at the time, was busy in the days after the disastrous rout preparing his men for the possibility of a renewed Rebel drive. "We took it for granted," he later wrote, "that the Rebels would be on our heels and accordingly prepared to defend our posts."

Among his problems, however, were the short-termers in his command. They were "extremely tired of the war and wanted to go home," he reported. "Some of them were so mutinous, at one time, that I threatened to open fire on them, if they dared to leave camp without orders."

Sherman kept his men busy and under control with drills, exercises and roll calls that only he, in person, could dismiss. But then came the open, highly visible defiance of an officer from New York, a lawyer in civilian life, who had the nerve to approach Sherman after reveille one morning. He announced, as if the matter were already settled, that he was going to New York that very day. Sherman replied, "I do not remember to have signed a leave for you," and would have moved on.

But that was not the end of the encounter. Not at all. As "a good many soldiers" stopped to listen, the errant officer said he had signed up for three months, his three months were up, and he was going home. Sherman realized that if this officer could defy him, the onlookers also would. "So I turned on him sharp and said: 'Captain, you are a soldier and must submit to orders till you are properly discharged. If you attempt to leave without orders, I will shoot you like a dog!'"

For the moment, that was an end to their conversation, and later the same day, Sherman spotted a carriage approaching with both President Lincoln and his Secretary of State, William Seward, sitting side by side inside the open hack. Sherman had posted himself by the roadside by the time they drew abreast. They stopped and he asked if they were going to his encampment. Lincoln said, "Yes, we heard that you had got over the big scare [of First Bull Run], and we thought we would come over and see the boys."

Sherman joined them in their carriage to show the way, while one of his men was sent racing ahead to alert Sherman's command that the President was coming.

On the way, Sherman was pleased to discover that Lincoln "was full of feeling and wanted to encourage our men." But when he announced he wished to address them, Sherman asked Lincoln "to discourage all cheering" and said there had been enough of that "to ruin any set of men." What was needed now, Sherman said, were "cool, thoughtful, hard-fighting soldiers—no more hurrahing, no more humbug."

Lincoln "took my remarks in perfect good nature," then delivered "one of the neatest, best and most feeling addresses I ever listened to, referring to our late disaster at Bull Run, the high duties that still devolved on us and the brighter days to come."

Before finishing, Lincoln assured the troops that they could appeal to him in person to right any wrongs done to them. That was when Sherman heard again from the New York captain who had buttonholed him that very morning. The man's "face was pale and his lips compressed" as he pushed his way forward to the presidential carriage and addressed Lincoln with words that Sherman would never forget. "Mr. President," said the New York advocate, "I have a cause of grievance. This morning I went to speak to Colonel Sherman, and he threatened to shoot me."

Lincoln coolly glanced from one man to the other, Sherman later related, then stooped low and told the complaining officer in a perfectly audible stage whisper, "Well, if I were you and Colonel Sherman threatened to shoot, I would not trust him for, by Heaven, I believe he would do it." And that was that. Lincoln did not even ask what their dispute was all about.

HEAD OF THE PASSES

If First Bull Run (First Manassas) was the first major land battle of the Civil War, a stinging defeat for the Union at that, what was its equivalent on water? And who came away the victor?

One early sea battle between North and South came on October 12, 1861, at the Head of the Passes at foot of the mighty Mississippi River below New Orleans. Here was both an early clash and an historic engagement for an ironclad. Here, too, Lilliputians did their best to entrap a few "Gullivers."

The action that took place probably would have come about at some early point anyway, but it was U.S. Navy veteran George N. Hollins who had the aggressive instinct to move events along to their climax.

The great river, a pulsating artery leading into the heart of America, was vital to commerce and crucial to either side's military strategy. Who controlled the Head of the Passes below New Orleans controlled access to and from the seas beyond.

Leading to the Gulf of Mexico from the lower Mississippi was a fan of outgoing channels. Above the fan, however, was a single channel, a bay actually, handle to the fan, navigable to large ships—the Head of the Passes.

No surprise, then, that the Union Navy moved quickly to establish a blockading flotilla there consisting of four ships—the screw steamer *Richmond* as flagship; the paddlewheel steamer *Water Witch*, and the sailing vessels *Preble* and *Vincennes*.

The *Richmond*, carrying 16 guns, encountered problems crossing the delta sandbars before reaching the small bay that was the Head of the Passes, but she did, and as of September 29, all four Federal warships were on station as a blockading force—a cork in the river's mouth. The South, of course, was bound to strike back, to try to drive off the enemy warships—or tamely accept their presence as a choke-point to commerce in and out of New Orleans.

As one indication of the trouble soon to come, a small steam-powered towboat mounting a single 15-pounder gun, the Confederate gunboat *Ivy*, had taken on the four Federal warships by herself on October 9 and left their gun crews fiercely gritting teeth, since her lone gun outranged all 41 guns aboard the Union ships. She withdrew, no harm done to either side, but there was lesson enough—in her range—for the Federals to take heed.

To the north up in New Orleans, largest city in the South, meanwhile, was a busy man planning the real trouble for the Federals, former U.S. Navy officer Hollins. Just entering his sixties, the Baltimore native had been going to sea with the U.S. Navy since he was 15, but that didn't stop him from immediately quitting his hard-earned rank as a naval captain to join the Confederate naval service . . . also as a captain, it so happened, but with no assurances for his future security.

Hollins, a veteran of the Barbary Coast Wars and other conflicts, distinctly was a man of bold action. Before taking up his Confederate posting to New Orleans in mid-1861, he had spent a short interval leading a raid against the Federal steamship *Nicholas* on the Potomac River. Former subordinates would have been startled to see their commander dressed as a woman to board the vessel and achieve surprise during the raid.

After arriving in New Orleans and taking note of the scanty naval resources available to the Confederacy there (as, indeed, everywhere else), Hollins did not hesitate when he heard a local entrepreneur was building an ironclad ram with plans to hire it out to the Confederate Navy for a handsome profit. Hollins wasted no time on troublesome detail—he simply sent his steamer the *McRae* alongside the ram and had it seized by a boarding party.

The addition of the ram *Manassas* gave Hollins a small flotilla consisting of the ironclad, his own flagship the *McRae*, and a handful of seagoing tugs and river towboats, with only a few guns among them. The chief weapon of the *Manassas*, meanwhile, was not her immovable 32-pounder bow gun but her ram of heavy armor.

All the while, of course, it had been the intention of Hollins and his superiors at New Orleans to clear the Federals out of the Head of the Passes . . . but until all was ready in mid-October of 1861, the Rebels had not been able to offer much protest to the Union blockade. With "acquisition" of their ram, though, the time for action had come.

In the early morning darkness of October 12, 1861, *Manassas* slipped into the bay that was the Head of the Passes undetected, the Rebel gunboats strung out behind her like ducklings following their mama.

Aboard the Federal ships, all was quiet, all was calm. "Despite the lateness of the hour [it was about 3:45 a.m.]," wrote John D. Pelzer in the December 1994 issue of *Military History* magazine, "a supply schooner had been lashed alongside the squadron's flagship, the USS *Richmond*, and the warship's crewmen were busy onloading coal." At the same time, on the sloop-of-war *Preble* nearby, Commander Henry French, the skipper, was asleep in his cabin.

Things would not remain so quiet for very long.

On *Preble*, a midshipman burst into his skipper's cabin to announce, "Captain, there's a steamer alongside of us!" And indeed, as French saw moments later from a gunport, there was a shape in the darkness just 20 yards away—"like a huge whale in the water," he later said.

It was the ram *Manassas*, and the monster was headed for the unsuspecting *Richmond*, beyond *Preble*. In fact, it was almost immediately that *Manassas* crunched into the port side of the *Richmond*. She backed off, then tried again . . . but by now, *Richmond* and her naval companions all were firing at the ram—and moving on, aiming for South West Pass and the open sea beyond.

The firing presented quite a spectacle to onlookers such as a Confederate aboard the *McRae*, a mile distant. "Instantly the heavy broadsides of the United States ships blazed forth as they shot holes in the darkness," he said.

As the Northern vessels picked up speed, the ungainly *Manassas*—armored by plating made from rail ties and somewhat damaged by her own ramming lunge—fell behind and, in fact, ran afoul of a marsh.

That left the ducklings to pursue the heavy Federal ships alone, and they did, releasing three fire rafts in the process. The rafts didn't prove much, but the speedy little Confederate gunboats could chase and brave the fire of the behemoth Federal warships ahead because the *Ivy* on October 9 already had shown that the Federals didn't have long-range guns, hadn't she? Thus, on this morning just three days later, the smaller Reb boats could pursue fairly closely without fear of retaliation . . . and their own few guns might score a lucky hit or two.

And then, for the Federals, disaster struck. They reached the same sandbars that had been crossed with difficulty coming into the river delta. Now, the Yankee *Richmond* and *Vincennes* both became hung up on the sandbars, helpless prey.

"While return fire from the Northern warships fell well short, the Confederate rounds burst all around the stranded Northern ships," wrote Pelzer. "Only the tiny steamer *Water Witch*, with its rifled 12-pound howitzer, had sufficient range to engage the enemy."

In short order, the captain and crew of *Vincennes* abandoned their ship . . . but then the fortunes of war intervened. The river current turned *Richmond* so that her broadside faced the Rebel gunboats, while outside the bar a still-mobile Federal warship, the *Santee*, could approach, maneuver and fire on the smaller gunboats.

They had to turn back, but with both *Richmond* and the *Vincennes* knocked out of action for a time—and the Head of the Passes cleared for Southern river traffic—Hollins and his flotilla had achieved a resounding victory. A "gallant exploit," proclaimed the New Orleans *Daily Picayune*.

The euphoria would burst when the great port city fell to the Yankees in April 1862, but for the time being the Confederacy had a naval feat to rank alongside its victory at Bull Run, just north of Manassas, Virginia—the very reason, of course, for the name given the ironclad ram whose actions had stimulated the Federal rout below New Orleans.

Heart in the Throat

He started out as the moderator at a meeting of war-fevered citizens. In Galena, Illinois, it was not so much the firing on Fort Sumter that stirred things up, but Lincoln's appeal for 75,000 troops. "As soon as the news of the call for volunteers reached Galena," he wrote, "posters were stuck up calling for a meeting of the citizens at the courthouse in the evening."

They say people in the South were *hot*, were fire-eaters. Well, take a look at Galena, and, by extrapolation, much of the North! "Business ceased entirely; all was excitement; for a time there were no party distinctions; all were Union men, determined to avenge the insult to the national flag."

No surprise, then, that the courthouse that night was packed. But . . . who would lead the meeting?

"Although a comparative stranger," continued Ulysses S. Grant many years later in his *Personal Memoirs*, "I was called upon to preside; the sole reason, possibly, was that I had been in the army and had seen service [at West Point and in the Mexican War of the 1840s, that is]."

And so, with "much embarrassment and some prompting," Mexican War veteran Grant "made out to announce the object of the meeting," then subsided while others, the postmaster and a pair of local politicians, made speeches. Afterwards, the townsmen formed a company of volunteers and elected their officers and non-coms. Grant turned down a captaincy before the vote, but offered to help in any way he could.

A few days later, in fact, he went with the volunteers when they traveled to the state capital at Springfield to find a duty assignment. In the meantime, Grant already had been helpful—

by drilling the locals and advising the towns*women* on how to design the U.S. Army infantry uniforms they volunteered to make for their menfolk. Grant was so busy after that first courthouse meeting, in fact, that he never did return to the family leather goods store where he had been working as a clerk—not even "to put up a package."

At Springfield, meanwhile, he and the men from Galena found the governor and his legislature so overwhelmed with volunteers that they authorized the creation of ten short-term regiments on top of the six previously established as the state's quota for a somewhat longer term—the new outfits to serve one month paid by the state, but available to go into Federal service if needed.

The Galena company soon was swallowed up by the 11th Illinois Volunteer Infantry, and Grant prepared to return home, his duties done. He thought.

He was staying, it seems, at the same hotel in Springfield as Governor Richard Yates. The very evening that Grant was ready to leave, after first finishing supper, the governor stopped Grant at the front door and asked him to come see him the next morning. When Grant did, he was offered a post in the State Adjutant General's office—his first job would be mustering in the ten new regiments. Grant took the post and over the next few weeks did the mustering required, visited St. Louis for a few days, sought a more permanent Federal post from the U.S. Army's Adjutant General in Washington, tried to see fellow West Pointer George McClellan, already considered a Union Army "comer", and generally just stirred around looking for a way to reunite himself with the U.S. Army and join in the war effort.

Finally, after Lincoln called for 300,000 more troops to serve a full three years, or the duration of the war, Grant was appointed colonel of one of the ten new regiments—the 21st Illinois—since its men didn't have confidence in the commander they had selected beforehand. Grant had from about June 15th until mid-July to work with his new command before he and his men were sent into camp in Missouri, close by the Mississippi River. After a quiet two weeks, Grant next was ordered to "move against" a Southern colonel's command at Florida, Missouri, about 25 miles south.

Even though he had seen considerable combat during the Mexican War, Grant was anxious as he marched his men southward. Noting the countryside and houses along the way were all deserted, Grant felt "anything but easy." The only sign of life he and his men saw on the entire march were two horsemen on an intersecting road. "As soon as they saw us they decamped as fast as their horses could carry them," he wrote later.

Grant and his men marched on, over hill and dale, quite literally, he expecting the worst at every step. They followed a creek, with ominous hills on either side that insisted upon rising "considerably," to a hundred or more feet.

They neared their goal at last. "As we approached the brow of the hill from which it was expected we could see [Confederate Colonel Thomas] Harris' camp, and possibly find his men ready formed to meet us, my heart kept getting higher and higher until it felt to me as though it was in my throat. I would have given anything then to have been back in Illinois, but I had not the moral courage to halt and consider what to do; I kept right on."

So it was that Ulysses S. Grant, future leader of all the Union armies in the Civil War, the general most widely credited with bringing about the victory over the South . . . so it was that he and his command of a thousand marched right over the brow of the hill into . . . the unknown!

And what did they find? Nothing. Harris and his own command were gone. The marks of their encampment were still visible, but they, every one, had decamped for parts unknown, as Grant immediately realized.

"My heart resumed its place," he later wrote. And it did so for the remainder of the Civil War, he added. For Grant suddenly realized his potential enemy had been "as much afraid of me as I had been of him."

Here was a valuable lesson that Grant would never forget. "From that event to the close of the war, I never experienced trepidation upon confronting the enemy, though I always felt more or less anxiety."

Good Times . . . And Bad

For Candis Goodwin of Cape Charles, Virginia, slavery apparently wasn't half bad. In fact, once recalling the games of her childhood, she said years later, "Dem was good ole times."

Her white people, she said in an interview in the 1930s, were good to her. They didn't beat their slaves. As a child, she was just like one of their own children. She played with them, ate with them, slept with them.

Her mother worked in the kitchen, and Candis had no work except "nursin' de babies." The white and black children often played in the woods together. They would make houses out of brown pine needles and "grass" out of the needles that were still green. Then they'd go over to the Missus' dairy and "steal anything we want an' tek it to our houses in de woods."

Candis used to play all sorts of pranks on "ole Massa Scott." At night, she said, everybody would be sitting around the big fireplace in the living room, the small slave girl, too. It would get late, and the Massa would leave his chair to wind up his clock, and the little black girl then slipped up behind his chair, "an' quick sneak his cheer f'om un'er him." And when he finished with the clock and eased himself back into the chair there was . . . no chair! And . . . "he set smack on de flo'."

Then there was trouble—but not really. "Doggone you lil cattin'. I gwan switch you," he'd threaten. "I jes' fly out de room. Won't scared though, 'cause I knows Massa wont goin' do nottin' to me."

The small girl knew about slave whippings . . . elsewhere. Her Massa Scott, she said, allowed none of that on his place. "He say tain' right."

Nancy Williams of Norfolk, Virginia, on the other hand, had a "singing" uncle in the slave days, an Uncle Jimmy who, "usta sing an' pray all de time he wukin' in de fiel's," and he wasn't so fortunate. Her Uncle Jimmy might have been born of God, she recalled in a 1930s interview, and like Jesus Christ Himself, Uncle Jimmy paid a high price for his devotion.

Her uncle lived and worked on a plantation next to her own,

she relates. He belonged to a master so mean he couldn't find over-seers to "treat de niggers mean 'nough." None was so mean as the master himself. And all the time, there was her Uncle Jimmy who would sing and pray as he worked the fields, and most of the over-seers who came and went at "Ole" Tom Covington's plantation really didn't bother the singing slave man named Jimmy.

But Covington eventually found an overseer who apparently was mean enough, and one day this "ole mean devil" was sitting by, on a stump, as the blacks worked a field. Nancy Williams herself apparently among them. Her Uncle Jimmy as usual was "jes a'singin' an' praisin' his God," but the new overseer didn't like that. He told the slave man to stop the singing; he said he wasn't working, he just was singing.

"Uncle Jimmy ain' said nottin'—jes' keep on plowin 'dat cawn an' a-singin'."

The overseer obviously was becoming plenty mad, but before doing anything about it, he went up to the main house to consult his boss, the Master. Nancy Williams, who couldn't have been present there, too, but who possibly had sources, relates their conversation:

—I got a nigger down in the field who can't be working 'cause he's just singing all the time.

—Kill the nigger if he won't work. Go back down there and kill him! What's a nigger for if he won't work?

And now, the other slaves watching, the overseer returns to the cornfield, all right. He returns, and he takes Uncle Jimmy across the field to a place by some fence, and there he makes the slave dig a hole in the ground with his bare hands. Then, they put straw in the bottom of the hole. And then, pour in some tar, it appears. And then . . . the overseer "chained" Uncle Jimmy and threw him into the hole and lit a match to the whole business. Nancy and unnamed others still watching—"peepin' threw a crack in de fence."

And as they watched, the flames licked up . . . but even the fire didn't "stop" Uncle Jimmy. "Ise fixin' t die to live agin' in Chris'," he said. And as the flames mounted and mounted, he began to preach and to pray. The flames were getting hotter,

hotter . . . and Uncle Jimmy sang. He sang:

> *God is de spring of all my joy.*
> *De life of my delight.*

And as the song faded away, he died, the other slaves still watching through the fence.

STAGGERING STATS

As just a few staggering stats from the American Civil War, please consider the fact that it encompassed, by best estimates, 10,455 battles, fights, engagements, actions, skirmishes, shooting affairs . . . whatever you wish to call them. By state, the leader far and away was Virginia, with 2,154 such military events recorded, while many states, chiefly in the North of course, had none.

Next to Virginia, the fratricidal war's most fought-over state was Tennessee, with 1,462 official "events". Next, in descending order (and some of these may surprise) were: Missouri, with 1,162; Arkansas, with 771; West Virginia, with 632; Louisiana, with 566; Georgia, with 549; Kentucky, with 453; and Alabama, rounding out the "top ten," with 336. The famous "valley of humility between two mountains of conceit" did not make the top ten with her 313 combats, . . . but North Carolina indeed can be ranked as No. 11 in this category, and her sister state, South Carolina, one of the two "mountains," ranked next with 239 combat affairs. To finish out the 18 states that hosted the most Civil War battles, Maryland came next, with 203; then Florida, with 168; Texas, 90; Indian Territory, 89; California, 88; and the New Mexico Territory, last with 75. (Despite Gettysburg, Pennsylvania hardly ranked in the *number* of battles fought on its soil.)

Those are the stats for the states as ranked and listed by the able historical compiler (and researcher for Bruce Catton) E.B. Long in his *The Civil War Day by Day, An Almanac 1861-1865*, which cites events of the war on a daily basis from start to finish. Consider also that the roster he cites is not really complete until you add odd, sporadic items such as the guerrilla actions in Kansas,

John Hunt Morgan's raid into Ohio, or the Confederate bank robbery in a small Vermont town near the Canadian border.

Still, the "stats" of the war contribute much to our understanding as to how and why it ended—had to end—the way it did. Horses . . . now take horses, until the modern age an indispensable item for any army on the move (forward or even backward, for that matter). In horses, alone, the North began the war with roughly 163 million to the South's 84 million, or twice as many.

More obviously, look at the navies, at ships. At the outset, the North, 90 ships. The South, 0. Both forces soon ballooned, naturally. The Federals built or purchased 624 more vessels (not all of the original 90 were serviceable, actually), and the South finished the war with an estimated 500 vessels having served in the "Lost Cause."

Even more crucially, what about manpower? Well, just as the population of the North, an estimated 31.4 million, was greater than that of the South, an estimated 12.3 million, so, too, the disproportionate size of their respective military forces—roughly 1.5 million to 2.2 million men served the Union as soldiers or sailors, to the South's 750,000, or half as many at best.

Consider the country's centers of gravity another way, look at the Nation's nine cities with more than 100,000 inhabitants as of the 1860 U.S. Census. Of the nine, only New Orleans was distinctly Southern, although Baltimore and St. Louis had their divided loyalties, true. The two Confederate capitals, Montgomery, Alabama, and Richmond, Virginia, by contrast, could claim population counts of only 36,000 and 38,000, respectively. Charleston, where the shooting really began, barely outdid those two with 40,578 folk.

And what about slavery, that divisive and evil institution that would cause such heartache all around? Were there really that many slaves in the middle of the 19th century? If you consider something like 4 million a sizeable number of human beings, there really were that many, yes. Oddly, though, while nearly all slave owners were in the South, 64 slaves were counted as living in the North. And, another odd stat, the South's slaveowners included a handful who were, themselves, black.

Not all blacks in the South were slaves, of course . . . just most of them. Free blacks numbered an estimated 262,003 in the South—a few more, actually, than the 225,967 free blacks who lived in the North.

Middles

Hello, Washington

The Washington of the Civil War period was far removed from the beauteous city of today—it, in fact, was distinctly primitive, even slovenly to look at, with unfinished Capitol dome, half-built Washington Monument, and even worse . . .

Even worse, in the words of Ohio's Representative Albert G. Riddle, it was "as unattractive, straggling, sodden a town, wandering up and down the left bank of the yellow [*yellow*!] Potomac, as fancy can sketch."

Perhaps Riddle exaggerated ever so slightly, but he offers factual observation, too. Pennsylvania Avenue, he later wrote, "twelve rods wide, stretched drearily over the mile between the unfinished Capitol and the unfinished Treasury building on Fifteenth Street, west, where it turned north for a square, and took its melancholy way to Georgetown . . ."

Worse, "illy paved" with cobblestones, Pennsylvania Avenue "was the only paved street of the town," averred Mr. Riddle. "The other streets, which were long stretches of mud or deserts of dust and sand, with here and there clumps of poorly built residences with long gaps between them, passing little deserts of open lands, where their lines were lost, wandered from the highlands north towards the Potomac, and from the Eastern Branch (Anacostia) to Rock Creek."

Worst of all, certainly!: "Not a sewer blessed the town, nor off of Pennsylvania Avenue was there a paved gutter."

It sounds unbelievable to us today, but Riddle very firmly stated: "Each house had an open drain from its rear, out across the sidewalk."

The result of course was not too pleasant for residents or visitors, to say little of the hygienic aspects. "As may be supposed the Capital of the Republic had more mal-odors than the poet Coleridge ascribed to ancient Cologne."

Just for added atmospheric color, Riddle also noted the open canal running from Rock Creek to the Anacostia River, a branch of the Chesapeake and Ohio (later Tiber Creek), as a breeding ground for tadpoles, mosquitoes and malaria.

In another vein, the Ohio Republican found that, "Political-ly, the city—the fixed population—was intensely Southern, as much so as Richmond or Baltimore." Indeed, "very few men of culture, and none below that grade, were Republicans at the advent of 'Lincoln and his Northern myrmidons,' as they were called in 1856-61."

The new political and social set ushered into town by Lin-coln's so-called "advent," Riddle among them, changed all, it would seem. Fresh blood, heroic deeds and the inspiration of men facing hostile forces—and overcoming them—"excercized [sic] an irresistible influence upon the population, and at once and forever silenced the open utterance of sedition and rebellion."

Be that as it may, another visitor to the beleaguered capital city of the 1860s was a young Union officer, a future Congress-man himself, destined to be President of the re-united United States, James A. Garfield.

In an outing with Kate Chase, daughter of Lincoln's Trea-sury Secretary Salmon P. Chase, in October 1862, Garfield saw that "the city is surrounded by a nearly complete circle of hills." They had a choice of crossings over the Potomac River. "In cross-ing over into Virginia there are three famous bridges, the Long, the Aqueduct, and the Chain Bridge—the last being furthest up-stream, and around which there have been many skirmishes dur-ing the past year. The great [Chesapeake and Ohio] canal which comes in here from the west, formerly crossed the Potomac and made its southern and eastern terminus at Alexandria. The water has been let off and it is now used as a bridge from Georgetown to Virginia. Hence the name [Aqueduct Bridge]."

The Union troops had been busy since their rout at First Bull Run. "The heights around Washington are all crowned with for-midable fortifications, mostly heavy earthworks and are called Forts. We passed through Georgetown and over the Aqueduct Bridge and went via Arlington Heights, the home of Lee, the rebel General in Chief. He owns a large tract of land there and has a quaint old pillared residence on it with a touch of the Norman Castle style about it. He married a Custis, one of the Washington family."

So much for the grand Arlington House, it seems. "From there we went by Bailey's Cross-Roads to Fairfax Court House, about 18 miles through a country completely devastated, it having been in turn held by both armies several times during the last eighteen months. Fairfax is an old town built mainly of stone and brick, and seems to be nearly or quite one century old."

And from a tour later the same year, more Garfield observations . . . more, that is, on the future site of today's Arlington National Cemetery—"We took the carriage and went across the Potomac to Arlington Heights, thence to Alexandria, then to Fairfax Seminary, back to Alexandria, drove the carriage on board a steamer and came back to Washington by water. General Lee's House at Arlington Heights was built by George Washington Custis whose daughter Lee married. It is a quaint old building, built in the castle style, and the walls of the main hall are ornamented with the skull and antlers of stags and paintings of the chase, also several battle pictures of the Revolution. It is now the headquarters of General Heintzelman. [General Samuel P. Heintzelman, at the time commander of Union defenses in northern Virginia, across the Potomac from Washington proper.]"

No Panacea For Politicians

Imagine a member of Congress riding to the nation's capital in an unheated railroad boxcar, a national legislator wearing his unlaundered shirts and socks for days at a time and foregoing a Christmas recess. Imagine a capital where the seasonal turkey would cost $125 whole . . . where the legislative pay at any time of year barely covered the cost of a boarding house.

Imagine . . . but such really were the experiences of Georgia's Warren Akin and other members of Congress during the Civil War—the Confederate Congress sitting in Richmond, that is.

The Confederate States of America enjoyed three Congresses in all—the Provisional Congress that first met in both Montgomery, Alabama, and Richmond, Virginia, to draw up the new Confederate government, plus two more Congresses meeting exclusively in Richmond. Members of the "Provisional" were selected at the secession conventions held by their respective states. This body was unicameral--one deliberative chamber only. The next two Congresses were bicameral with an *elected* membership.

The Provisional body, for the record, first convened in Montgomery on February 4, 1861. It assembled for five sessions in all over the next year, then dissolved itself with final adjournment in Richmond on February 17, 1862. The next day, the First Congress took over.

Meeting in Richmond, it held four sessions, then faded away in February 1864 to make room for the Second (and last) Confederate Congress, which met in two lengthy sessions, from May 1864 to March of 1865.

After that, it was all over. In fact, the last Southerner elected to the legislative body never could assume his seat. Nathaniel W. Townes of Texas had won the right to take the House seat of a deceased Confederate Congressman, but Townes' special election of March 13, 1865, came too late—Appomattox was just weeks ahead.

Of the 267 other men who collectively made up the Confederate Congress, about one-third had been U.S. Congressmen before the Civil War changed their lives and political careers. A clear majority, for that matter, had political experience on federal, state or local level.

Their lot in the more permanent Confederate capital of Richmond was not so enviable, noted history professor Bell Irvin Wiley in his book *Letters of Warren Akin: Confederate Congressman* (University of Georgia Press, 1959). The legislators were asked to do their job in a fragile house of glass in the midst of wide-ranging war against a powerful enemy. "The ultimate result," wrote Wiley, "was frustration and failure; and in the long time that intervened between the hopeful beginning and final defeat, most Congressmen were subjected to considerable abuse by journalists, members of other departments of government, state authorities, constituents, and the public in general."

To make matters worse for many, their home districts were being overrun by the dreaded Yankees. Many a Congressman's family "at home" no longer *was* at home—they were refugees living elsewhere, "in exile." One member with exactly that problem was a former U.S. Senator from Alabama, Clement C. Clay, Jr. Now a Confederate Senator, Clay and his family were forced to flee from their home base of Huntsville. As he plaintively wrote to a fellow Senator: "My home & parents & most of my kindred [are] in the hands of the enemy & I an exile wandering about like a troubled spirit seeking rest." (Fortunately for the rest of the Confederacy, Clay's earlier efforts to have Huntsville picked as the permanent Confederate capital had been to no avail!)

House member Warren Akin's experience was strikingly similar. A lawyer and state legislator from Cassville in northern Georgia, Akin at first kept to a relatively normal course despite the outbreak of war in 1861. By early 1864, however, he and his family had moved to Oxford, southeast of Atlanta, in anticipation of Federal incursions. But they then had to beat a hasty retreat farther east, to Elberton, in his native Elbert County. The Yankees, meanwhile, burned down his home and law office in Cassville in May 1864, then returned six months later to fire the rest of the town (except for three houses occupied by persons too infirm to flee). Atlanta, of course, fell to the invaders and Akin himself was fortunate to escape capture by George Stoneman's cavalry raiders.

By this time, summer of 1864, the 52-year-old Akin had been elected to serve in the Second Confederate Congress that began its sessions in Richmond in May of 1864. This meant Akin had to leave wife Mary Verdery, their seven small children—and six or seven slaves—on their own in a troubled, besieged land. Nor was he very well compensated for his lengthy absences from home and law practice. His monthly pay of $690 in Confederate money, he once wrote, would cover his boarding house costs and other basic needs, with only "a little left to take home." Even the $690-a-month sum didn't come until almost the end of the Civil War. At first, noted historian Wiley in his book of Akin letters, the Southern Congressmen only received $8 a day and 10 cents a mile as a travel allowance. An 1862 increase gave them $2,760 per annum in legislative salary, plus 20 cents a mile for official travel. Finally came the $690 a month, still no panacea.

Lodging and meals were the high-cost items during Congressional sessions, which customarily lasted for weeks at a time. "Some of the Congressmen stayed in hotels," noted Wiley, "and a directory published in 1864 shows that the Exchange, the Ballard House, and the Spotswood were favorite places of abode. A few legislators bought or rented houses in the capital. But the majority of them lived in boarding houses or private homes."

And not always happily. A.M. Branch of Texas wrote home in May 1864 that he was paying $600 a month for his lodging and two meals a day—"which is pretty high board." Likewise, Missouri's Thomas A. Harris once lamented that his pay of $10 to $11 a day fell far short of his actual needs. "Board alone," he wrote in April 1864, "without washing, clothing or incidentals of any kind, is at hotels, $30 and at the most mediocre boarding houses from $8 to $12 per day. With my family, my absolute expenses average $50 per day & you know that I live plainly & with rigid economy."

Speaking of laundry, Akin often mentioned that subject and his enforced frugality. His letters reveal he wore his shirts for three or four days at a time and his socks for a week, to save laundry costs. He seemed always to be darning his own socks, and he once commented: "I carry and use my handkerchiefs until they are soiled so much I am ashamed to use them."

As the war wore down all elements of Southern society, Richmond had become a dangerous place for the average citizen— even a legislator, it seems. One reason the Confederate House voted against extending its meeting time into the evening hours was the members' fear of muggings in the streets of the capital city.

By late 1864, various societal amenities—such as passenger train service—had deteriorated so much that Georgia Congressman Akin, once Speaker of the House in his own state legislature, had to travel in a railroad boxcar for the last leg of a trip back to Richmond. "I was just 9 ½ hours going from Greensboro, N.C., to Danville, Va.," he wrote, "a distance of 48 miles [I] travelled in a box car in the night and slept on some corn sacks, but as it was not very cold I made out pretty well."

If he could exhibit a cheerful Spartan attitude on his travel difficulties, Akin at the same time did despair over the larger portent of his plight—and that of the Confederacy. "I don't know how long I am to support my family, if this war continues long," he wrote to his wife. "Everything I have been working hard for so many years will be *eaten up* and in my old age myself, family and children will be left without the means of support."

The only answer, he added, was to trust in God—"and do the best I can."

BRAVE DEED RECORDED

Before the Union fleet bulled its way upriver and set stage for the fall of New Orleans, how were things ashore in the Big Easy? What were the local conditions after a year of War Between the States in this town of truly multi-cultural past?

In a word or two, pretty sad. A city of futile images and yet determined to go on.

George W. Cable—call him a young man, call him an old boy—was there. He saw what was to be seen with keen eye. He saw at the Coliseum Place the daily dress parade of the Confederate Guards. And so well turned out! "Long, spotless, gray, white-gloved ranks that stretched in such faultless alignment down the hard, harsh turf of our old ball-ground."

Fine, except that these were not exactly front-line troops. *Those* fellows, the *young* men of the city, had long since passed on to distant fields. This, here and now, was the home guard—"Gray heads, hoary heads, high heads, bald heads." These, bravely turned out as they might be, smart-looking as they might be . . . these were "the merchants, bankers, underwriters, judges, real estate owners and capitalists of the Anglo-American part of the city."

Not that the "Anglos" held any monopoly on local patriotism, either. Elsewhere, down at the famous Levee (or steamboat landing) there drilled "a superb body of Creoles..in dark-blue uniforms." Their commands and their manual were in French.

Other ethnic groups also were vital, since, "as a gendarmerie they relieved just so many Confederate soldiers of police duty in a city under martial law, and enabled them to man forts and breastworks at short notice whenever that call should come."

The city had lost its normal bustle. People were hiding valuables. "Gold and silver had long ago disappeared." Commerce had slowed, and where there had been business conducted or goods manufactured there now was armament . . . or nothing. For a short while after war began, even after the Union clamped on its blockade outside the mouth of the Mississippi, the Levee had kept busy, but no longer. "Its stir and noise had gradually declined, faltered, turned into the commerce of war . . . "

And even more of the young men had gone off to that war. "The brave steady fellows, who at entry and shipping and cash and account desks could no longer keep a show of occupation, had laid down the pen, taken up the sword and musket, and followed after the earlier and more eager volunteers."

From those early days, too, there had come the sad, the dismaying, returns. The town "had never been really glad again after that awful day of Shiloh." The city "had sent so many gallant fellows to help Beauregard, and some of them so young . . . "

And now, in spring of 1862, war was coming nearer and nearer . . . "For now even we, the uninformed, the lads and women . . . knew the enemy was closing down on upon us."

Still, was not every gray-haired man and boy ready to do his duty? Were not the fortifications ready? "But there was little laughter. Food was dear; the destitute poor were multiplying terribly . . . The Mississippi was gnawing at the levees and threatening to plunge in on us. The city was believed to be full of spies."

Finally the day came that all had expected . . . and feared. Heralded by alarm bells! Sure enough, the Union warships were moving up the river. Mobs gathered at the levees. They watched—and waited—as firemen threw burning bales of cotton into the river, cast loose ships and boats of all kinds and sent them, burning, into the jaws of the Federal monster.

To no avail. "'Are the Yankee ships in sight?,' I asked of an idler. He pointed out the tops of their naked masts as they showed up across the huge bend of the river . . . Ah, me! I see them now as they come slowly round Slaughterhouse Point into full view, silent, grim, terrible; black with men, heavy with deadly portent; the long-banished Stars and Stripes flying against the frowning sky."

Not long after, Cable heard roars and shouts and curses outside the store he worked in. "Kill them!" were the shouts. "Hang them!" Or, "Hurrah for Jeff Davis!"

It was a mob, with a weapon in every third pair of hands. And in the center, two men—two officers of the United States Navy—strode on, undeviating, "never frowning, never flinching, while the mob screamed in their ears, shook cocked pistols in their faces, cursed and crowded, and gnashed upon them." And so, "through the gates of death," walked these two Union men to the City Hall to demand and receive the surrender of New Orleans, April 25, 1862. Just about the bravest deed our witness ever did see.

COMPLETE CONQUEST REQUIRED

It was, said Ulysses S. Grant afterwards, "the severest battle fought at the West during the war, and but few in the East equalled it for hard, determined fighting." He was recalling Shiloh, *Bloody Shiloh*.

It had lasted two days, and that was enough. "I saw an open field, in our possession on the second day, over which the Confederates had made repeated charges the day before, so covered with dead that it would have been possible to walk across the clearing, in any direction, stepping on dead bodies, without a foot touching the ground."

Close to the Federal line, the Union and Confederate dead were "mingled together in about equal proportions." But, sadly for the South, the rest of the field was its dead.

The battle took place in April of 1862 on the western banks of the flooding Tennessee River, a place called Pittsburg Landing, a church nearby, the small Shiloh meetinghouse. Here, in Tennessee near the Mississippi border, in cold, cold rain and mud, came the two armies for an early showdown—40,000 Johnny Rebs under Albert S. Johnston come to fight 42,000 under Grant.

The fighting raged, and even some of the generals would not walk away unscathed. Johnston, for one, died—after being wounded in the leg, he could have tended to it and lived. Instead, he stayed on his horse, kept his boots on and bled to death. On the Union side, Grant's subordinate William Wallace also was mortally wounded.

Before the shooting died down in the second day's fighting, for that matter, Grant himself survived a Confederate ball that plucked its way through the air to his very side, but struck his metal sword scabbard, "just below the hilt."

Not quite so fortunate—but a survivor—was Union General William Tecumseh Sherman. "A casualty to Sherman that would have taken him from the field on that day [Sunday, April 6] would have been a sad one for the troops engaged at Shiloh," wrote Grant later. "And how near we came to this! On the 6th Sherman was shot twice, once in the hand, once in the shoulder, the ball cutting his coat and making a slight wound, and a third ball passed through his hat. In addition to this he had several horses shot during the day."

A horse, actually, was the cause of Grant's own greatest physical discomfort at Shiloh—his mount slipped on a muddy incline two days before and fell, "with my leg under his body." Grant's ankle was so swollen afterwards that his boot had to be cut off; and he had to get around on crutches for the next two or three days.

One result was that the commander of Union forces at Shiloh spent the crucial night between the two days of fighting still in pain from the ankle injury and well aware that the Confederates had pushed back the Union line in the first day of fighting, while also capturing a Union general, Benjamin M. Prentiss and 2,200 of his men in one fell swoop. That night, one would think, there was much to discourage U.S. Grant.

"During the night," he, himself, related later, "rain fell in torrents and our troops were exposed to the storm without shelter." As was their commander, it seems. "I made my headquarters under a tree a few hundred yards back from the river bank. My ankle was so much swollen from the fall of my horse . . . and the bruise was so painful, that I could get no rest. The drenching rain would have precluded the possibility of sleep without this additional cause."

Sometime after midnight, Grant was so uncomfortable he sought shelter in a small log cabin nearby. But it had been turned into a field hospital, "and all night wounded men were being brought in, their wounds dressed, a leg or arm amputated, as the case might require, and everything being done to save life or alleviate suffering." In the end, Grant could stand it no more. "The sight was more unendurable than encountering the enemy's fire, and I returned to my tree in the rain."

Next day, Grant's anticipated reinforcements arrived, swelling the size of the Union force, and he counterattacked against the now-outnumbered and tiring Confederates. By mid-afternoon on April 7, they were in retreat . . . and, in Grant's view, that was what counted. Not who won the first day or phase of battle, but who won the final spasm in the battlefield.

In the harsh hours before the shooting did die down, meanwhile, both sides had experienced desertions from the front lines. Grant took a surprisingly forgiving and philosophical view of the "stragglers," as these men were called, even though they were enough of a problem for him to form his cavalry in a line at the rear to halt the runaways. "When there would be enough of them to make a show, and after they had recovered from their fright, they would be sent to reinforce some part of the line which needed support, without regard to their companies, regiments or brigades," he wrote in his memoirs.

At one point in the first day's fighting, Grant found "as many as four or five thousand stragglers lying under cover of the river bluff, panic-stricken, most of whom would have been shot where they lay, without resistance, before they would have taken muskets and marched to the front to protect themselves."

Grant's fellow Union general, Don Carlos Buell, was furious with the malingerers. "I saw him berating them and trying to shame them into joining their regiments," wrote Grant. "He even threatened them with shells from the gun-boats near by."

Grant was not nearly so perturbed, even though Buell's tongue lashing had little effect. Said Grant: "Most of these men afterward proved themselves as gallant as any of those who saved the battle from which they deserted."

He asserted also that the Rebel stragglers at Shiloh were just as numerous, and the only difference was that they "left the field entirely" while "on the Union side, but few of the stragglers fell back further [sic] than the landing on the river, and many of these were in line for duty on the second day."

Indeed, one of the major positive results of the Union victory in Grant's view was the confidence it gave the largely green, inexperienced troops of his Army of the Tennessee. While the battle also gave the Union control of the middle Mississippi River line, it opened Grant's eyes to a central truth. "Up to the battle of Shiloh," he later said, "I, as well as thousands of other citizens, believed that the rebellion against the Government would collapse suddenly and soon, if a decisive victory could be gained over any of its armies." The fact is, Grant, himself, already had gained such a victory at Forts Donelson and Henry not far away, and still the Confederacy fielded its hard-fighting armies. It lost, if narrowly, at Shiloh, and still "not only attempted to hold the line farther south . . . but assumed the offensive and made . . . gallant effort to regain what had been lost . . . " As one result, however, the Confederacy created a monster, its own nemesis, in the form of Grant, as he now resolved upon the outlook and strategy by which he would lead the Union armies to ultimate victory just three years later. For Grant now "gave up all idea of saving the Union except by complete conquest."

SECESSION FROM SECESSION

Once upon a time—during the American Civil War, that is—there was a community within the thoroughly excited, newly-born Confederacy that was *not* so happy with the recent course of events, that was thinking, of all things . . . secession of its own!

The community was Winston County in north Alabama, a town named Houston serving as its county seat. The populace here, often called "hill people," was *not* to be counted among the South's plantation owners or slave-owners. Far from either category, the Winstonites were against Alabama seceding from the Union, and they sent a young schoolteacher named Chris Sheets to represent their point of view at the state's Secession Conference in Montgomery in January 1861.

A maverick among the fire-eaters and other secession-minded delegates to the convention, Sheets argued long and vociferously for the hill country's point of view. As cited in Alabama writer Drue Duke's anecdotal history *Alabama Tales*, the hot debates in Montgomery led to name-calling . . . and, for Sheets, even worse. "When Sheets refused to sign any papers of oath that the Secessionists offered him [after voting for secession], tempers flared more violently. 'I am an American,' Sheets declared, 'and an Alabamian, I don't need to sign anything to prove who I am.'"

He might as well have spoken to the wind. "At that point, he and the remaining few who sided with him were seized and dragged off to jail," writes Duke. "A few of the non-secessionists were able to slip away and hide."

Naturally, news of their emissary's incarceration and other rough treatment "downstate" did not sit well with his fellow residents of Winston County. "The hill people grew more angry each time they heard it repeated" and, "Sheets came to represent a real martyr to the people of Winston and the surrounding counties."

Nor did matters rest there. As the Confederacy and the Union came to actual blows, their respective loyalists in Winston were at odds, too. "Friends and neighbors who had known each other for years were now on opposite sides of the issue and weren't even speaking to each other. Church congregations, even denominations, split. Family members argued their conflicting beliefs, and young brothers left home to fight against each other."

Here, deep in the South, the split rending the country had

been duplicated in microcosm. Some in Winston, though opposed to the idea in principle, wished simply to go along with Alabama's secession, to keep the peace in their own community, but others, Sheets among them, weren't willing to let matters lie there. They issued a call for a "Neutrality Meeting" on July 4, Independence Day, and 2,500 to 3,000 persons, including "people from all over the South," turned out for the conference at Looney's Tavern. The talk soon turned to secession—secession from Alabama, that is! "The Free State of Winston" would be the result.

But secession from a state that already had bolted from the Union, pointed out one speaker, J. L. Meeks, would mean that Winston had no representation in any governmental entity beyond the county borders. It would be "much wiser," he argued, "to declare ourselves neutral and ask that our rights as neutral citizens be recognized."

By Duke's account, those present were then asked to approve a declaration proposing "that the people continue to respect Old Glory and to . . . take up no arms against the flag." At the same time, the people of Winston would ask "both the Confederacy and the Union to respect their rights and leave them alone to settle their own affairs in their own way."

The declaration was approved by a loud and enthusiastic voice vote, it seems. And if no Free State of Winston ever did emerge, "the hill people still proudly recall the day they took a strong stand in the face of great danger," writes Drue Duke.

Soldier A-Courting

He had small white hands, and he always looked clean, newly washed. But he was a big man, broad in the chest, proud in mein. He could be charming to the ladies, but he also knew what it was to be very firm, even to fight a duel. When a man in his Kentucky hometown balked at taking his own wife and children to church, the preacher spoke with John Hunt Morgan, who then spoke with the recalcitrant husband.

The preacher had one way of speaking, and Morgan another. He simply told the wayward soul, "I've come to give you a sound thrashing—if necessary." It seems the offender started going to church right after that.

Morgan came from Lexington in the bluegrass country, where cavalier attitude and behavior were rife, where men (and women) thought with such independence that the town fed both the Confederate and the Union armies numerous hot-bloods intent on fighting for their respective beliefs. Here, for instance, three grandsons of Henry Clay cast their lot with the Union and four with the Confederacy. Among other citizens, Dr. Robert Breckinridge, himself a Union man, gave two sons to each side (and a son-in-law to the Southern cause), while U. S. Senator John J. Crittenden's two sons each became a general on opposing sides.

Indeed, this was Mary Todd Lincoln's home territory and her own half-sister's husband, Benjamin H. Helm, was a Confederate general whose death at Chickamauga was sincerely mourned in the White House—the Union White House. No such splits, however, within John Hunt Morgan's family, which saw all six Morgan "boys" join the Confederate ranks. And one of them, John, soon became famous as a Confederate raider, a dashing war hero to rival Virginia's colorful icons "Jeb" Stuart and John Singleton Mosby.

Indeed, it is debatable whether either Stuart or Mosby inflicted as much damage, overall, on the enemy in personnel and materiel losses, or had as great an impact on enemy strategy. It is absolutely non-debatable, of course, that only John Hunt Morgan took an invading force—raiding party, if one must be technical—as far north as a point in Ohio only 100 miles south of Lake Erie.

It also can be argued that only the charming and courageous John Morgan would have courted an intended bride with quite the flourish that he displayed when based for a time in Murfreesboro, Tennessee, home of the two Ready sisters, Alice and Martha (called Mattie). Morgan, in his frequent visits in town, met their father, "Colonel" Ready, who promptly invited the cavalryman home for dinner, sending ahead a message: "Tell Mattie that Captain Morgan is a widower and a little sad. I want her to sing for him."

Mattie, it should be pointed out, was no aging spinster nor a callow country girl, either—but rather a winsome, 21-year-old who, as daughter of a former U. S. Congressman, had lived in the Federal capital as a leading, albeit young, socialite of the single variety. And it was true—Morgan, a captain destined to become a general in just eight months' time, was a widower, his invalid wife Rebecca having died at the time of First Bull Run in July 1861.

After that first dinner at the Ready mansion in early 1862, Alice eagerly confided to her diary that their visitor was modest but pleasant and agreeable. He didn't look the part of "the daring reckless man he is."

It wasn't long before John Morgan spent his free time riding horseback with Mattie or making other visits to the Ready household. But soon, in February, the Confederates had to pull out of Murfreesboro (following a farewell dinner at the Ready home), with Morgan and his men left behind as a screening and scouting force. For his dashes and raids against the Federals, his daring "visits" inside Union-held Nashville, and like escapades, Morgan by then had achieved such a reputation that a crowd was known to collect outside the Ready door, a block from Courthouse Square, at word that Morgan was there.

His own division commander, William Hardee, warned Morgan to be more careful, or he could be killed or captured. Said Morgan: "Sir, it would be an impossibility for them to catch me."

While operating out of Murfreesboro after that, Morgan sent challenging messages to pro-Union Louisville editor George D. Prentice by splicing into the Union telegraph lines. And in March he set out one day to ambush and capture a Union general on the roads outside Nashville—the notion being that any general would do. Pretty soon Morgan and his men had rounded up 85 assorted prisoners, but none was a general. Morgan sent them to the rear, and waited some more. He then bagged another 11.

On the way back to Murfreesboro, some of the prisoners were lost to a pursuing Union detachment. Morgan was a bit late in making his reappearance. People began to worry—the two Ready sisters in particular were on pins and needles as they hied off to church that Sunday morning. In church, though, they received word that Morgan and one of his officers were awaiting them with 38 Yankee prisoners. As Morgan biographer Cecil Holland said in his book *Morgan and His Raiders*, the two young women just couldn't stay in church after that. "We felt it would be mockery to remain and pretend to hear the sermon," one of the sisters later explained.

Shortly, Morgan and his compatriot appeared in front of the Ready home with the prisoners and escorts, 60 to 70 horsemen in all. Ladies, said the colorful raider, we present you with your prisoners. What disposal should be made of them? And the reply, "You have performed your part so well we are willing to entrust it all to you."

Next, Morgan and Company were off to the Union-held railroad town of Gallatin, he promising more trophies upon return. Meanwhile, the Federals were moving ominously close to Murfreesboro itself.

At Gallatin, Morgan and his men performed their wrecking work on the rail facilities and obtained intelligence by approaching the telegraph operator in the guise of Federal officers.

The operator accepted them at face value, then foolishly boasted that he was ready to face John Morgan if the Reb ever appeared in Gallatin. Morgan's companion of the moment then told the man the startling news. "Sir, let me introduce you to Captain Morgan."

Back in Murfreesboro, meanwhile, the Union army at last had arrived, taking possession quietly but decisively. Fortunately, Morgan found out before riding blithely into town himself to visit his newfound love. Mattie, assuming she wouldn't see Morgan for a time, wrote him a farewell note to be sent by messenger. Then, she received word he was at a village eight or ten miles away. Would it be safe for him to slip into town? The Union troops were encamped about eight miles out of town in another direction, so she sent back word to come ahead, then waited on tenterhooks, wondering if she had invited him to his doom.

Suddenly, he was there, at the front door—Morgan, a fellow officer and five prisoners, more "trophies" for the ladies, who of course once again told Morgan to dispose of them as he knew best.

Morgan, in fact, stayed until dawn while his men and his prisoners waited for him to complete his visit with the fair Mattie. By Ready family tradition, that is the night they became engaged, although they would not see each other for another eight months, much less go ahead with their marriage plans. But that ceremony—and a colorful, widely heralded one it was, too—finally did take place, with the young Morgan a general by the time of their wedding day.

BATTERY DISBANDED

Few, yesterday or today, have ever heard of the 13th Independent Battery, Ohio Light Artillery, organized and mustered into the service of the Union Army at Camp Dennison, Ohio, on December 20, 1861, one year to the day after South Carolina seceded from the Union. Few at any time since the battery's first and only appearance in battle have heard of it because its furious division commander, Brigadier General Stephen A. Hurlbut, disbanded the unit, scattered its men, gave away its guns and ordered its officers home, accusing all of cowardly performance in battle . . . even if it was their first combat experience.

By Hurlbut's angry account, the battery personnel ("ignorant of duty and drill") set up their guns on Sunday, April 6, 1862, and then . . .

"A single shot from the enemy's batteries struck in [Captain John B.] Myers' 13th Ohio Battery, when officers, and men, with a common impulse of disgraceful cowardice, abandoned their entire battery, horses, caissons, and guns, and fled, and I saw no more of them until Tuesday."

The facts, as related by others, may have been somewhat less stinging. For instance, Thomas Jeffrey, a young enlisted man in the battery, later wrote that he and his companions spent most of the time after their unit's formation in December 1861 in marching drills, because only one practice cannon was available at their camp for the use of several artillery batteries.

On March 1, 1862, the battery at last received "guns and horses." Just four days later, the battery was ordered to the front. The front would be Pittsburg Landing on the Tennessee River; the battle awaiting him and his comrades, Shiloh.

How did they get there from Ohio? "They [he and his companions] marched to Cincinnati and by railroad to St. Louis, then by steamboat down to Cairo and up the Ohio and Tennessee Rivers to Pittsburg Landing."

The entire trip took nearly a month—leaving March 5, the 13th Ohio Battery arrived just six days before the fighting erupted on Sunday, April 6, near the Shiloh meetinghouse. "From the time of receiving their guns and horses to their arrival at Pittsburg," wrote Jeffrey later, "they had not had their horses hitched up more than a half dozen times."

On that "terrible first day," as he later called it, Jeffrey's artillery battery was "prompt to respond" as the fighting began, but had to wait for an hour or more in camp for orders. They came at last, carried by an aide to General Hurlbut—move up to the front.

"After going forward a mile or more the Captain was ordered to place his battery in position in a narrow belt of timber to the right of an open field," wrote Jeffrey years later. Myers objected, saying he wanted to place his guns in the open field. "The staff officer peremptorily ordered him to place it in the timber."

It may be, too, as other accounts have it, that the inexperienced Myers mistakenly held back when his supporting infantry, four regiments under Brigadier General Jacob Lauman, dashed ahead. Hurlbut later accused Myers of holding back, "either from ignorance or some other cause."

In the lines opposite, meanwhile, a very proficient artilleryman was preparing his own guns to support a Confederate charge against Lauman's position. This was Captain Felix H. Robertson, commander of an Alabama battery—and a West Point graduate who had gone with the South. He had in his sights the 13th Ohio Battery. The results, seconds later, apparently was Hurlbut's "single shot" or more.

As Jeffrey tells it: "As they [his battery] undertook to obey the order [to go into the trees], the enemy opened with both infantry and artillery which resulted in their becoming hopelessly entangled among the trees and logs, the horses shot down, the men in disorder. So complete was the destruction that but two of the team with one gun and its caisson escaped from the general disaster."

Said a friendly onlooker, Union Lieutenant Cuthbert W. Laing of the nearby 2nd Michigan Battery: "They had just got unlimbered when one of their caissons was shivered to pieces, and the horses on one of the guns took fright and ran through our lines. All then left the battery without firing a shot."

Other Union artillerymen, it seems, ran forward, cut loose the surviving horses and spiked the guns left behind by the 13th Battery, which suffered one man killed and eight wounded.

The day wore on, with at least four Confederate assaults against Lauman's "Hornets Nest" sector in the Federal line, which gradually was pushed back—but at horrendous cost to the attacking Rebels. Said an Indiana officer, "The advance was made up to within some 10 yards of my line and the slaughter among the enemy in its front was terrible." General Lauman recalled, as did U.S. Grant later, "The ground was literally covered with their dead."

Young Sergeant Jeffrey, meanwhile, wrote that his battery's one undamaged gun and "detached pieces of other batteries did efficient work in the repulse of the enemy on the evening of that terrible first day at Shiloh." Battery members, he wrote later, regrouped at "their old camp" after the battle ended the next day, "having recovered their guns and equipments except horses."

They were in for a shock. "A few days thereafter they were surprised by an order from General Hurlbut for the muster out of their officers and the assignment of the men to the Ninth, Tenth and Fourteenth Ohio batteries."

Even years later, Jeffrey could not understand Hurlbut's attitude. "Why this was done I do not know," he wrote. "No doubt General Hurlbut thought he had sufficient reason, but the only apparent reason was that they officers in attempting to obey orders had lost their battery."

According to Jeffrey, later in the war an officer himself, an official investigation by the Ohio Adjutant General's office "fully exonerated Captain Myers from blame," and according to Jeffrey further, "The treatment of Captain Myers and his officers by General Hurlbut has been denounced as outrageous by all who knew of the affair."

In the meantime, though, the war continued. Jeffrey found himself assigned to the 14th Ohio Battery, which now took over the old 13th's remaining equipment. The 14th served honorably through the rest of the war—at Corinth, Mississippi, in the Atlanta Campaign, the Battle of Nashville and the campaign against Mobile, Alabama.

At Resaca, Georgia, one day, the battery was asked to "knock out" some Confederate snipers in distant trees. "It took us but a short time to knock them out," and the onlooking General James B. McPherson "remarked that in all his military experience it was the first time he had ever seen artillery used for the purpose of sharpshooting."

Another time, the battery had marched so long, through such completely stripped Confederate countryside in parts of Georgia and Alabama, that its horses starved to death. Later still, the 14th Ohio covered 4,500 miles just in the final five months of the war.

If Jeffrey didn't see much of the war with the ill-fated 13th Ohio, he and a number of his old compatriots certainly did with the 14th Ohio.

"GRANNY" LEE

Crucial battle outside Richmond. The commander's preparations not always the best. The enemy's superiority in numbers overwhelming. The commander suddenly wounded, incapacitated. The second in command available to take over. But . . . not well, not up to the job. The enemy virtually at the gates to Richmond.

Who to call in? Well, there is that desk-bound fellow, that veteran of engineers. That . . . that "Granny" fellow. Why not him? Robert E. "Granny" Lee. Bring him forward to the rescue . . . *if he can.*

Difficult to believe nowadays, but there was a time during the Civil War when the South's Robert E. Lee—now undoubtedly greatest icon of them all—was held in some contempt, was unknown to many, was called "Granny" Lee by others for what were deemed his slow, tentative ways.

Better acquainted associates knew or suspected his fighting qualities . . . but not everyone, not yet.

In part, it was his own fault for being so gentlemanly in manner, true. And he indeed had begun his Civil War career as a deskbound planner, rather than a field commander. He had experienced combat in the Mexican War, true, and he was in charge of the military unit sent, pell mell, to arrest John Brown at Harpers Ferry in 1859, but all small-unit action, however successful—small potatoes in scope. Otherwise, his background largely was in engineering, defensive fortifications, and the like. A West Pointer himself, he had been superintendent of West Point for a time, true . . . but again, it was not the equivalent of major field command in war.

At the outset of the Civil War he became commander of Virginia's forces, initiated their recruitment and training and began gathering a coterie of brilliant officers such as Thomas J. "Stonewall" Jackson. With First Bull Run in July 1861, the Confederate forces showed they could win battles. The resultant acclaim went to the two commanders with the troops—Pierre Gustav Toutant Beauregard and Joseph Johnston. Lee, chained to his desk in

Richmond, was not on hand, although Jefferson Davis, President of the Confederacy, had gone up to Manassas to see things for himself. It was Lee's planning, in significant part, that positioned the Confederate forces, and the training programs he had instituted that prepared many of the troops for their first combat, but few were aware . . . he did not, in all the excitement, receive public credit. And yet, when the Southern forces failed to chase the Union troops into Washington and perhaps lost opportunity for a bold stroke ending the war, Lee was criticized for not seizing that opportunity.

Hardly had the smoke cleared than Lee, as an aide and advisor to Jefferson Davis, was dispatched on a thankless errand that would not—repeat, NOT—redound to his credit as a commander of men.

He was sent into the mountains of southwest Virginia to "iron out the differences between Generals Henry A. Wise and John B. Floyd, two temperamental former governors of the state, and General W.W. Loring," writes Virginius Dabney in his *Virginia: The New Dominion*. Lee's charge was to achieve coordination among the three separate commands and to end the various rivalries among the three generals, and yet Lee did not have real authority over the "feuding prima donnas," adds Dabney. The gracious and genteel Lee probably was the wrong man to send on this errand—"What was needed was a knocking together of heads rather than attempts at tactful persuasion . . . "

Unsurprisingly, he was unable to achieve the harmony needed among the three commanders. Thus, "when many of Virginia's western counties went over to the enemy that winter, Lee got much of the blame."

And perhaps fairly so. "Lee's gentlemanliness, his humility, his unwillingness to be sharply categorical and critical in expressing his views, would plague him throughout much of the war."

Meanwhile, now fully bearded for the first time, Lee returned to his Richmond desk job accompanied by "sneers from the press, which referred to him derisively as 'Granny' Lee and 'Evacuating' Lee."

His next assignment also lacked the color and sometime

glory of combat command—he was sent south for the tedious work of developing fortifications for Charleston, Savannah, and the North Carolina coast, returning to Richmond once again in March of 1862. By now, writes Dabney, "His reputation with the public was in tatters, and few could have foretold the future that awaited him."

The Union's George McClellan, meanwhile, had mounted his Peninsula campaign (between the James and York Rivers), intended to reach and seize the Confederate capital of Richmond . . . eventually. The slow-moving and overly cautious McClellan had been sparring for some weeks with the Confederate field commander, Joseph Johnston, with neither one of the two finding the bold stroke necessary to knock the other out of the game.

McClellan, ironically enough, had seized upon White House Landing on the Pamunkey River, 20 miles east of Richmond, and turned it into a "small city of supply," in the words of Virginia historian Clifford Dowdey. Circles within circles—the plantation here once belonged to George Washington's wife Martha Custis, and it now belonged, by inheritance, to Robert E. Lee's son "Rooney." At the moment McClellan seized upon it as a supply depot and staging base, moreover, Lee's wife, Mary Custis Lee—a war refugee since being forced to leave her Arlington House to Federal troops the year before—was staying at her son's plantation on the Pamunkey River. McClellan, though, graciously allowed her to pass through the lines with an officer escort to her own side—a relief for the distantly onlooking but helpless Lee.

The McClellan-Johnston sparring finally led in a few more weeks' time to the clash of giants, Johnston's 60,000 men versus McClellan's 100,000 overall, at Fair Oaks, just a few miles east of Richmond. Johnston, though, was twice wounded on the first day of battle, and Gustavus Smith, second in command, was not well enough to take over. Unshackled from his desk at last, Lee was sent forward to salvage the situation at the gates of Richmond.

What then followed was Lee's surprisingly aggressive, often brilliant leadership in the Seven Days Battle that forced McClellan to give up his dream of seizing Richmond, although, true, Lee of necessity began his new stewardship by digging in—now being dubbed the "King of Spades" as a result.

By the end of the Seven Days, however, Robert E. Lee had acquired an entirely new image—attacking again and again, albeit at great cost in human lives, he had saved Richmond. In the process, he had created his famous Army of Northern Virginia, which he would command for the rest of the war and take into Maryland and even Pennsylvania before it was all over.

In the meantime, as various innovations made their appearance, a Lee-inspired siege gun placed on a railroad flatcar now came into action under his subordinate John Magruder—"the first piece of railroad artillery ever used in warfare," according to historian Dowdey.

Observation balloons already had made their debut, and down in Hampton Roads the Confederacy's *Virginia* (originally the frigate *Merrimac*) and the Union's *Monitor* had traded blows (neither one greatly harmed) in history's first duel between ironclads. In like vein, the Confederacy soon would develop a submarine vessel; the belligerents would sow roads with "torpedoes" (early mines, actually), and the Gatling gun would just miss widespread use as an early "machine gun."

In sum, a new kind of warfare was dawning, added challenge for the gentlemanly Lee, whom Dowdey aptly named a product of "old America." Wrote Dowdey, too, of the watershed moment when Lee took command: "At the Seven Days, when the Army of Northern Virginia was born, the old America died, and the Union [that] Lincoln and McClellan tried to restore became as lost in time as the traditional society [that] Lee sought to preserve."

STIRRING WORDS FOUND

Mine eyes have seen . . . it was dark and before the dawn one morning in Washington, D.C., just two city blocks from the Lincoln White House, when the New York-born woman in a hotel room took up pen and began to write down the words.

Mine eyes have seen the glory of the coming of the Lord;

For days she had struggled to find those words. For days she had seen the soldiers from her hotel window; she had heard the tramp-tramp of marching feet and she had heard and re-heard their old camp-meeting song, again and again. Only they called it "John Brown's Body," in reference to the crazed abolitionist who had tried to seize the U.S. Army arsenal at Harpers Ferry in 1859.

Now, in 1861, Julia Ward Howe hardly needed the Reverend James Freeman Clarke's urging to write fresh lyrics for the haunting tune that the soldiers obviously loved so well. "I have often prayed that I might," she told Clarke, who was with Julia and her husband, Dr. Samuel Gridley Howe, on a visit to Washington and the 12th Massachusetts Infantry Regiment. The Howes were Boston residents, and Clarke was their pastor.

The fact is, Dr. Howe was far better known at the time than his wife Julia. A committed human rights activist, this proper Bostonian had spent time in a Prussian prison while attempting to help Polish refugees; he had spent six years of his life as a fleet surgeon and even guerrilla fighter with Greeks fighting Turks, and at home he had taken up the cause of the insane and retarded, the blind and the deaf. It was only natural, then, that he would seek out and marry a woman who was a committed feminist, peace advocate and abolitionist, becoming, with her, co-editor of the anti-slavery journal *The Commonwealth*. After taking up wife Julia's great cause, Samuel Howe plunged into activities such as working against the forced return of escaped slaves, joining hands with the Free-Soilers of Kansas, even developing vague ties with John Brown . . . ties close enough to force Howe to flee to Canada after the Harpers Ferry affair.

With the Civil War underway by 1861, however, he was back home and serving as a New England regional director of the U. S. Sanitary Commission, that good agency that sent doctors and nurses into Union-held battle zones to care for the wounded and injured of either side.

He had been dispatched to Washington by the governor of Massachusetts to make sure the Commonwealth's young soldiers were being taken care of in proper and healthy fashion. Julia and the Reverend Clarke accompanied him, and it was from her

Willard's Hotel window that she could see the Union campfires dotting the city environs every evening, could hear the tramp of many thousands of feet, could catch the strain of that song afloat in the air, again and again. Quite often it took the form of a march, thanks to the adaption by the bandmaster of the 12th Massachusetts, it is said.

The tune cried for more acceptable, stirring words.

She awoke one of those tumultuous, early-in-the-war mornings in Washington, not far from where slept Lincoln, awoke an hour or so before dawn, the room still dark. The words suddenly had come! As a mother, she had learned beforehand how to write down her thoughts in the darkness of the children's nursery at home, and she now snatched up both pen and a piece of paper—stationery from her husband's Sanitary Commission. She scribbled rapidly, before the words forming in her head, marching to the distant drumbeat, could fly, fly away. They didn't, and soon her lyrics had flown across the country, had soared in a million hearts.

How far and wide did her song travel, how lasting was it? At Libby Prison in Richmond two years later, in mid-1863, a black well-wisher slipped word to the Union prisoners held there of the great victory at Gettysburg. They sang in thankful jubilation— they sang Julia Ward Howe's *Battle Hymn of the Republic*, its new words by now well known, repeatedly sung and even published for all to see, learn or memorize, in the *Atlantic*. And in Washington itself not long after, a former prisoner from Libby Prison told an audience one time of that memorable and moving moment at the prison. The storyteller, a chaplain McCabe of the 122nd Ohio, then sang Julia Ward Howe's song before the Washington audience, a rendition so heartfelt that onlookers shouted, wept, sang with him and burst into wild applause when it was over. And Lincoln . . . Lincoln, too, was there, *exclaiming*, wrote Julia's daughters many years later, exclaiming, "Sing it again!" And "the tears rolled down his cheeks."

JACKSON'S ODD FAILURE

It never has been fully explained, and many of Thomas J. "Stonewall" Jackson's fellow Southern officers could not quite forgive him for his lethargy, delays and downright nutty behavior when called to the aid of Robert E. Lee in defense of Richmond in June of 1862. After all, here was the man labelled "Stonewall" for his forthright stand at First Bull Run hardly a year previous; here was the brilliant leader fresh from running rings around the Federal foe in the Shenandoah Valley campaign, probably just as famous among military men and historians today as Napoleon's First Italian campaign.

Here was the great, if eccentric, leader all right, on his way to take urgent place in Lee's line-up for the first real counteroffensive against the massive Federal foe threatening from just six to ten miles outside of Richmond. Here was the genius of the Valley campaign, missing from Lee's line-up, at the middle of one day taking to a chair on a porch, reading a novel briefly, then going inside for a nap!

E. Porter Alexander, probably the leading artillerist of the Confederacy and a superb postwar memoir-writer, stated that difficult-to-forgive case against Jackson most bluntly. "Lee's instructions to him were very brief and general, in supreme confidence that the Jackson of the Valley would win even brighter laurels on the Chickahominy River east of Richmond," wrote Alexander later. Jackson's role was made easy for him, Alexander maintained. "The shortest route was assigned to him and the largest force was given him. Lee then took himself off to the farthest flank, as if generously to leave to Jackson the opportunity of the most brilliant victory of the war."

And what did Jackson do in response? He repeatedly turned up late for his assignments, or not all. Alexander asserted: "His failure is not so much a military as a psychological phenomenon. He did not try and fail. He simply made no effort . . . He spent the 29th of June 1862 in camp in disregard of Lee's instructions, and he spent the 30th in equal idleness at White Oak Swamp. His 25,000 infantry practically did not fire a shot in the two days."

Jackson's delays, naturally, were soon noticed by his companion commanders in the field, as Lee unfurled his battleplan to push and shove George McClellan's great host away from Richmond in what became known as the Seven Days Battle. John Magruder, for instance, informed by Lee that Jackson would be crossing the Chickahominy alongside Magruder's own command, was stunned to hear from a subordinate, "I had hoped that Jackson would have cooperated with me on my left, but he sends me word that he cannot, as he has other important duty to perform."

Possibly, Alexander surmised, Jackson on one day was holding off because it was Sunday, the Sabbath, and Jackson was known to be fanatically religious. But in the past he had fought on Sundays.

As his part in Lee's plans to *discourage* McClellan from Richmond and its precincts, Jackson was expected to join in the battle opening the Seven Days affair on June 26, his assignment to flank the Federal right and cut off McClellan's umbilical cord to the huge Union supply depot at White House Landing on the Pumunkey River near West Point, Virginia.

It was an extraordinary gamble that Lee had devised. With McClellan and his superior numbers obviously preparing to besiege Richmond and pound the city with huge guns that could only be moved up by rail or by barge, Lee would leave a token force demonstrating at his newly dug fortifications and attack the Federal left with the divisions headed by A.P Hill, James Longstreet and D.H. Hill. The risk was that McClellan might see through Lee's ruse and walk into Richmond past the defensive line with small token force to be maintained by "Prince John" Magruder. In addition, Lee was willing to split his army and advance on either side of the Chickahominy with its swamps and tributaries, a plan making coordination difficult. Luckily for all, McClellan was so timorous that he never saw his great opportunity—instead, in wailing tones, he repeatedly asked Washington for more and more reinforcements and, in the end, predicted his far from irrevocable defeat.

In the meantime, Jackson inexplicably did not appear at his assigned "jump-off" position on June 26, and A.P. Hill launched his portion of Lee's counteroffensive without waiting any longer. That rash move dragged along Longstreet and D.H. Hill in support, and Lee was thus committed to his plan without all his commanders in place.

Jackson at last arrived, 12 hours late, but perhaps he could still carry his part of the attack the next morning. In the meantime, A.P. Hill's attack was repulsed, but McClellan was alarmed enough to prepare for possible movement of his vulnerable supply base to Harrison's Landing on the James River below Richmond.

The next day, June 27, Jackson was again late in taking position, but the Confederates at last mounted an advance that was concerted for the most part, and by nightfall collapsed the Federal right as originally planned. McClellan that night made the fateful decision to retreat to the James. A long-tailed column of 100,000 or more men by this time, the Federal host began its rearward march the very next day, June 28, with the White House landing base left to the Rebs once again.

Here, Lee was presented with opportunity to pursue and strike a harsh blow destroying the Union's greatest army on the spot—in the river swamps east of Richmond. But things kept going awry for the Confederacy's newly appointed field commander, even in the midst of a strategically great victory.

Lee briefly lost contact with McClellan, and it wasn't clear for some hours that the Federal commander actually was headed for the James. Then, in mounting pursuit at last, Lee was frustrated by the mistakes of his subordinates (not only Jackson, but other subordinate commanders as well). As stated by historian Bruce Catton in his *Terrible Swift Sword*, "Magruder proved an inexpert tactician, [Benjamin] Huger moved much too slowly, and Jackson, most inexplicably, missed a crucial assignment."

And so, by July 1, "the head of the Federal column had reached Harrison's Landing and the protecting gunboats [out on the James River waters] . . . " When Lee caught up at Malvern Hill, the Federal guns on the high ground were simply too much for the attacking Confederates—"that afternoon and evening saw one of the most tragic and hopeless attacks of the war, with Magruder's and D.H. Hill's divisions and elements from other commands trying heroically to do the impossible," adds Catton's account. Throughout the Seven Days, quite obviously from all accounts, Stonewall Jackson had not covered himself with glory. Years later, in fact, South Carolina's rough, tough cavalryman Wade Hampton would inform Porter Alexander of a visit to Jackson at a crucial point in the Seven Days to tell Jackson he had complied with orders to build a temporary infantry bridge over a small stream in their path. A key Federal force could be attacked just beyond.

Hampton said he found Jackson seated on a fallen pine and made his report. "He drew his cap down over his eyes, which were closed and after listening to me for some minutes, he rose without speaking . . . " Hampton's complaint was that if Jackson had proceeded, they might have defeated the Federal force just beyond, and thus the "Federal army would have been destroyed . . . "

Jackson's own brother-in-law, D.H. (Daniel Harvey) Hill, on the other hand, sought to explain his "inaction" by blaming the exhausting rigors his troops had been through in their Valley campaign, his pity for his own men, and their reduced numbers. "He thought that the garrison of Richmond ought now to bear the brunt of the fighting."

To which Alexander retorted, in his *Military Memoir of a Confederate*, that the veterans of the long Peninsula Campaign "had suffered just as many hardships and done even more severe fighting, as the casualties will attest."

Further argued Alexander, to show a natural pity or affection for one's own men "by shirking battle" was "no real kindness to them, apart from the tremendous consequences to the army and the nation." In sum Jackson's failure was a "lapse of duty."

It wasn't long before the "old Jackson" reasserted himself and fought with skill and bravery by Lee's side up to his flanking movement at Chancellorsville a year later that won the battle . . . but cost Jackson his own life, after his wounding by his own troops who fired into the darkness while he returned from a reconnaissance in front of them.

And so what did happen to the rightly vaunted Stonewall outside of Richmond in June of 1862?

Perhaps historian Clifford Dowdey was on the correct trail

when, in the 1960s, he investigated the latest medical findings on the effects of stress. As he pointed out in his 1964 book *The Seven Days: The Emergence of Lee*, Jackson had been under extreme stress for the ten weeks of his whirlwind Shenandoah Valley campaign. When he led his forces to Richmond in response to Lee's call, "not only were his naturally limited physical powers extended . . . but his total organism [had been] exposed to the prolonged stress of danger, sustained alertness and the urgent need of constant decisions affecting the cause he represented as well as the lives of the men entrusted to him."

It did not help Jackson's condition that on his way to Richmond he left his marching columns to ride ahead by horseback—"he foolishly made the fourteen-hour night ride to Richmond from 1 a.m. to late afternoon on the 23rd, and then, without rest or food—taking only a glass of milk—made the return ride through a second night from about seven in the evening until mid-morning of the 24th."

All that was exhausting enough, but no doubt, as Dowdey adds, "His judgment had already been affected when he made the all-night rides on successive nights." In Dowdey's view, Jackson was the victim of stress exhaustion, his mental and physiological resources already depleted beforehand. Still, "In Stonewall Jackson's world, no general would have considered such an ailment as stress fatigue, even if he had been aware of the reactions to stress." While all certainly knew the effects of strain and loss of sleep, "a leader was supposed to be above the limitations of the flesh . . ."

Obviously, not even a Stonewall Jackson could be that superhuman. Wrung out by his Valley exertions, he simply had been asked to resume the strain of march, command and battle too soon . . . too soon again.

HELLO, RICHMOND

For Richmond, these were giddy, crowded days. High drama side by side with everyday events. Real, classical tragedy together with the pathos and even the occasional human comedy. And all so tightly packed into short, short time-frame.

One potentially bright moment in the capital of the new and separate country was the inauguration of Jefferson Davis as Permanent President, no longer provisional. But . . . an event not quite as gay as the prior ceremony held in Montgomery, Alabama, the year before. For one thing, it was pouring down rain on this bleak 22nd of February in 1862 (George Washington's birthday, at that). The umbrellas of the assembled crowd struck the onlooking Constance Cary as "an immense mushroom bed." Wrote this teen-aged girl also, "As the bishop and the President-elect came upon the stand, there was almost a painful hush in the crowd." They felt the gravity of the occasion and although a shout went up when Davis "kissed the Book," the crowd quickly dispersed with no real show of elation.

And then there was that awful story about Mrs. Davis— Varina—on her way to the inauguration that day. Her coachman drove her carriage at "snail's pace", reported Constance Cary later, and escorting her were four more black men, two to a side, all wearing white gloves and black clothing, all stepping slowly and somberly. It was just like a funeral procession, and indeed, the coachman said he thought that's what she wanted. "This is the way we do in Richmond at funerals and sich-like," he explained.

Earlier that winter, horrible weather had afflicted the Old Dominion, and in January scarlet fever had struck Richmond, a lethal threat to any child. Confederate General James Longstreet was in northern Virginia opposite the Federal lines when he received word to hurry to his family's side in Richmond. Wife Louise and their four children were staying with friends . . . and all four youngsters had come down with the fever.

Longstreet arrived in the capital in the final days of January, just in time to see their 12-month-old Mary Anne lose her battle with the disease. A day later, January 26, James, only four, died. And after him, on February 1, six-year-old Augustus succumbed as well. Only 13-year-old Garland survived the fever's onslaught. The Longstreets were so devastated that Brigadier General George Pickett, later to lead Pickett's Charge at

Gettysburg, had to make the funeral arrangements. They say that Longstreet was never the same again, and little wonder.

Soon, Richmond itself heard the not-so-distant sound of guns. As May was about to give way to June, the weather at least no longer bleak, the Battle of Seven Pines (Fair Oaks) began. It was May 31, and, "Every heart leaped as if deliverance were at hand," noted the teenaged Cary girl. As the same time, she added, "Hardly a family in the town whose father, son or brother was not part and parcel of the defending army."

For the city's civilians, its leaders, war planners and soldiers alike, darkness brought a pause in the cannon fire, but they slept that night "lying down dressed upon beds." Early next morning, "the whole town was on the street."

For now came the wounded, in from the great battle just beyond the city. "Ambulances, litters, carts, every vehicle that the city could produce went and came with a ghastly burden; those who could walk limped painfully home, in some cases so black with gunpowder they passed unrecognized." By afternoon, "the streets were one vast hospital." In homes and other buildings, hastily converted into temporary hospitals, mutilated men suffered or died . . . or both.

A couple of days after the "first flurry of distress," the young diarist saw "flitting about the streets" and hurrying to the hospitals from the homes of the affluent, "smiling, white-jacketed negroes, carrying silver trays with dishes of fine porcelain under napkins of thick white damask, containing soups, creams, jellies, thin bisquit [sic], eggs a la creme, broiled chicken, etc., surmounted by clusters of freshly gathered flowers."

Then, too, "day after day we were called to our windows by the wailing dirge of a military band preceding a soldier's funeral." *Day after day*. "One could not number those sad pageants: the coffin crowned with cap and sword and gloves, the riderless horse following with empty boots fixed in the stirrups . . . "

It wasn't always thus, of course. In the early days, only a year before, Richmond's beginnings as a new nation's wartime capital were heady, confusing, thrilling. "Noise of drums, tramps of marching regiments all day long, rattling of artillery wagons, bands of music, friends from every quarter coming in," wrote noted diarist Mary Chesnut back in July 1861. "We ought to be miserable and anxious, and yet these are pleasant days. Perhaps we are unnaturally exhilarated and excited."

Perhaps so. "A young Carolinian with queer ideas of a joke rode his horse through the barroom of this hotel [the Spotswood]. How he scattered people and things right and left!"

Then too, right after news of the Federal defeat at First Bull Run, Mary Chesnut could report: "Mrs. [Jefferson] Davis' drawing room last night was brilliant, and she was in great force. Outside a mob collected and called for the president. He did speak. He is an old war-horse—and scents the battlefields from afar. His enthusiasm was contagious . . . "

And a few days after that: "At the fairgrounds today—such music and mustering and marching—such cheering and flying of flags. Such firing of guns and all that sort of thing. A gala day: double distilled 4th of July feeling." Only it was August 1, 1861, in the capital of the Confederacy. And soon, the joyful event, the glad excitement, would give way more and more often to grim tidings, friends and relatives with wounds, others widowed or dead, depending upon their gender.

Mary Chesnut's fellow South Carolinian Frank Hampton died at Brandy Station, largest cavalry engagement ever staged in North America. She and several other ladies visited their fallen soldier's open coffin at the State Capitol. "How I wished I had not looked! I remember him so well in all the pride of his magnificent manhood. He died of a saber cut across the face and head and was utterly disfigured."

In Richmond, too, despite the united war effort, not all was harmony among the principals. There came a moment of tension, for instance, between Longstreet and General Ambrose Powell Hill (A.P. Hill), both West Point graduates, both among the generals responsible for the Confederate victory in the Seven Days campaign outside Richmond in June 1862. A Richmond newspaper editor, greatly impressed by the Virginia-born Hill, wrote a series of articles giving Hill *exclusive* credit for a major aspect of the Southern victory. Longstreet, outraged and feeling publicly humiliated, persuaded a more-than-willing aide to write to a rival paper pointing out the discrepancy.

Hill, upon that report reaching the public, felt humiliated in his turn . . . and so the affair went, with Hill asking to be transferred out of Longstreet's command, then ignoring, then *refusing* a Longstreet order, then being placed under house arrest. He finally challenged fellow Confederate general Longstreet to a duel, but Robert E. Lee at last stepped into the dispute and ordered Hill transferred to Stonewall Jackson's command at Gordonsville.

That cooled the argument, but Hill naturally still visited Richmond from time to time. On one such occasion, he was called into the chamber of the Virginia House of Delegates to receive an official accolade from that body for his battlefield prowess.

Another time, all Richmond was agog over the visit of a Confederate hero—and brother-in-law to Hill—who recently had escaped from Union custody, John Hunt Morgan, the cavalry raider revered for his breakout from the Ohio State Penitentiary.

Hill, accompanied by "Jeb" Stuart and Georgia's John B. Gordon, visited the Confederate capital in early January of 1864 to greet the famous Kentuckian. They appeared at a public reception in front of the Richmond City Hall at noontime one day, and the next day Hill and Morgan visited Richmond's Libby Prison to chat with Union prisoners held there. They attended church with fellow Confederate officers on still the next day, at St. Paul's Episcopal. Morgan next would pay a visit of his own to the Virginia legislature and appear at a ball held in the Ballard House.

Diarist Mary Chesnut mentions the Morgan visit, which also included the former Vice President of the United States, John Breckinridge, now a Confederate general and soon, in less than a year's time, to be the Confederacy's Secretary of War. She saw Richmond Mayor Joseph Mayo introduce Morgan at the City Hall affair. "These huge Kentuckians fill the town," she wrote. Shortly after, she added: "The City of Richmond entertains John Morgan. HQ is at free quarters. Tonight [January 12] there will be a great gathering of the Kentuckians. Morgan gives them a dinner."

She had known Morgan's wife, the former Mattie Ready, before the war. "A graceful girl and a Kentucky belle in Washington during the winter of 1859. We were glad to meet again once more under altered skies."

All was not so festive this same week in the Jefferson Davis household, though. Two slaves, a man and a woman, had fled. "The president's man Jim that he believed in, as we all believe in our own servants—'our own people' as we are apt to call them—and Betsy, Mrs. Davis' maid, decamped last night," wrote Mary Chesnut on January 9 or 10, 1864. Saying it was a miracle that the pair had resisted temptation so long, Chesnut added: "I do not think it had ever crossed Mrs. D's brain that these two would leave her." Richmond during the war. City under siege, city of visiting heroes and escaping slaves. City of riderless horses and funeral dirges. And . . . circles within circles. Said Mary Chesnut's own maid (and slave) Molly: "I like Mrs. Davis, but Betsy did give herself such airs because she was Mrs. President's maid."

Loyalty Charge Dismissed

It was "an evil hour," Justice George M. Savage of Henrico County, Virginia, told the court in adjoining Richmond—an evil hour when, sorely tempted, he did "take the hated oath."

But then, the circumstances had been mitigating to large degree, and perhaps his fellow Southerners could forgive and forget. He had succumbed to temptation at a moment of great duress involving not only himself but his family.

It all began, it seems, on Friday, May 23, 1862, the eve of the Battle of Fair Oaks that led to the Seven Days campaign, which in turn ended the Union Peninsula campaign.

Explained Henrico farmer-citizen-justice Savage: "Two Yankee pickets came to my door and enquired for milk and butter; I told them I had none to spare. They then enquired as to when our pickets left. I replied; I did not know exactly. One was very insolent, remarking that the rebels were cowards and would not stand. I replied that that was a matter on which we could not agree. They very soon left."

One thing led to another, as the Yankees very next day arrived in force, "some coming into the house and insulting me and my family."

After a skirmish took place about a mile away, the Northern visitors "appeared with their wounded." Savage told them they could not use his house as a hospital but they were welcome to his barn.

On Sunday, May 25, Union Major General Erasmus D. Keyes (and staff) appeared as well. Polite, Keyes said he would like to use the house as his headquarters, and to this Savage did not object. "He then introduced the subject of this war. I replied that on this subject I did not care to converse, as I was sure we would not agree."

But Keyes insisted, and Savage then stated his pro-Southern views "frankly and fearlessly as I have over and over again expressed them among my own people."

Keyes was so impressed, he turned to his staff and declared, "This gentleman is an honest and candid man, and I wish you to see that his property is thoroughly protected."

Unfortunately, Keyes soon left, to be replaced by Union Major General Samuel P. Heinzelman.

Until now, the situation for Savage and his family had not been *all* bad. His crops and his property "were not much damaged," and the Union officers, "with some exceptions, were tolerably civil." At same time, "I could not at any time go fifty yards from my house without being denounced by the men as a 'damned rebel and secesh.' "

Then came the Battle of Fair Oaks on May 31, when Joseph Johnston counterattacked the Union's George McClellan (with Johnston wounded and relieved of command in the process). The Yankee wounded now "came pouring in like an avalanche," recalled Savage. They just about took over the whole house, and when he appealed to the Union adjutant on the scene, that officer said, "he had no protection to give, nor did I deserve any." And, "I was a damned secessionist, and had been instrumental in bringing about this state of things and my head ought to be cut off, and the sooner I got away, the better."

118

With that warning, Savage on Monday, June 2, did send away his three children, and the next day his wife "had to leave," as well. By July 4, the day that Savage petitioned the court in Richmond to forgive him for taking the Union loyalty oath, his family still was absent from home, and the home still was being used as a hospital, although McClellan and his host of 100,000 or so had retreated from the Richmond area.

What had taken place on Savage's farm in the interim was close to indescribable. Starting with the night of May 31, he said, the Yankees "forced nearly every lock on the place and stole very nearly all my stores, together with crockery and innumerable articles of furniture, forced my corncribs and took all the corn, all long forage, ground and cut all my oats and wheat and hay, burned my enclosures of every description, destroyed my fruit trees, took the boards from my buildings for every use they could apply them, broke up and destroyed my farming implements, stole two horses, about 80 hogs, some sheep and cattle and appeared to try how much they could damage me."

Savage's wife was so distraught she twice was confined to bed, and on June 12, he, himself was taken ill. He improved, however, and on June 16 returned home—a mistake, it transpired. "On the night of that day I was arrested on the order of General McClellan, taken to his headquarters, where I remained until the next day, without being able to learn what charge there was against me."

He was told on the 17th that he would be locked up at Fort Monroe, overlooking Hampton Roads. Savage asked to see his wife first, with Federal officers present, simply to let her know what was happening to him. Otherwise, he said, in her delicate health, his incarceration could have serious impact on her. When the Federals refused Savage's request, he caved in, "profoundly convinced that to be taken up under these circumstances would kill my wife." He caved in and took the Union oath, but "without kissing the Book" and while declaring his allegiance still lay with the South.

That apparently satisfied his Yankee tormentors (who had visited similar destruction upon the Henrico County farm of a free black woman named Isabella Adams), but he next had to defend himself before the court in Richmond against the charge of disloyalty to the Confederacy. In his court paper Savage earnestly and formally said: "I do here declare that I have not at any time up to this hour knowingly said or done anything the least prejudicial to the Southern cause, and that all my sympathies, interest and feelings, are today, as ever, with the South and I now hold myself ready and willing to do whatever the interests or laws of the Confederacy may require of me, and in conclusion I do hereby declare upon my honor and conscience that at the time of taking the [Union] oath I did not regard it, nor do I now regard it, as binding upon me, but laboring under a profound conviction that the life of my wife would be sacrificed, leaving three little children in the power of a merciless enemy, I was tempted in an evil hour to take the hated oath."

So be it, charge of disloyalty to the Confederate dismissed . . . by order of the court!

POIGNANT MOMENTS IN BATTLE

Here was fighting indeed. Confederates on the offensive, Union men on the defensive, in large and strategic sense. But tactically, as the men actually collided in the field, it was the men in blue who had sortied out at the moment, who were on the attack. Small arms and artillery traded shots. The Confederate mounted infantry at one point climbed down from their steeds—some of them mules—to repel the Union infantry that had crossed the river between the two forces.

"As we were in the act of dismounting," wrote Virginia-born Alfred U. Peticolas, lawyer and future judge serving his "Victoria Invincibles" as sergeant, "[B.A.] Jones' horse was shot in the thigh, [Sergeant Charles A.] Wooapple's was crippled, and a ball tore a small peel of skin from my right thumb, which bled profusely."

But Confederate Sergeant Peticolas hadn't seen anything yet!

This was war, and war truly is hell. The enemy approached

in strength just 600 yards away from where he and his compatriots had take position lying under the bank of the river. The men in blue were firing most rapidly. The shooting "began to play havoc with our horses." Sam Hyatt's went down, Louis J. Berkowitz' went down, and so did a number of others. And next came the men themselves. "One man on my left . . . was shot through the back, as he raised to load, by a flank fire, and fell with heart rending groans." Amazingly, though, the same man had directed a companion to load his gun, then . . . "he [the wounded soldier] fired at them again, although he had a wound which proved mortal."

Peticolas, himself, was loading and shooting as fast as he could while also taking careful aim at his quarry, though "their balls whistled with deadly intent around my head," Nearby others were hit. Corporal Al Field took a wound in the arm and exclaimed, "Oh, God, I'm shot." A man named S. Schmidt was struck in both upper legs by a single Minié ball, but by far the most grotesque casualty was William H. Onderdonk, who was struck in the mouth, "his tongue nearly shot out." The wounded Onderdonk certainly must have felt desperate. As Peticolas tells the story, "He pulled out a part of it [the mouth, the tongue or other tissue] which was hanging ragged . . . and cut it off with his knife."

As Onderdonk was carried off the field, the fight went on. The Rebs were shooting with greater accuracy than their Yankee brothers, and soon the Blues were driven back across the river. The Confederate howitzers "opened upon their retiring column with killing effect, and they broke lines and ran back out of range."

One of the Confederate soldiers asked his captain's permission to go forward and kill a wounded Yank who was still shooting from behind a tree. Captain David Nunn assented, but the wounded Union man then "begged so hard" that he was merely disarmed.

The fight was not yet over. All around were dead and wounded horses. Sergeant Peticolas' own mule was shivering from the effects of a wound that proved fatal once the battle was over.

The Confederates now regrouped—both sides in fact spent considerable time simply maneuvering for position. The Confederates present numbered about 2,000 and the Union force 2,000 also. About eveningtime, the Yankees crossed the river, artillery in tow, and advanced in strength. Their eight guns were heavier than the Confederate force's four six-pounders, and their small arms were longer-range pieces, too. "As long as we laid behind the sand banks our own lives were in comparative safety," wrote Peticolas in his journal, but "every few moments some one would be wounded or killed and our horses were being badly shot to pieces."

Soon six of the Union guns were brought up within "point blank range of us and began to play grape and shell upon us." In response, the Reb battery commanded by Captain Travonian Teel moved two guns to within ten yards of where Peticolas was lying and began firing back at the Union guns. "And now the battle was indeed hot."

Hot, and on the left the Confederates slowly but surely were being driven back, back . . . and back. "In two minutes, a raking fire up our line on the side of the bank would slay the last man of us. The bombs and grape were bursting and flying all around us and [nearby] Colonel [Thomas] Green, and sweeping the trees and the bottom far behind us."

It was a critical moment, and Green, a regimental commander, realized it. "We must charge that battery, boys," he said, and when some of the men before him instead ran for their horses to flee, he chased after them while shouting: "Back, men, back! Would you disgrace yourself and your country here? Remember you are Texans!" For most were that, Texans.

With other officers sounding the same call to charge, about 200 of the Johnny Rebs ("a mere handful," said Peticolas) responded. "[They] started up and with a wild yell dashed forward through the shower of Minié balls and grape toward the belching cannon and solid lines of infantry supporting them [the cannon]." Major Samuel A. Lockridge, "a heart of iron," led the Confederate charge, with three captains close behind brandishing their sabers and shouting, "Come on my boys, don't stop here."

The short-range Reb guns now were felling the Yankees at such pace that they wavered, then turned and ran, "and we poured in our deadly fire upon them."

Then came one of the most poignant moments of the battle.

Major Lockridge, reaching a Union cannon, put his hand on it and exclaimed, "This is mine!"

"At that moment he was shot dead," wrote Peticolas later. "His last words were: 'Go on my boys, don't stop here!'"

The Yankees had a poignant moment of their own, as they defended their artillery battery, "brave to the last," in the words of Peticolas. So brave were the men of Captain Alexander McRae's battery that one of them touched off the ammunition in a battery caisson just as the Rebs swept into the battery's position, sacrificing his own life in the process.

"Two guns were loaded when we took them," wrote Peticolas. "A gunner was just about to touch one off. One of our men, who had just killed one of the artillery men, was up on the caisson. He leveled his pistol at the gunner, who in an instant thrust his fuse into the caisson box, which blew up with a dread explosion."

By other accounts of the same action, McRae, himself Southern-born, saw and heard Major Lockridge and supposedly shouted at his Union troops, "shoot the son of a bitch!" Which someone quickly did. Then, too, a Union soldier from Colorado recalled the second part of the battery incident narrated by Peticolas: "When the battery was gone," wrote the Union survivor, "one of the battery boys sprang up on a magazine which was near, cried 'Victory or death' and then coolly fired his pistol into the ammunition. One long, loud crash and all was over for that brave boy."

So it went in the fighting of the Civil War, not only in the East or along the Mississippi and in adjoining states, but also in the far Southwest. For in the Battle of Valverde of February 21, 1862, the river in question was the Rio Grande, and the territory being fought over was New Mexico. The winner, for this moment in the New Mexico campaign, mounted by the South's hard-drinking, blustering adventurer-general Henry H. Sibley, was . . . well, no one in particular. The losers, though, were the 170 killed and 310 wounded, casualties distributed about equally to each side.

Unnecessary Tragedies

Murders three . . . It was late September 1862, and in the Galt House hostelry in Louisville, Kentucky, a coterie of Federal flag rank officers was astir between 7 and 8 o'clock in the morning. Their overall commander, Don Carlos Buell, had not yet gone downstairs for breakfast, reports Roy Morris, Jr. in his *Sheridan: The Life and Wars of General Phil Sheridan*. Among those staying at the Galt House was a longtime U.S. Navy officer-turned Army general, William "Bull" Nelson, who had led a reinforcing division at Shiloh the previous spring. Another general on hand, brooding over running clashes with his superior, Nelson, was the lesser-ranking Brigadier General Jefferson Columbus Davis.

"Bull", it seems, was an apt nickname for the hulking, sharp-tongued Nelson, described by Civil War historian Morris as "coarse, profane and physically imposing." He could easily offend, it seems further, "neither noticing nor caring what impression he left in his bullish wake."

The North's Jefferson Davis also had enjoyed a lengthy military career, starting with the Mexican War of the 1840s, but at low rank for most of the time. He had been vaulted from lieutenant to colonel at the outset of the Civil War by his good friend in high office, Governor Oliver P. Morton of Indiana. Serving in the battles of Booneville, Missouri, and Pea Ridge, Arkansas, he then joined Buell's command in defense of Louisville . . . and a series of confrontations with Bull Nelson soon followed. Their dispute had led Nelson to order Davis "out of town" toward the end of summer 1862, recalls Morris in his biography of their fellow Union officer Phil Sheridan (uninvolved in the unhappy affair).

But Davis, obviously, was very much *in* town the early morning of September 29. "At the prompting of his close friend, the ubiquitous Governor Morton," writes Morris, "Davis had approached Nelson that morning and demanded an apology."

Nelson, unarmed, was not to be cowed in the least. "Go away, you damned puppy," he bellowed. "I don't want anything to do with you." Davis reacted immediately. He had "nervously" been crumpling up a calling card in one hand, and now he "angrily flipped it into Nelson's face." Nelson reacted, too. He smacked Davis in the face, sending his fellow general reeling backward.

"With the imprint of Nelson's hand still visible on his cheek, Davis borrowed a pistol from an obliging bystander and shot Nelson once in the chest."

For all his bulk and imposing physique, (six foot five, more than 300 pounds), Nelson was human—one bullet at close range was all that was needed to bring him down. "Tom," he said to another Union general, Thomas Crittenden, "I am murdered." His last words . . . and indeed he had been.

Davis was placed under house arrest, but he won his release by Christmastime with the posting of a $5,000 bond in Louisville. As events turned out, Davis never would be tried for the slaying of fellow Union general Nelson, thanks to the intercession of his good friend Governor Morton and the press of wartime events. Davis went on to serve in the Battles of Murfreesboro, Chickamauga, Atlanta, Savannah and the Carolinas campaign as both a division and corps commander. He remained in the Army until his death in 1879 at age 51.

* * *

Murders three . . . In the South, meanwhile, shock and consternation over another murder—an elderly white woman in South Carolina murdered by her slaves. Betsey Witherspoon was her name, and by her family's accounts, she had long pampered and "indulged" her slaves.

In mid-1861, however, the Witherspoons discovered that in her absence on a trip, her slaves had "borrowed" her china, linens, and silverware for a "ball" held some 15 miles from her Society Hill plantation. Her son John Witherspoon, visiting his mother one evening after her return, told her slave William that he would be back the next day, "and give every one of you a thrashing."

That night, his mother died in her bed . . . of natural causes, it first appeared. According to diarist Mary Boykin Chesnut, writing about her own second cousin Betsey, investigation—and the key confession of a slave—instead revealed a chilling scenario orchestrated by William.

In the middle of the night, long after the Widow Witherspoon had gone to sleep, William and her maid Rhody stole into her bedroom and smothered her with a bedspread. They thought it would appear she had simply died in her sleep, like her kinswoman Elizabeth not long before. The slaves then started to dress their victim in a clean nightgown when . . . she started up, conscious again.

Mary Boykin Chesnut does not say exactly how her cousin now died, but she does say the unfortunate woman "begged them hard for life," and, "She asked them what she had ever done that they should want to kill her. She promised before God never never to tell on them. Nobody should ever know. But Rhody stopped her mouth with the counterpane. William held her head and hands down. And the other two [slaves] sat on her legs."

Her children began to suspect foul play when they saw bruises on their mother's face and neck. They then found blood on a candlestick on her bedside table. They found bloody fingermarks on the underside of her bedspread. Further searching turned up bloody rags. Then they found that their mother's cache of gold pieces, kept in a trunk, had been stolen. Finally, a detective called to the plantation home questioned a young, frightened-looking slave named Romeo, and he "told every particular from beginning to end."

There was talk of a lynching in response but the murder victim's son John "will not allow anything wrong or violent to be done," wrote second cousin Mary Chesnut. The suspects would be "tried as the law directs." Oddly, she also noted, it was the maid Rhody who had first pointed out the blood on the bedspread. "They suppose she saw it, knew they would see it, and did it to avert suspicion from herself."

But Rhody seemed to want to call attention to herself. After the blood was found, the victim's daughter-in-law Mary Witherspoon wouldn't accept the obvious. "I wish they would not say such horrid things," she cried. "Poor soul, she died in peace with all the world. It is bad enough to find her dead. Nobody even touched a hair of her head. To think, any mortal could murder her. Never! I will not believe it."

To which, Rhody looked "strangely" into Mary's eye and

said, "Well done! Miss Mary. You stick to dat, my Missus. You stick to dat."

Postscript: The perpetrators later were convicted and hanged, Mary Chesnut also reported in her diaries of the Civil War period. And violence still begat more violence, as some time after the trial, a Captain W.H. Wingate, who had "stood by" the murderous slaves during their trial, shot and killed the victim's grandson, Captain George Williams, in cold blood, reasons unclear. By Chesnut's account, the abolition-touting Wingate came up behind Williams as he sat in a chair at a railroad station waiting to leave with his troops and shot the young officer, "before the very faces of his soldiers." No surprise that "it was very hard to rescue Wingate from the hands of George's men, who wanted to shoot him instantly." Oddly, the jury convicting this murderer recommended mercy and he merely was banished from South Carolina as his punishment.

* * *

Murders three . . . "Oh, you coward!" How many times in the course of human affairs have such words led to violence, physical injury and even death? So it was in Norfolk, Virginia, destined to be occupied by Federal troops from May 1862 until war's end, a difficult period for the port city's old-line, pro-Confederate white citizenry, to be sure. Surely they winced at the parade by local blacks upon the effective date of Lincoln's Emancipation Proclamation (January 1, 1863). And cringed, no doubt, at the sight of black women trampling the Confederate flag and at reports of an effigy of Jefferson Davis being buried in a local cemetery.

Such events, in any case, formed the background when a white Union lieutenant marched a company of black soldiers past an esteemed and widely loved physician of Norfolk, David Minton Wright.

Here was a man dedicated to saving human life, a man "who had been heroic in his treatment of patients during the deadly yellow-fever epidemic of 1855," recalls Virginius Dabney in his *Virginia: The New Dominion, A History from 1607 to the Present*. And yet, yet . . . at the sight of the Union officer and company of blacks something within the doctor snapped. Fists clenched, obviously agitated, he uttered those always fateful words. "Oh, you coward!"

The accosted officer, Lieutenant A.L. Sanborn, stopped and said, "You are under arrest."

It happened just that quick. "Whereupon Wright drew a pistol and fired twice at the Union officer, wounding him fatally. It was a rash and inexcusable act."

It was also one that would haunt Norfolk for months, even years. First, Dr. Wright underwent trial before a military commission. Next, he was convicted and even sentenced to death. Followed by a sensation! His daughter Penelope, visiting him in his jail cell, exchanged clothing with her father, and he briefly escaped.

But not for long. Discovered, he was returned to his cell, confined, and the dread plans proceeded. Finally, in October 1863, the public hanging took place in the middle of the race track in the city's fairgrounds. "Thousands watched," reports Dabney, "as was the custom in those days, but 'few old citizens could be recognized,' since the 'better classes' were said to have stayed at home." Nor was that really the end of the affair, since "his death cast a pall over Norfolk for years."

KNIGHTS OF THE REALM

Few if any schools of the 19th-century South were held in such high esteem as the University of Virginia in Charlottesville, founded within many a Southerner's own lifetime by Thomas Jefferson, and now, four decades later, a magnet for the elite of the Old South, the *plantation* South.

But let a University historian describe the students to be found on Thomas Jefferson's gorgeous campus—"Grounds" is still the proper name—at the outbreak of the war. Except for a small minority, wrote Professor Philip Alexander Bruce, the few hundred students at the University "were representative of the very best element of the Southern communities."

And how so? According to Bruce's multi-volume centennial history of the school (1818-1918), "they belonged to the widely known families which had always controlled the social and political destinies of that broad division of the country [the South]." Such prestigious background—good breeding, in effect—meant more, in his opinion, than mere social status. "Imbued to the fingertips with the free, virile, and chivalrous spirit which had been nurtured by the plantation system, they were at once democratic and aristocratic."

While that combination may seem unlikely to some, Bruce probably is correct when he notes that the young scions at the University came from a rural environment and were quite accustomed to manly pursuits such as riding horses, hunting, fishing, tramping in the countryside, and getting along in all kinds of weather.

They made good soldiers, not only because of these useful skills, and a general self-reliance in the field, but also because of their "high sense of personal honor and unshakable devotion to country." It hardly needs to be said that they held a special feeling for home and family tradition. They lived on or in properties passed down since Colonial days. "The history of these houses—their heirlooms, their surroundings, their occupations, their atmosphere—had left a permanent impression on the spirit of the young men who went straight from these thresholds to be educated in the University of Virginia."

And there was explanation for their ultimate allegiance not to Union, but to home state. "Their loyalty to their respective states," wrote historian Bruce, "was a passion as ardent as that which the Swiss felt for their mountains, or the Highlanders for their glens."

When 515 University students joined the Confederate Army in 1861, only a handful of students were left at the school, which soon became a giant de facto Confederate hospital. Of the school's 9,000 alumni as of 1865, about 2,500, or more than a fourth, "took an active part in the hostilities . . . about 500 of the University alumni perished in the service."

Many more were wounded—the students showing up later

in the Civil War period, in fact, were *recovered* wounded—young men too maimed or disabled to fight again, but still able to get around as students. The conversion to a military hospital filled the school's dormitory rooms and even Jefferson's famous Rotunda, originally the school's library. In a dormitory room, at one point, a wounded Federal prisoner languished with two recuperating "Rebs".

"Hello," said a surprised visitor one day, "how did this Yank get in here." Never mind, said the "Yank's" companions. "Leave him alone. We are brothers now through suffering."

While most of the University's casualties were 20 and over in age, quite a few were not—16 were under 20, eight under 18, nine under 17 and three under 16.

Bruce's account, at the same time, reflects a romantic glow as it turns to University heroes, after saying that *all* its sons "were equally unselfish, equally devoted, and equally brave," and *all* again, "with equal cheerfulness, offered up their lives upon the altars of their native commonwealths."

Despite his unabashed jingoism, Bruce then does tell the stories of remarkable and inspiring young men. It is significant, though, how often the allusions to knights of old crop up—and not always in his words alone.

Take young Dabney Carr Harrison, who at nine "had read Hume's *History of England*;" who at fifteen had entered the sophomore class at Princeton; who had "a countenance classical;" who by nature "was at once frank, cordial, and fearless;" who in manners was "singularly gentle and refined;" who attended law school at the University for two years, but then became a minister . . . who at 27, as war broke out, was the University's chaplain.

He remained a man of God as the war's toll mounted, especially among the First Families of the South. "The war had now begun, and in a short time, the news arrived that two of his cousins, men of brilliant promise and graduates of the University, Holmes and Tucker Conrad of Winchester, had been killed. Then followed the announcement that a third cousin, Carter H. Harrison, had fallen, then that his own brother also had perished."

That was it for University Chaplain Harrison. "'I must take

his place,' was his quiet response to this last fateful message."

As a soldier, a captain in fact, the young minister then performed with courage but said, "I can fight for my country, but I cannot hate my enemy." It was reported that he never ordered his men forward . . . he led them, from in front.

And the outcome? "He fell at last, shot through the lung, after three bullets had passed through his hat, and one across his temple, leaving a bloody streak in its course."

Dying, he said he was "content and happy, trusting in the merits of my Saviour, Jesus Christ." A "short, feverish sleep" silenced him for a while, but he then started up, with apparently a final cry. "Company K! You have no captain now, but never give up, never surrender."

A fellow minister, the Reverend J.M. Atkinson, reacted with the same romantic viewpoint as that imbuing Bruce's history. Said Atkinson: "Among the deified heroes of ancient song, in the golden record of Grecian fame, in the stirring chronicles of the medieval knighthood, in the ranks of war, in the halls of learning, in the temple of religion, a nobler name is not registered than his, nor a nobler spirit mourned."

But Dabney Harrison was not alone. There was, for instance, Randolph Fairfax, "the grandson of the ninth Baron Fairfax, of Cameron . . . sprung from a family which had been conspicuous in England and America through eight centuries . . . " A student who joined Virginia's Rockbridge Artillery, this martyr served so well and so conscientiously until his death in battle that Robert E. Lee wrote the young man's mourning father, "I have watched his conduct from the commencement of the war, and have pointed with pride to the patriotism, self-denial and manliness of character he has exhibited."

Another to be installed in the University's pantheon of heroes was a professor—Lewis M. Coleman, who taught ancient languages. An artillery major, he was fatally wounded at Fredericksburg.

Still another University hero was Cotesworth Pinckney Seabrook of South Carolina, who used to walk "many miles" into the mountains near the University to conduct religious services "for the mountaineers." Said a close friend from both college days and the soldierly ranks: "He seemed raised up from among the medieval dead and set in the midst of us, to give proof that the spirit of knightly courtesy, constancy, and valor had not departed from our times." This amazing young man, who hurried home to volunteer as soon as South Carolina seceded, managed to survive major battles of the war—Second Bull Run, Antietam, Fredericksburg among them—and the first clash at Cold Harbor. After that engagement, he wrote, almost unbelievably, "We had the satisfaction of charging through grape, canister, and bullets for half a mile."

He wrote to his mother to have no fear for him, since he had no fear for himself. The next day, at Chancellorsville, he was killed—another romanticized martyr from the ranks of those privileged by birth, background and education, to defend tradition, chivalry as they saw it, a way of life they thought their right and their responsibility, too.

Six-Year-Old's Flight

When Martha Harper was "'bout" six years old, there loomed a good night for her escape from the Master's farm to rejoin her mother and father in Richmond. The white overseer's daughter was getting married, and all round the Ryland place in Saluda, Virginia, the white folks were getting ready for a big time. Who among them would be thinking about what the slaves were up to?

It was about 8 p.m. when a friendly slave named Bill crept up to a window in Martha's quarters and beckoned. The proverbial coast was clear. As instructed in advance, she ran out the door, and Bill handed her over a fence to her Uncle Jack, who was waiting with another man.

The two men ran through the woods while taking turns carrying the little girl on their shoulders. About midnight, however, four hours after their start, they heard the yelp of bloodhounds!

Somebody was after them after all!

It was a frightening, traveling sound that was steadily drawing closer. The little girl knew the significance. "My poor heart started jumping as the sound neared and neared," she related many years later.

She was sure they'd all be caught any moment. But her Uncle Jack reassured her. "Dem's Ryland's hounds," he said. He had outdistanced them before, and he would outdistance them this time.

The two men bent to it and ran faster, faster . . . faster. They reached the Pamunkey River, where Uncle Jack took the child high on his shoulders and waded the deep stream. He just "ploughed" through the water to the other side. There, the small party of fugitives paused for breath under some brush and watched as the pack of hounds and their slave-hunting masters reached the shoreline left behind and the dogs muddled about in confusion over the lost scent. As the blacks held their breath, the white posse turned downstream. In minutes, the pursuers were gone.

The two men and the girl went on, and after a time they found a place in the thick, hardly trammeled woods of those days to hide out for the coming day. They did the rest of their traveling that way—rest and hide by day, travel by night . . . until one morning, they had reached a farm in Hanover County, outside Richmond, where Martha's father had left his wagon for them. The two men placed Martha under a pile of vegetables in the wagon and told her to hush up while they proceeded toward nearby Richmond—and the two sets of military lines ahead of them.

"When they got to the Yankee lines, Uncle showed Father's pass, and they let us pass through the lines. Outside of Richmond, he had to show it to the Confederates, and they let him pass into the city because he was bringing provisions."

Soon the wagon had turned down old Brook Road; soon it turned into St. James Street. Martha's waiting mother suddenly, at last, saw the horse-drawn rig coming. "She screamed so loud that they must have heard her all over Richmond."

DAVISES EVERYWHERE

So many people, so many involved in so many ways! All across America, *from* all across America, the Civil War sucked up so many different people, pulled them into the maelstrom and spit them out again, changed forever. Heroes, fools, rogues, knaves and innocents all were affected, whether they wanted to be or not.

Take one family name, and just notice. No, not Smith, Jones or Brown, but another fairly commonplace name—Davis.

There was Jefferson Davis of course. President of the Confederacy and a mainstay of the history books, yes. But how about the ten men named Davis who won the Medal of Honor for their gallantry during the Civil War? Not so well known today are they? Except possibly among descendants or by hometown historians.

All ten were Union men, naturally, and they were visible enough to be decorated for their exploits. As always happens, many others, named Davis or otherwise, were not—the system is far from perfect and never will be.

Confederates named Davis (or otherwise) naturally did not exactly qualify for Union decorations, and so few among us today will recall Private John Davis of the Confederacy's "Quitman Rifles," Kershaw's Brigade, at Chancellorsville (May 3, 1863). A compatriot, Dr. Augustus Dickert, called this particular Davis "one of the bravest men in our regiment." Said Dickert: "He was reckless beyond all reason. He loved danger for danger's sake. Stepping behind a tree to load—he was on the skirmish line—he would pass out from this cover in plain view, take deliberate aim, and fire. Again and again he was entreated and urged by his comrades to shield himself, but in vain."

Finally, a Union sharpshooter's bullet found the little-known John Davis.

Others by the same name were better known in their day, though none quite on the scale of Jefferson Davis. Not even . . . *the Union's own Jefferson Davis*! Yes, the U. S. Army brigadier and Mexican War veteran who became notorious throughout the Union for the moment, in September 1862, when he shot and killed fellow Union general William Nelson, at the Galt House hostelry in

Louisville, Kentucky, as climax to a personal quarrel.

Among other Davis nameholders who achieved notice during the Civil War was Confederate President Jefferson Davis' nephew, Mississippi State Senator and lawyer Joseph Robert Davis, who led a brigade in Pickett's Charge at Gettysburg and served later at the Wilderness, Spotsylvania, Cold Harbor and Petersburg, surviving all before returning to more normal life as an attorney. This Davis at first encountered difficulty winning confirmation from the Confederate Congress for his nomination to brigadier general. Opponents charged his Uncle Jefferson with nepotism. It *was* true that he had served his uncle in Richmond as an aide-de-camp for about a year.

Two Davis men named George served in the war also—on opposite sides. George Davis of North Carolina at first opposed secession, but then served in the Confederate Congress as a state senator. He later served the Confederacy as its last Attorney General (appointed by Jefferson Davis), and he was in the party of high government officials who had to flee Richmond when their capital fell to the invading Union Army in April 1865. George Davis, later separated from the Jefferson Davis entourage, was captured at Key West, Florida, spent a year as a Federal prisoner, then resumed his law practice, later declining an appointment to North Carolina's supreme court. (It didn't pay enough.)

The other George Davis, a Vermonter and thus a Union man, was one of those ten Medal of Honor winners, his earned at the Monocacy River, Maryland, where in July of 1864 he helped to hold off Jubal Early's Washington-bound force at a pair of bridges. Davis was the last man to hurry across a key rail bridge, stepping gingerly on the cross ties under heavy fire, as his small delaying force withdrew. He had begun the war as an enlisted man and he left it as an officer, after suffering severe injury from the collapse of a log cabin during the siege of Petersburg.

Two more *Union* men, both fine cavalry officers and combat standouts, were Hasbrouck and Benjamin F. "Grimes" Davis —the second a native of Alabama. In September of 1862, just before the Battle of Antietam, both were at Harpers Ferry as Stonewall Jackson enveloped the town and placed it under siege.

Coordinating efforts, they formulated and led a bold break-out by the Union cavalry in the darkness of night, a long file that snaked across the Potomac and into the Maryland heights beyond. In the process, they came upon Confederate General James Longstreet's reserve ammunition train of 97 wagons—opportunity enough for Grimes Davis! Using his Southern accent (and hoping that his uniform couldn't be discerned in the dark), he ordered Longstreet's teamsters to fall in with the silent column of horsemen headed north. They did, and in the morning's light, they discovered they were prisoners of the two Davises . . . Union men!

Both later served at Chancellorsville, among other engagements of the Civil War. Grimes Davis, unfortunately, did not survive the subsequent cavalry battle of Brandy Station, where he had been leading a brigade; his Harpers Ferry sidekick Hasbrouck, also a brigade commander before war's end, did survive the conflict but then disappeared at sea in 1870.

Let us not overlook still more Davises of Civil War fame. Sam Davis, for instance—Confederate spy and heroic figure who, like Nathan Hale of another day, refused upon capture to divulge what he knew about his confederates . . . and was hanged for his efforts.

—Or naval officer Charles Henry Davis, who led the Union forces on the upper Mississippi that captured Memphis. He was a founder of the National Academy of Sciences and a career naval officer to his death in 1877 as a rear admiral.

—Or Florida native Edmund J. Davis. Texas lawyer and judge, who raised a "Texas" cavalry regiment in Mexico, fought for the Union throughout the war and later became a Reconstruction Governor of Texas.

—Or also a politician, Abraham Lincoln's fellow Illinois attorney, presidential campaign manager and later U. S. Supreme Court appointee, David Davis. Ironically, this Davis could have wound up a president himself. Why? Well, in 1877 he left the bench and entered the U. S. Senate, where he eventually became the body's president pro tempore. He held that post when Chester Arthur, as Vice President, succeeded the assassinated Civil War veteran James Garfield as President. With no Vice President actually in place during the time that Arthur served in the White House, David Davis would have been next in line if Chester Arthur died. As it happened, and as yet unknown to most, Arthur did suffer from a terminal kidney disease, but he served out his term and died a year later (1886), at the age of 56.

CAPITALISM AT ANDERSONVILLE

"We had not long been prisoners," wrote a survivor of the notorious Confederate prison called Andersonville. Not long at all, he later said, not long in those conditions of deprivation and near-starvation before he discovered a remarkable fact of prison life. Call it, in fact, *capitalistic* life. Free enterprise . . . even in an appalling prison!

"We had not long been prisoners before we discovered that men here, as in other conditions of life, in order to 'get on' and preserve life, must adopt some trade or business," wrote Warren Lee Cross. *Business? Trade!* Yes, indeed. Even in a prison so bad that ration time was like a gathering of wolves. Caged, starving wolves at that! "These rations consisted of Indian meal, and sometimes of bacon. As a whole there was a large quantity, but when subdivided among 20,000 or 30,000 men it gave to each one but a small quantity."

The rations arrived via the North Gate. "A street or path, to which was given the name of Broadway, led from the gate through the stockade from east to west. Here, at ration time, was gathered a motley crowd. With eager, hungry eyes, they watched each division of the food, the sight of which seemed to have a strange fascination for the hungry wretches, long unused to full stomachs. They crowded to the wagons to get a sight of each bag of meal or piece of meat."

These were searing scenes, hard ever to forget. "The attempt to grasp a morsel which sometimes fell from the wagon, the piteous expression of disappointment on their pinched and unwashed faces if they failed, the involuntary exclamations, and the wistful hungry look, had in them a pathos not easily described."

Then, you see, came the moment of trade. "After the drawing of rations, a dense throng of prisoners always gathered near the North Gate to trade. One with tobacco cut in pieces not larger than dice might be seen trying to trade it for rations. Another could be heard crying out, 'Who will trade a soup-bone for Indian meal?,' 'Who'll trade cooked rations for raw?' 'Who'll trade beans for wood?' While others with small pieces of dirty bacon an inch or two in size, held on a sharpened stick, would drive a sharp trade with someone whose mouth was watering for its possession. But for its misery, the scene would often have been intensely comical."

It was far from comical, naturally, but the fact is, trade, *business*, if you wish, apparently did flourish. Necessity, wrote Gross, produced ingenuity, produced amazing adaptation . . . "Some [men] set up as bakers, and bought flour, and baked biscuits which they sold to such as had money to buy. The ovens which were built showed such ingenuity as to extort expressions of surprise from the Confederates who occasionally visited us. The soil contained a red precipitate of iron, which was very adhesive. This was made into rude bricks by mixing the earth with water, and the oven was built of these over a mould of sand. After being left to harden in the sun for a few days, the sand was removed, a fire was kindled, and the oven was ready for use."

Other entrepreneurs made wooden buckets to hold water, "whittling out the staves and making the hoops with a jackknife." Still others managed to obtain from mysterious "outside parties" sheet tin, "generally taken from the roofs of railway cars, and, with a railway spike and a stone for tools, made small camp kettles, without solder, by bending the pieces ingeniously together." These remarkable containers were popular with "those who had money." And they were badly needed. "As no cooking utensils were possessed by the prisoners, except such as they brought into prison with them, these tinmen were benefactors."

Some prisoners tinkered with broken-down watches, "the object of their owners being simply to make them 'go' long enough to effect a trade [often with the purchaser a Confederate]."

Then there was the crowd who "fried flapjacks of Indian

meal, and sold them hot from the griddle for ten cents each." One real success story—call it survival—came from "the camp beer made of Indian meal soured in water." The beer, "proclaimed by the vendors to be a cure for scurvy," was considered a refreshing drink. As for that success story . . . "a certain enterprising prisoner added ginger and molasses to the compound, and made, as he termed his success, a 'boom' by selling it. He became so rich as to buy food, and so regained his health and strength."

Not many were so fortunate at Andersonville, where so many Union prisoners met their death. It seems that in some cases, however, a touch of free enterprise had its good effect. Said this survivor: "We had not long been prisoners before we discovered that men here, as in other conditions of life, in order to 'get on' and preserve life, must adopt some trade or business." In short, said he, free enterprise . . . *in order to preserve life.*

Jaws Of Death

His commanding officer, Braxton Bragg, had ordered it done, and so the division commander led his men into the jaws of death. It was the Charge of the Light Brigade all over again, but this advance was at the Stones River, outside Murfreesboro, Tennessee, and the guns on the high bluff opposite were Union.

On foot, John Cabell Breckinridge's division, "with guns loaded and bayonets fixed, marched with steady step to the assault," wrote a perceptive Northern onlooker.

A proud Confederate agreed. "A more imposing and thoroughly disciplined line of soldiers never moved to the attack of an enemy than responded to the signal gun stationed immediately to our rear."

On the high bluff on the west side of the river, Union artillerymen stiffened behind their 58 guns.

On the eastern ground opposite, the advance continued. "Every man vied with his fellow man in steadiness of step and correct alignment," recalled the Confederate participant, "with the officers giving low and cautionary commands, many knowing that it was their last hour on earth . . . "

There would be momentary interruption. "Suddenly the ground shook as if rocked by a fearful earthquake, and the fifty-eight cannons emptied their double-shotted contents on this living human mass in front of them; but a few seconds intervened, and again and again the fifty-eight cannons spread death into Breckinridge's men."

It was too much, and in minutes the Rebels were streaming back in rout.

Before his assault of January 2, 1863, Breckinridge had argued in vain with his commander Bragg that they faced a trap. Moments before the assault, the Kentuckian told a fellow general that the attack was being made "against my judgment." He asked that if he should be killed, "I want you to do justice to my memory and tell the people that I believed this attack to be very unwise, and tried to prevent it."

Now, with the assault over, riding to the rear, past the dead and the dying, many from his native Kentucky's "Orphan Brigade," "with tears falling from his eyes, he was heard to say in tones of anguish, 'My poor Orphans! My poor Orphans!'"

This was John Cabell Breckinridge in an hour of agony, outside of Murfreesboro, Tennessee, the same officer who hated to commit the youthful cadets of the Virginia Military Institute to the Battle of New Market. And in triumph or tragedy, hardly such a unique soldier there ever was, even in the fratricidal American Civil War.

Stones River came as 1862 passed into 1863. Only finger-countable months before, Breckinridge had served the *Union* as Vice President, under James Buchanan. He ran for President against one Abraham Lincoln in 1860 as the nominee of the Southern Democrats. He then took his seat as a U.S. Senator from Kentucky, but after joining the Confederacy was expelled, post-haste, from the Senate.

His gallantry, however, rarely failed him or his men, and few generals of either side attended so many of the war's major battles—Shiloh; defense of Vicksburg; Chickamauga; Baton Rouge;

Chattanooga-Missionary Ridge; Cold Harbor. In most, as at Stones River, he appeared in a subordinate command role, but as an overall commander, he prevailed over the enemy at New Market, at the second Battle of Kernstown and, again in Virginia, at Lynchburg.

Later, as Secretary of War, he was a mainstay for the Confederacy in its dying hours, helping to direct the evacuation of Richmond and to organize Jefferson Davis' flight south. Davis was captured, but Breckinridge made his way to Florida and escaped to Cuba in an open boat.

He returned to America from England under amnesty in 1868—still and well remembered for the fairness with which he had presided over the Senate in those difficult years just before the Civil War.

BRIDE LEFT BEHIND

The bride wore lace, the groom wore his general's uniform . . . as did the clergyman performing the wedding ceremony in Murfreesboro, Tennessee, in December of 1862. Actually, the clergyman, one Leonidas Polk, also wore his Episcopal bishop's vestments, with his own general's uniform peeping out from beneath.

Standing by as the groom's very proper groomsmen were a corps of Confederate generals—Braxton Bragg, William Hardee, John C. Breckinridge and Benjamin Cheatham, while many other officers and two regimental bands filled the bride's happily bedecked home, and outside hundreds of soldiers filled the streets, built bonfires, sang and cheered.

The bride's father, a former U.S Congressman fresh from a prison cell in Nashville, held nothing back in providing a memorable wartime affair for his daughter and her guests. Their supper ranged from turkey to ham, chicken, duck and various delicacies, plus plentiful bottles of wine for toasts to the happy couple.

For cavalry raider John Hunt Morgan, his marriage to Mattie Ready was the culmination of a heady week that had begun with his signal victory over a large Federal force at Hartsville, Tennessee, followed by his award of a brigadier's star from President Jefferson Davis in person, and an unusually warm commendation from the usually reserved Bragg. "To the brave officers and men composing the expedition the General tenders his cordial thanks and congratulations," Bragg's official orders had read. "He is proud of them and hails the success achieved by their valor as but the precursor of still greater victories."

The site of Morgan's wedding, Murfreesboro, was in the eye of a storm that kept sweeping back and forth—a town buffeted by Confederate, then Union, then Confederate forces, with the townspeople largely Southern in their loyalties.

Just eight months earlier, Morgan had been forced by a Yankee occupation to quit his courting of Mattie Ready in person. Now, he and his fellow Rebs were back, but who could tell for how long . . . whatever the case, he would marry her between activities of his own, his cavalry raids.

In his absence of eight months, Morgan's future father-in-law, Colonel Ready, once a member of the U.S. House in Washington, had been imprisoned for refusing to take the Federal oath of allegiance . . . but now he was free again, the Rebs were in town, and on December 14 they just had themselves a spectacular wedding, as Morgan and Mattie became man and wife, to the words intoned by Confederate Lieutenant General Polk, an Episcopal bishop in civilian life.

Spectacular, yes . . . but allowing no time to linger. War still called, and in six days' time, Morgan was off again, on his Christmas Raid of 1862-1863, 14 days consumed, 500 snow-covered miles traveled, four engagements and countless skirmishes fought, with 2,000 Union prisoners taken, four bridges, 25 miles of railroad tracks and $5 million in Federal stores all destroyed.

As one result of this Morgan excursion, however, he missed the big Battle of Stones River at Murfreesboro over New Year's— a tilt that meant Bragg's Rebels must move out as William S. Rosecrans and his Union legions moved in.

While Mattie persevered under the Federal occupation that now resumed for the better part of a year, Morgan, naturally, was kept busy fighting the war in other quarters, his most spectacular foray of all about to take place. That, in summer of 1863, would be his famous (and unauthorized) raid into Ohio, an incursion that took Morgan and a steadily dwindling band to a point 100 miles south of Lake Erie at its high point, the Federals in hot pursuit. He then was captured . . . but no, the story didn't stop there. A few months later, he and a handful of his men further electrified an admiring public in the South by escaping from their confines in the Ohio State Penitentiary. Morgan then wended all the difficult way back to Confederate territory . . . and to his anxious Mattie, still more a bride than a real wife.

Audible, Not Visible

Was there ever a storm like that at Murfreesboro (Stones River), Tennessee? Except some other battle hot and heavy, true. And yet, yet, from the accounts of those there, those who saw, heard . . . *survived*, you could wonder, was there ever fighting like this?

Acting as his unit's sergeant major, for instance, was Union Private Henry A. Castle, with his regiment deployed for the moment—the afternoon of December 31, New Year's Eve, 1862—in a railroad cut up at the front line. Oblique to the front line, in fact. And he saw a Confederate officer spot exactly where Castle and his compatriots were "and then gallop off." To fetch his artillery, of course. And in short time, sure enough, here came a Rebel battery right within Castle's view.

It wouldn't be long before the Rebel guns began firing down his rail cut, and so Castle as acting sergeant major pelted off to notify his regiment's commander, a major. But the major had been wounded and carried off the field. Castle then sought out his next in command chain, the adjutant, but he too, had been carried off.

With no one to give him orders for the moment, Private Castle then marched his company "double quick out of the defile, trusting the rest to follow."

143

They did, naturally, and just in time, "as just then the shells came shrieking through the straight and narrow gorge with a venom that would have left few unscathed in five minutes more."

Castle's next step was to tell the four captains still with his regiment that they had no overall commander. In response, they dispatched him to the brigade commander, clearly visible sitting on his horse just 200 yards away. Castle started out on the errand, to settle the matter of seniority among the captains, "but before I had made half the distance, he, the last of our brigade commanders, was shot before my eyes and fell to the ground a corpse."

Another Union private, George H. Daggett, found himself during the same battle in a strange, horror-tale woods.

It was a patch of cedars, about 200 acres, a ground covered with rock—all slabs, boulders and fissures. No soil, oddly, and tree trunks so thick and close as to be almost impenetrable—"so near together that the sunlight was obscured and the vision extended but a short distance horizontally."

The Union men who retreated into this shelter at one point had no idea what was going on just outside the cedar woods. All they knew came from "avalanches of sound which assailed us from every direction."

The Confederate enemy poured artillery and musket fire into the wooded patch, while, close by, other Union forces were fighting off other Rebel forces. "Thus on all sides we were stormed at and stunned by the conglomeration of fiendish noises that came seemingly from every point of the compass."

Then, too, "Not the least terrible of these sounds was an occasional explosion of the hot, fierce, indescribable Rebel yell."

Echoing Daggert's impressions, an onlooking Union officer was aware that the Confederate left was desperate to overrun the cedar woods and reach the Nashville Turnpike beyond, thus to cut off the Union force there. Union General William S. Rosecrans rushed forward some reinforcements into the woods, but under the pressure of the determined Confederates, they would be inadequate. The Union officer couldn't see into the woods and estimate what was happening. All he knew, was that "Nearer and nearer came the storm; louder and louder the tumult of battle."

Rosecrans had massed more men along the turnpike, and well that he had, for quite suddenly "10,000 fugitives [Union troops] burst from the cedar thickets and rushed into the open space between them and the turnpike."

Among the fleeing men many fell to the fire from behind of their Rebel pursuers, but "fresh crowds . . . burst from the thickets" to replace the fallen—to overrun their prone forms in the field. For long moments it appeared the routed regiments even would overrun the Union line formed along the turnpike.

Indeed, "It was with the greatest difficulty that some of the regiments, which had been massed together as sort of a forlorn hope, could prevent their ranks from being crushed by the mass of fugitives." And the pursuers? Where were they? Still largely hidden from sight, in the deep deep woods, but not for long. For now, just as suddenly, they too burst forth. "At last the long lines of the enemy emerged from the woods with a demoniac yell, intended to strike terror into the souls of the 'Yankees'."

They burst out of the forest, and from the awaiting Union line there came a "dazzling sheet of flame." In that response, "An awful roar shook the earth; a crash rent the atmosphere." The advance ranks of the Rebel charge "seemed to melt away like snowflakes before a flame."

Then, in seconds, a vast cloud covered the field—"smoke which hid everything from the eye."

While in one quarter the fleeing Union men still fled, in this covered field a fierce battle ensued before the onlookers . . . yet remained invisible to them. "The combat under that great cloud of smoke was somewhat similar to that in the woods. No one knows exactly what occurred. There was a shout, a charge, a rush of fire, a recoil, and then all for a time disappeared." Yet, there was no doubting what was happening inside the obscuring vapors. "For 10 minutes the thunder of battle burst forth from the cloud."

Finally, the officer-onlooker's battalion was able to advance; his men found "no Rebels between the woods and the turnpike except the dead, dying and disabled." Those there were in the hundreds, on ground soaked and reddened with blood. "Since the annihilation of the 'Old Guard' in their charge at

Waterloo, there has probably been no instance of so great a slaughter in so short a time as during this repulse of the Reb left at Murfreesboro."

Left was certainly key to the entire day's events, since each of the warring sides had decided, in advance, to employ his own left against the enemy's right, which in theory would have produced a revolving-door effect. The Confederates, however, under their commander Braxton Bragg, gained the initial advantage by beginning battle an hour ahead of the Union timetable.

On the Union left that morning, breakfast was still a very recent memory and the troops barely had begun to cross the Stones River, with the town of Murfreesboro as their goal, when, reported Union officer William D. Birckham, "some firing" was heard on the right, "but not enough to indicate a battle."

Not yet, that is, for soon after and suddenly, "All hearts were thrilled by a sound sweeping from the right like a strong wind sweeping through a forest." The Rebel left had hurled itself against the Union right, of course.

And the sound was the "din of battle." It swelled up rapidly, then came a tide of fugitives from the thickets. "You have seen cinders from burning buildings flying when the conflagration was still invisible. You could hear the roaring flames and crackling beams. Seeing the cinders, you would say, 'There is a fire.' You had not yet felt the blast, but its avant-couriers were unmistakable. These teamsters [wagon crews] Negroes, soldiers, flying before it were cinders from the flames of battle." That early development of course spoiled the Union plan to advance with the left, since the Union right already was giving way to the Rebel left. Later, after the charge through the cedars and the equally invisible battle under the cloud of smoke, the trend again reversed itself, and the Rebel left was beaten back . . . all at great cost to both sides.

In the midst of it all that day, good Kentucky men on the Rebel side at one point met good Kentucky men on the Union side—many of them old friends and neighbors from the same county. "As soon as they came near enough for recognition," related Union Colonel Charles S. Greene later, "they ceased firing, and began abusing, and cursing, and swearing at each other, calling each other the most outlandish names."

For a time the Kentuckians paid no attention to the violent battle all around them, but that couldn't last. "By mutual consent they finally ceased swearing, and charged into each other with the most unearthly yell ever heard. The muskets were thrown away, and at it they went, pulling and gouging." And why not? Pulling and gouging, yelling and cussing, at least was not killing each other.

The Confederate Third Kentucky was "getting the best of it" when the outsider 9th Ohio intervened and took many of the Confederates prisoner. "As the late belligerents were conducted to the rear, they were on the best terms with their captors, laughing and chatting and joking; and they all became jolly as possible."

SPANK THE BOYS

Intrepidly he pushed on. And on! "Severely wounded," it says here—in his citation for the Congressional Medal of Honor—"and exposed to a heavy fire from the enemy, he persistently remained upon the field of battle until he had reported to . . . [General William Tecumseh] Sherman the necessity of supplying cartridges for the use of troops under command of Colonel Malmborg [Company C, 55th Illinois Infantry]."

Well, let's face it, and no disparagement intended, but many a man performed similar brave duty when called upon, rather than fail his comrades in battle. After all, in the ideal, such is every soldier's duty. To ignore the storm of shot and shell and to press on.

Every man's duty even when struck in the leg by a Minie bullet while on the way with a crucial message for General Sherman, you could say . . . as was the case that day in May 1863 at Vicksburg for Orion P. Howe, native of Portage County, Ohio As was the case, indeed, for the brave and persistent Orion P. Howe—except that he was no average Union soldier. And not even a man.

Not yet, anyway. At age 14, he was his Illinois company's

drummer boy, one of thousands, perhaps even 40 thousands or more, of boys, mere boys, who marched off to war with the Union and Confederate armies.

In the Union forces alone, an estimated 300 such youths served at the age of 13 or even younger. Indeed, by another reliable estimate, a startling 25 *kids* began their army tours at the age of 10 or less! One was the redoubtable Johnny Clem, also known as "Johnny Shiloh" after his drum was knocked to pieces by a shell at Shiloh. Only 9 when he

"joined up" (a bit unofficially, it seems), Johnny not only became a lance sergeant by the time he was 12, but he didn't muster out of service for 55 years! It was 1916 before he finally retired, by that time a major general and the last Civil War combat veteran still in active service in the U. S. Army.

Certainly many such youngsters slipped into Civil War units by the wink of someone's eye or by various, sentimentally intended chicanery—and most were drummer boys, buglers, musicians.

In young Clem's case, the recruiters visiting his home of Newark, Ohio, in 1861 turned aside the small lad trying to join their 3rd Ohio Regiment. Naturally. One even said, "We can't use infants here." As David Mallinson reported in the magazine *America's Civil War*, however, Clem hid in the baggage car of the train carrying the 3rd Ohio to camp at Covington, Kentucky. Then came a switch. "Once there, he attached himself to the 22nd Michigan and became the drummer for Company C."

At Shiloh in April of 1862, his drum was hit as he tapped the advance for Company C. But there was more to come. "Drumless, Clem went into the battle of Chickamauga carrying a musket cut down to size," it also seems. Left alone at one point, he used the weapon to wound a Confederate colonel who "rode up and yelled for Johnny to surrender."

After that they called him "the Drummer Boy of Chickamauga." Taken prisoner just three weeks later, and released in a few more weeks, he was able to serve as an orderly in the headquarters of Union Major General George H. Thomas and carry dispatches for Thomas in the Atlanta campaign, during which the youngster's horse was shot down beneath him.

Rejected by West Point after the war for his lack of schooling, the young veteran appealed to President Ulysses S. Grant, the youth's commander at Shiloh. Grant relented and Clem was allowed a commission as a 2nd lieutenant in the Regular Army.

Others from the ranks of youthdom did manage to gain entrance to the military academies, it should be noted. One was Orion Howe, the 14-year-old given the Medal of Honor for his bravery at Vicksburg. Sherman recalled the wounded youth's message so well, he gladly appointed him to Annapolis, but Howe struggled with the books and bowed out after two years.

Another appointee received his boost from none other than Abe Lincoln, who often showed interest in the welfare of the Union's drummer boys. Young Robert Henry Hendershot, also of a Michigan regiment (the 8th), came to Lincoln's attention as "the Drummer Boy of the Rappahannock," a sobriquet given after the teenager crossed the icy Rappahannock River on December 11, 1862, (Battle of Fredericksburg) by hanging onto a boat carrying Union soldiers across under heavy Confederate fire. Losing his drum to a piece of flying shrapnel on the far side, he took up a musket, found a Reb soldier and took him prisoner.

After the boy's discharge, Lincoln asked War Secretary Edwin Stanton to find a job for "the gallant drummer-boy Robert H. Henderson." The result was a messenger's berth in the U. S. Treasurer's office, but later still Lincoln endorsed Treasurer Francis E. Spinner's recommendation of Henderson for appointment to the U. S. Military Academy at West Point. At that time, Lincoln wrote: "I know something of this boy, and believe he is brave, manly and worthy."

The U. S. Congress late in the war acted upon the reservations of many who felt mere children should not be thrown into war. As might be expected, the boys did not always live to become men. Congress acted in March 1864 to prohibit the enlistment of anyone under 16—action finally taken after a young Cincinnati boy was killed in battle at Resaca, Georgia.

Most men in the Union Armies, all but 1.5 percent, fell into the age bracket of 18 to 46, with an average age of 25.8 years at the time of enlistment. Only hundreds served at age 15 or less, but the numbers begin to jump into the thousands right after that. At age 16, for instance, 2,758; at age 17, 6,425; at age 18, 133,475, the largest age group among all Union soldiers.

The real youngsters not only served as musicians (and mascots!) but as "gofers," too. They were seen in camp as barbers and water carriers, and on the battlefield, they tended to the wounded—or even took a wounded man's place in the line.

If the enemy didn't perchance kill or wound such a youngster, his own compatriots might! Some boys were sentenced to death for desertion. Lincoln once took up the cause of such a youth the day before his scheduled execution. "I am unwilling," wrote the President, "for any boy under 18 to be shot; and his father affirms that he is yet under 16." Another time, informed of a 14-year-old facing the firing squad for desertion, Lincoln wrote to War Secretary Edwin Stanton: "Hadn't we better spank this drummer boy and send him home?"

Perhaps Lincoln on such occasions was thinking of home life in the White House itself, where son Tad sometimes wore a Union officer's uniform tailored to fit his diminutive stature, where Tad and brother Willie subjected an unfortunate toy soldier named "Jack" to occasional "execution" and where a playful Lincoln once wrote a "pardon" sparing Jack from still another firing squad. More sadly, Lincoln's obvious empathy for the boys in service may have reflected the fact that his beloved Willie died of fever in early 1862, long before the war ended.

Injury Added To Insult

On the morning of July 2, 1863, disputing Confederate officers George Moody of a Louisiana artillery battery and Pichegru Woolfolk of a Virginia artillery battery were scheduled to duel with rifles at 10 paces . . . except that this was Gettysburg and events overtook their disagreement and postponed their duel forever.

A Confederate legislator, Henry Cousins Chambers, did attend a duel, however—in his case, rifles at 50 paces. He killed his political rival William Lake in the process. Chambers then took his seat in the Confederate Congress—and no one rose to oppose him in the next election.

It was a violent period, with people often killed over insult, honor, politics and the slavery issue for years before the Civil War broke out. Abraham Lincoln once accepted the challenge to a duel by sword . . . only it was called off at the last moment by mutual agreement. Even during the Civil War, not all the passion and violence were directed at the enemy.

Nathan Bedford Forrest, preeminent as a cavalry leader for the South, was a notoriously violent man. Well known among Civil War buffs and historians even today is his angry threat directed at Braxton Bragg, a senior Confederate general. Face to face and very personal indeed, Forrest called Bragg "a damned scoundrel" and said, "If you ever again try to interfere with me or cross my path, it will be at the peril of your life."

Not so well known is the time that Forrest and a fellow officer in the Confederate Army did "come to blows" . . . with truly dismal result. The scenario began when a youthful artillery officer was placed in charge of two recently captured Union artillery pieces. The young lieutenant was Andrew Willis Gould, first serving with his cousin, Colonel Alonzo Napier's Tennessee Cavalry Battalion, and next with Morton's Tennessee Battery.

Then came a fire-fight on April 30, 1863, at Sand Mountain—Gould had to withdraw too quickly to take his two guns, but he apparently did spike them at considerable personal risk.

All that Forrest heard, unfortunately, was that Gould had lost the two precious guns. A pending command slot went to another officer and Forrest questioned Gould's courage. The unfairly maligned young man confronted Forrest at Columbia, Tennessee, on June 13, 1863, and a heated argument followed in the hallway of the Masonic Building. Gould suddenly struggled to pull his pistol out of the pocket of his lengthy coat of linen, while Forrest, anticipating trouble, reached into a pocket of his own for his penknife.

Gould was unable to free his weapon, which suddenly went off with an ear-splitting bang. Forrest at almost the same moment was opening the penknife with his teeth and lunging at Gould.

The pistol ball lodged in Forrest's left hip with painful impact that produced visible reaction . . . but Forrest with one hand still managed to grab Gould's hand holding the now freed pistol and push it up into the air while at the same moment, with the other hand, plunging the penknife into the younger officer's ribcage.

For the next few minutes at Columbia, pandemonium! Gould ran from the building into the street. Other officers rushed Forrest, stunned, into a nearby doctor's office. Meanwhile, two more doctors, one of them a relative, saw Gould staggering in the street and pushed him into a nearby tailor's shop.

The first doctor, Forrest's, made the mistake in his haste of blurting out that the hip wound could be fatal—and now Forrest really was enraged. "No damned man shall kill me and live," he shouted, jumping to his feet and taking to the street in search of Gould.

In the tailor's shop, Gould looked well enough—he could stand and he could talk—but blood squeezed out of his puncture wound with every breath. One doctor tried to help him while the other hurried off for his surgical instruments.

In the street Forrest was still raging. "By God, he has mortally wounded me and I'll kill him dead before I die," he roared again. One officer told Forrest "that damned scoundrel is not much hurt," but a local citizen said Gould was "bleeding profusely" and likely to die.

Forrest told the citizen to get out of his way. By now Forrest had taken a pistol from the saddle gear of a horse tethered nearby and somehow had found another. He burst into the tailor's shop brandishing both weapons wildly and cursing. As Gould dashed into a back alley, one pistol went off, the bullet striking a bystander in the leg (a minor injury as it turned out). Pursuing Gould, Forrest found him supine in a clump of weeds, pushed at him with a foot and turned away. After commandeering Gould's two doctors, Forrest then learned that his own wound was not to be fatal after all.

With that welcome news, he suddenly told the doctors to hasten to Gould's aid and "spare nothing to save him." It is still unclear whether Forrest later visited Gould and granted him forgiveness, as some accounts would have it, but it is absolutely clear that in the aftermath it was Forrest who soon rode off into battle again—and young Gould who died just days after the ugly incident.

FAMILY AFFAIR

Ellet, Ellet, Ellet and Ellet . . . sounds like a firm of barristers or solicitors out of a Charles Dickens novel. But no, these Ellets, all related to be sure—a family enterprise at that—more accurately can be associated with operations on the Mississippi River during the Civil War.

All four Ellets, a father and son, a brother of the father and a nephew, were associated, more precisely, with the Union's ram fleet on the Mississippi, a tale that begins with the birth of the first Ellet, Charles, in Bucks County, Pennsylvania, in 1810. Always called Charles Ellet, Jr., he grew up to be an engineer, railroader, inventor and bridge-builder. As one engineering feat, for instance, he built the first wire suspension bridge in the United States— across the Schuylkill River at Fairmount, Pennsylvania. He then spanned the Niagara River (*below* the famous falls) and at Wheeling, Ohio, in 1849, he erected a bridge of 1,010 feet over the Ohio River—at that time the world's longest single-span bridge.

While helping to build a Virginia rail line across the Blue

Ridge in the 1850s he also had on his mind an odd naval vessel— sort of an ironclad ram. No one in the United States seemed to be too interested . . . until the Confederacy produced the ironclad *Virginia* in 1862 (previously the *Merrimac*), along lines suggested in Ellet's published proposals.

Now, Washington and the Lincoln Administration suddenly awoke to the possibilities of Ellet's design. In short time he was dispatched by no less than Secretary of War Edwin Stanton to the Mississippi River (where he had worked before on flood control projects) to establish a fleet of rams. This he did by fitting out nine steam vessels with armor and rams and then moving them down the Ohio River en route to join the Union Navy's Captain Charles H. Davis and his Mississippi Flotilla.

Ellet managed to skim safely by Fort Pillow on June 5, 1862, and the next day take on eight Confederate vessels guarding Memphis, Tennessee. Four of them were sunk by the Union rams, with Ellet's own *Queen of the West* ramming and sinking the enemy's *General Lowell*. The remaining Rebel vessels turned downriver and fled, with the Union craft in close pursuit. Ellet's ships managed to sink another of the Rebel vessels and capture two more, a total of seven Confederate ships eliminated in one fell swoop.

The Union that day suffered but one casualty—a mortal wound inflicted upon the man behind the Union rams, Charles Ellet, Jr. He died on June 21.

The Ellet name, however, did not die with him. Far from it! The inventor's son, Charles Rivers Ellet, a medical student at Georgetown when the Civil War erupted, had just joined his father in time to bypass the Rebel batteries at Fort Pillow and was with him for the river battle at Memphis the next day. In fact, the elder Ellet had dispatched son Charles, officially a medical cadet, and two fellow Union men on the dangerous mission of going ashore in Memphis and demanding the city's surrender. They faced an angry mob (but no Confederate soldiers) and had to ignore hurled bricks and even stray shots, but they did it—they marched to the post office, took down the Confederate flag and raised the U. S. flag in its place.

The younger Ellet soon after would risk his life again by

crossing disputed territory on foot outside besieged Vicksburg on his way to inform Admiral David G. Farragut that Memphis had fallen into Union hands. Soon, too, the younger Ellet, no longer a mere medical cadet, had been raised to colonel's rank and placed in command of his late father's ram fleet!

As a riverine commander, he didn't do so badly, either. He four times ran the Vicksburg batteries over the next four months, and on the fourth such excursion attacked and rammed the Rebel *Vicksburg* at the city's south landing. That was on February 2, 1863, and the very next day, he and the redoubtable *Queen* captured three Confederate supply vessels at the mouth of the Red River.

It was at the Red River, another time, however, that the younger Ellet ran into misfortune—ascending the river, the *Queen of the West* ran aground and came under fire by a hidden shore battery. He and the crew had to abandon their ram. Worse, he had gone ahead of his supporting gunboat, *Indianola*. When it appeared, the Rebels turned the *Queen*'s own guns on *Indianola*, which also wound up a casualty of the day's activities. Ellet had to escape on board the accompanying *De Sota*.

Note, meanwhile, that this young and relatively untried "sailor's" rank was *Colonel*. Oddly, he was not really a sailor (and neither had been his late father), but instead was an Army officer—technically he was commander of the Mississippi Marine Brigade. And the Red River incident only inflamed Army-Navy rivalries over control of the small ram fleet and the Marines.

That odd situation also involved the younger Ellet's uncle—brother of the late Charles, Jr.—one Alfred Washington Ellet, a brigadier general of volunteers who had been second to his brother in command of the ram fleet; who had been present for the Memphis battle, and who had taken command after his brother was mortally wounded. Alfred briefly was in command of the Marine Brigade itself, but after a time was sent with brigade infantry elements to join Union General William Rosecrans on the Tennessee River.

Adding to the not-always-so-clear muddle was a fourth Ellet who served on the Mississippi, John A. Ellet, a nephew to both older Ellets and cousin to the younger Charles. This younger Ellet, often in conflict with naval authorities, also was an army officer; he served as second in command to Cousin Charles with the Marine Brigade. He had lost the ram *Lancaster*, and he, eventually, would command the Union *Switzerland*, which Cousin Charles had taken over for a time after the *Queen* had been lost.

Now John Ellet ran afoul of Union Admiral David Porter—when Porter gave him orders, John Ellet wouldn't obey them without checking first with his *army* uncle, General Alfred Ellet. Young John avoided Porter's threats of arrest and court-martial by joining Farragut downriver and strictly obeying the latter officer's dictates.

Young Charles, meanwhile, replaced earlier by Cousin John in command of the *Switzerland*, went with the Marine Brigade's infantrymen to join Rosecrans. He then became ill, retired to his Uncle Alfred's farm in Illinois and died in the fall of 1863, age 20 or 21.

MISS KATE'S BRIEF RUN

She was young, vivacious—the belle of the ball among Washington society during the Civil War. Kate Chase, daughter and official hostess for the widowed Secretary of the Treasury, Salmon P. Chase. *Poor, star-crossed Kate Chase Sprague, as events later turned out.*

With the eruption of the war and the departure of so many prominent political figures hailing from the South, the Federal capital lost the prime movers of its social circles. For years Washington society had been Southern-tilted, peopled by luminaries such as Varina Davis, wife of the new President now ensconced in Richmond. In the past four decades, in fact, a majority of Presidents had been Southern-born slaveowners. As recently as the Zachary Taylor administration (he died in office in 1850), the White House itself had been home to slaves. In his case, the slaves were sequestered in the attic rooms and kept to the private family quarters, to avoid ruffling ever-more sensitive feelings in *ante-bellum* Washington.

So now, under Lincoln, the Union split in two, the social

order was far different. As Union officer James A. Garfield (destined, himself, to be a future White House occupant) wrote in 1862: "This is the transition period between the old, slaveholding, aristocratic social dynasty and the New Republican one." Instead of "transition," actually, it was a *leap* from one social order to the next, he added in a letter to his wife Lucretia. Further, "The old social dynasty has been one of the most powerful political elements in Washington and is the secret of a great many successes for the South. From the days of General [Andrew] Jackson . . . it has been a great power."

True, and guess where Garfield was when he wrote that thought in the fall of 1862 . . . why, at the home of fellow Ohioans Salmon P. Chase and daughter Kate! A perfect match, too, since the Chase duo and Garfield all were politically ambitious. (Garfield, for that matter, soon would be serving the first of nine terms as a member of the U.S. House of Representatives.) "Mr. Chase and his daughter Kate," wrote Garfield to his wife on September 27, 1862, "have insisted that I shall stay with them while I remain in Washington, and so I came here this evening with all my luggage."

Garfield previously had been staying at Willard's Hotel, progenitor to today's Willard at the same site, just two blocks from the White House. After leading his regiment, the 42nd Ohio Infantry, in battle, the young colonel was in Washington in hopes of securing a new command that would advance his political agenda after the war—if, as he himself wrote, he didn't get killed in the meantime.

Soon, Garfield and Kate were going on "sightseeing" sojourns into the wartorn Virginia countryside, as well as enjoying the social gatherings that took place in the Chase home on many an evening, with the high and mighty of wartime Washington much in evidence. Thus it was that they set out one Friday early in October to visit Union troops quartered near Fairfax Court House and to view the site of the Second Battle of Bull Run. "On Friday last," Garfield wrote to his brother Harry, "Miss Kate Chase and I took their carriage and pompous liveried driver and, allowing him to change his tall plug for a comfortable slouch, we set out for General [Franz] Siegel's headquarters at Fairfax Court

House . . . Miss Chase had prepared two large baskets of provisions, partly for a present to the General and partly for our use if we should go on to the battlefield."

On Sunday morning, the outing continued, with Garfield riding a borrowed horse in borrowed boots and Kate traveling in a carriage, with another German general's wife, Mrs. Carl Schurz. Still another foreign general, Hungarian-born Julius Stahel, quartered in nearby Centreville, Virginia, furnished a cavalry troop "to see that the country was clear and safe for us to go to the battlefield."

What the visitors found there, almost within earshot of Washington and just a month after the second Union debacle at Bull Run, was no pretty sight.

"We went on," wrote Garfield, "across Bull Run to the limit of the late battle for about five miles beyond Centreville . . . and General Schurz, who was in the engagement, gave us a fine description of the whole two days' work and the shameful and unnecessary retreat which followed. We saw hundreds of graves, or rather, heaps of earth piled upon the bodies where they lay. Scores of heads, hands and feet were protruding, and so rapid had been the decomposition of 34 days that naked, eyeless skulls grinned at us as if the corpses had lifted their heads from their deathbeds to leer at us as we passed by. Shells and round shot lay scattered all over the field and broken muskets and dismantled gun carriages were very plenty. Hats, caps, coats, equipment, letters and all that lately belonged to life were scattered around.

"I picked up a joint promissory note of $1,000, which would probably be valuable to the heirs of some poor skeleton. 'Your loving wife til death' was the conclusion of a letter which lay near the bones of a skeleton arm which reached through the side of its grave, and had doubtless one day not long ago clasped the loving wife, but now the 'til death' has opened for him the portal of the world where 'there is neither marrying nor giving in the grave.'

"We followed the path of where the fierce giants struggled and saw their battle tracks thick with graves. At last we stopped and took a glass of milk with the old Negro who lives on the eastern marge of the field on the bank of Bull Run (to be a sadly famous stream hereafter) and who saw both battles—of 1861 and 1862.

All along the road from the Run to Centreville, and even far this side toward Fairfax, are wrecks of burned wagons and artillery carriages."

Garfield and Miss Kate returned to the capital the next day, crossing the Potomac by way of the Chain Bridge, but not before enjoying another night as guests of the German officers and a rousing sing-song with them and Mrs. Schurz. The day before Garfield also saw the "formidable" fortifications that Confederate General Beauregard had built on a "lofty ridge" at Centreville, as well as "the thousands of log huts [previously] built and occupied by the rebels . . . "

After writing about such adventures with the popular Miss Kate, Garfield soon heard a plaintive response from a piqued Mrs. Garfield back in Ohio. "From your letters to others," she wrote, "I learn that you and Miss Kate are taking dinners out, visiting camps, *etc.*, and I have a good deal of woman's curiosity to hear about some of those doings; and is Miss Kate a very charming, interesting young lady?"

To which Garfield hastily replied that his socialite hostess Kate Chase "is a woman of good sense and pretty good culture, has a good form but not a pretty face, its beauty being marred by a nose slightly inclined to pug." Nonetheless, Garfield added, "She has probably more social influence and makes a better impression generally than any other Cabinet lady."

Garfield soon departed from the Washington scene for a time, to become chief of staff to General William S. Rosecrans, to become a hero, it also would transpire, at the Battle of Chickamauga, even though it was a defeat for Rosecrans and his Union forces.

After Garfield's leave-taking, Kate Chase continued her heady social life, and a major figure in that unfolding drama was William Sprague, the young (31) governor of Rhode Island who had come to Washington to fight as a militia colonel. He allegedly had irritated his Regular Army colleagues for his inexperienced blundering at First Bull Run, and he also had taken part, in a minor way, in the ill-fated Peninsula campaign against Richmond. He apparently preferred the Nation's capital to his own state capital, since he officially left his governship behind to serve in the U.S.

Senate as of March 1863, a Democrat considered supportive of the Lincoln administration. One reason for such support on his part may have been his relationship with Cabinet member Salmon Chase's daughter Kate, whom he married in the fall of 1863.

With his money (for he had considerable), her father's prestige and her own reputation as a vivacious Washington hostess, it should have been a marriage made in heaven . . . a heaven for the politically ambitious. But it wasn't.

Secretary Chase, for his part, allied with the Radical Republicans, was briefly considered a possible rival to Lincoln himself for the 1864 Republican presidential nomination, just as he had been in 1860. Chase did leave the Cabinet in June of 1864, only to receive surprise appointment (from Lincoln) at year's end as Chief Justice of the Supreme Court. There, he was considered a Lincoln ally, ironical in light of their earlier rivalry.

Daughter Kate weathered the intrigues of the Civil War period as the socialite whose marriage in late 1863 had been a high point of that winter's social season. Five years later, she was still active on her father's behalf, in stirrings aimed at giving him the party's presidential nomination for 1868, but to no avail.

Her husband, meanwhile, had become too fond of the bottle, it is said. Kate, in time, was linked by capital whispers to another Senate member . . . and who knows? Her fourth child was mentally disabled. Her husband lost his fortune. Her father died. Suddenly, by 1882, she was a divorced woman with little to show for all the glamour and glitter she once had known. Even her family's old friend Garfield, nine times a Congressman, then himself elected President, could be of no help, since he had been assassinated shortly after becoming President in 1881.

Kate Chase Sprague at the end of her life (1899) was to be found managing her own small dairy and poultry farm. Her one-time husband, Sprague, lived longer . . . a two-term Senator before all was said and done, he lived to the age of 85, and when he died in Paris, France, in 1915, he was the last governor of the Civil War era still surviving.

Escape From Success

The enemy's fire, said Commander William B. Cushing later, "was very severe." So severe that in one instant, "the whole back of my coat was torn out by buckshot, and the sole of my shoe was carried away." And in another: "My clothing was perforated with bullets as I stood in the bow, the heel-jigger in my right hand and the exploding-line in the left."

In seconds, though, he had placed his torpedo device, primitive by today's standards, and . . . it blew all right. "The explosion took place at the same instant that 100 pounds of grape [grapeshot], at 10 feet range, crashed among us, and the dense mass of water thrown out by the torpedo came down with choking weight upon us."

Cushing, a daring young officer of the Union Navy, had achieved his aim of delivering a mortal blow to the last of the Confederate ironclads, the CSS *Albemarle*. To accomplish the feat, he and his volunteer crew ran a steam launch eight miles up the Roanoke River in North Carolina to Plymouth, a hotbed town of Rebel soldiery and sailors.

The Union men came at night, of course, late on October 16, 1864, and they weren't spotted until close to the "dark mountain of iron" looming in front of them. Once they were seen, however, it seemed every gun in the world was shooting at Cushing and his men. At this point, too, Cushing discovered his target was surrounded at its mooring by a ring of logs meant to keep away intruders like himself.

Undeterred, Cushing, still under fire, slowed his launch to a full stop, backed off to give himself room to make speed, then went at the log booms head-on, "trusting to their having been long enough in the water to have become slimy—in which case my boat, under full headway, would bump up against them and slip over into the pen with the ram."

And that's exactly what Cushing managed to do . . . while also blowing up the *Albemarle* at the end of the his scoot over the logs—quite a feat of dexterity, to say nothing of coolness under fire, since Cushing in his standing position at the bow had his boat to control, his spar torpedo to place, his lines to yank and pull in order to detach and then trigger the torpedo. All of which was done most successfully, but with success a dangerous penalty. Once his craft vaulted the log boom, Cushing might succeed in blowing the enemy ship, or he might not, but as he saw from the very beginning, his steam launch "would never get out again."

The huge explosion that rent the *Albemarle* resolved any doubts—Cushing's Union vessel instantly was swamped and began to sink. At this time of year the water was cold, too.

Cushing shouted to his men to save themselves, then struck out in the water for the opposite shore. "The whole surface of the stream was plowed up by grape and musketry, and my nearest friends, the [Union] fleet, were 12 miles away."

Nearby, with a "great, gurgling yell," Cushing's fireman Samuel Higgins went under and disappeared. Nearby, too, the Confederates soon were out on the water in their own boats, picking up other members of the Union raiding party.

Cushing, his strength fast ebbing in the chill water, swam onwards in the dark. He tried to help another crewman he heard splashing just behind, but that man also "sank like a stone."

Cushing then forced himself to keep moving, keep stroking,

in the direction of the town side of the river. "At last, and not a moment too soon," he wrote later, "I touched the soft mud and in the excitement of the first shock I half raised my body and made one step forward; then fell, and remained half in the mud and half in the water until daylight, unable to even crawl on hands and knees, nearly frozen with my brain in a whirl, but with one thing strong in me—the fixed determination to escape."

The growing light disclosed he was at one end of a swamp on the edge of Plymouth—"not 40 yards from one of the forts." Daylight showed the rebel town to be "swarming" with excited, angry soldiers and sailors. "It was a source of satisfaction to me to know that I had pulled the wire that set all these figures moving, but as I had no desire of being discovered, my first object was to get into a dry fringe of rushes that edged the swamp . . . "

First, he would have to cross a belt of open ground, 30 or 40 feet in width, without alarming a sentry pacing back and forth on a nearby Confederate parapet. Cushing waited until the man turned, dashed for half the distance and then threw himself flat just as the sentry turned once more. The dash had placed Cushing between two paths—and with little cover, except the river mud that covered him from head to toe. "Soon a party of four men came down the path at my right, two of them being officers, and passed so close to me as almost to tread upon my arm."

To Cushing's great relief, they moved on. He resumed his journey to the deep swamp, crawling "inch by inch, toward it." Once in the swamp and out of sight, he rose to his feet, plunged and tore ahead for about five hours before he came to solid ground. His path then alternatively took him through thickets of thorns and briars "that cut into the flesh at every step like knives," or through mire so soft under his weight that he was forced to throw his body upon it at length, and haul himself along by the arms. "Hands and feet raw from the ordeal, thoroughly exhausted, Cushing found more trouble ahead—a party of Confederate soldiers busy sinking schooners in the river channel to block it. Cushing circled behind them in a corn field, then plunged into a woods. He found an old black man and paid him $20 to go into town and find out what had happened to the Rebel ironclad the night before. While awaiting the report, Cushing was able to rest.

The old man returned with welcome news—the *Albemarle* had "gone down." Happy, Cushing resumed his escape journey. He soon was in more swamp with thick underbrush, struggling around until he hit a road, a stream, a Confederate picket party of seven soldiers and, behold!, their small, flat-bottomed skiff, tied to the root of a cypress tree.

The pickets were eating, and as they did so, Cushing braved the chill waters one more time to cast loose the skiff, push it along for 30 yards to the first bend in the stream, then squirm aboard. He then paddled away furiously—"as only a man could whose liberty was at stake."

He paddled, unceasing, for hours—to the mouth of the Roanoke River, across the sound beyond, until at last he reached the first ships of his own Union fleet on blockade station. With a cry to the nearest vessel of "Ship ahoy," he fell, now totally exhausted, into the water in the bottom of the skiff. "I had paddled every minute for ten successive hours, and for four my body had been 'asleep' with the exception of my arms and brain."

The Union sailors of the picket ship *Valley City* pulled the remarkable Commander Cushing aboard, and soon "rockets were thrown up and all hands . . . called to cheer ship" at news of his safe return from his hazardous mission.

Faces In The Crowd

A secret agent so secret not even his own side knew of his existence! That was smalltime publisher William A. Lloyd's precarious situation the moment that Abraham Lincoln was shot. Only the late President, it seems, had been aware that Lloyd did a bit more than simply publish railroad and steamship guides for Southern consumption. It was in that guise, though, that Lloyd had been allowed to re-enter the break-away territory, live there and travel widely while ostensibly gathering material for his guidebooks.

By prior, *personal* arrangement with Abe Lincoln, Lloyd also was gathering information on forts and troop dispositions, along with any other useful intelligence to be gleaned in his travels throughout the South. In short, he was spying.

The oddity was that he was spying for Lincoln, and Lincoln alone. He was, by contract signed with Lincoln, the President's own man in the Confederacy. He was paid $200 a month and expenses for his services.

The trouble was, only two of Lloyd's employees (and possibly his wife) knew of the arrangement. When Lloyd returned to Washington at war's end, after four years spent in the Confederacy, Edwin Stanton, Secretary of War, was willing to reimburse him for expenses ($2,380), but balked at paying the $200 a month retroactively. After Lloyd's own death just three years later, his estate sued the government for his back pay. Like Stanton, the U.S. Supreme Court raised a central question: Where's the contract signed with Lincoln? Unfortunately, faced with arrest in the South one time, the contract in his hat, Lloyd had destroyed it. Sorry, case denied.

* * *

A mystery man was Boston Corbett, a sergeant in the 16th New York Cavalry who survived five years as a prisoner at Andersonville, who then—in April 1865—joined in the pursuit of John Wilkes Booth, and certainly saw the barn where Booth was trapped set on fire. Then, a shot. And Booth wounded. *Fatally!* Who fired the shot? I did, said Boston Corbett. God told me to. Perhaps Booth shot himself, perhaps not, perhaps Corbett did . . . but some say Booth's pistol-ball wound could not have been caused by Corbett's carbine. In any case, Corbett accepted accolades (and reward money) from War Secretary Stanton, then stumped the country as the "Avenger of Blood." With Corbett, it should be explained, anything was possible. Before the war, he castrated himself. Later, hired as a doorkeeper for the Kansas State legislature, he fired two pistols indoors one day in 1886. No one killed this time, but off to the insane asylum. From which he then escaped— never to be seen publicly again.

* * *

Mystery man of another sort was Confederate officer John D. Kennedy of South Carolina, who somehow lived after suffering wounds six times . . . after being struck by 15 spent balls. An attorney in civilian life, he watched the shelling of Fort Sumter, then appeared at First Bull Run, Yorktown, Fair Oaks and Seven Days, Savage's Station, Antietam, Chancellorsville, Fredericksburg, Gettysburg, Knoxville, Petersburg, Shenandoah Valley, and even Bentonville at the war's 11th hour. After all this action, he then returned to his lawyering but only lived to age 56.

* * *

The captain of cavalry, Confederate cavalry, that is, probably was unique. Not because the captain ran a hospital in Richmond; not because the captain never rode a horse into combat, but because she was a woman—Captain Sally Tompkins. A single, still young, wealthy woman when the war started, she arranged to use a recently vacated home in Richmond as an emergency medical facility when the wounded from First Bull Run began to flow back from the front lines. The city was simply overwhelmed, and Judge John Robertson was more than happy to lend his Richmond home at Third and Main Streets for use as a 25-bed medical facility, since he and his family were moving to the country. In short order, and not stopping with that battle, Sally Tompkins was running a hospital—Robertson Hospital—with a better survival record for its patients than most, if not all, other Confederate hospitals, thanks in large part to her obsession with cleanliness. When the government insisted a few months later upon closing all such private hospitals to centralize the management of scarce medical supplies (and keep track of the soldier-patients), she appealed to Jefferson Davis. Impressed, he appointed her a captain in the Confederate Army. "In that way, your hospital can be saved," he said. With a slave woman named Phoebe her close companion and faithful worker, Sally Tompkins kept her hospital going until war's end, with an astounding record of only 73 deaths among her 1,333 patients.

* * *

Each a grandson of Revolutionary War icon Paul Revere, Joseph Warren Revere and Paul Joseph Revere carved out entirely contradictory careers as Civil War soldiers and only one of them survived. Joseph, the older of the pair, had served in the U. S. Navy and in the Mexican Army prior to the Civil War. Twenty years younger, Paul was far less experienced in military matters. Each served in the Union Army, and each appeared at one or more of the war's major battles in the East—Joe at Chancellorsville, Paul at Ball's Bluff and Antietam, among others. Joseph didn't fare so well as a temporary divisional commander at Chancellorsville, however—he was court-martialed for withdrawing his command without orders to do so. The sentence was outright dismissal from the army, but President Lincoln allowed him to resign instead.

Young Paul, in the meantime, had been wounded and captured at Ball's Bluff. He was held as a hostage guaranteeing the safety of Confederate privateers detained by Union authorities. Released at last, he was wounded again at Antietam. Once more recovered from his wounds, he led the 20th Massachusetts at Gettysburg, where he was wounded again, this time fatally. Paul died two days after his wounding the second day of battle at Gettysburg . . . Joseph Revere lived until 1880, publishing a memoir of his career and traveling widely in the post-war period.

* * *

You don't hear much about Jay Cooke, a high school dropout, but where would the Union Army have found its funding without his success in selling government bond issues? Arriving in Washington as a financial adviser to Treasury Secretary Salmon P. Chase, Cooke wasted no time in obtaining loan guarantees from Northern banks. His Jay Cooke and Company, as the Federal government's *exclusive* agent, then sold more than $850 million in bonds during the early months of the war. "This money kept the army in the field," says Stewart Sifakis in his compendium *Who Was Who in the Civil War*. Some in Congress, compiler Sifakis also said, gave vent to their uneasiness over allowing the Ohioan what amounted to a monopoly, but Cooke nevertheless proved himself a wizard with money . . . and "has been credited with doing as much to win the war as the armies in the field." Toward war's end, he even advanced personal and company millions "to stabilize the market, which, due to the actions of speculators, was facing a panic." All this from a man who left school at the age of 14!

* * *

If Jefferson Davis, future President of the Confederacy, was one of Mississippi's two U. S. Senators at the time of secession, who was the other . . . and what became of him? Meet, please, Albert Gallatin Brown, South Carolina-born *ante-bellum* attorney and militia general in Mississippi after moving there as a child. A successful—indeed, outstanding—politician, he served in the state legislature, and in the U. S. House, then became Governor of Mississippi. Brown had been in the U. S. Senate for nearly ten years at the time he and Davis resigned their seats on January 12, 1861. Brown then went home, gathered together an infantry company and, as a captain with the 18th Mississippi, saw action at First Bull Run and Ball's Bluff. He returned to the legislative forum as an appointed member of the Senate in the First Confederate Congress (February 1862). There, as chairman of the Naval Affairs Committee, he argued that the legislature should have greater control over the war effort, even at the expense of some civil liberties. If that was not enough to explain his split with fellow Mississippi figure Jefferson Davis, Brown also urged the emancipation and arming of the South's slaves, an expanded draft, and using the Confederacy's money-making cotton fields for production of vitally needed food crops. At war's end, he urged the South to "shake hands" with the North and adopt a cooperative attitude during Reconstruction. For this, he was branded a "submissionist".

* * *

He was black, he was a freed slave, and he sang a number of Scottish songs with an authentic Scottish "burr," thanks to his onetime master, a Virginian of Scottish descent. For a time, John Scobell traveled with Union spymaster Allan Pinkerton's agent Hattie Lawson (white and female) in the role of her servant. When she was arrested in Richmond in March 1862, her "manservant" Scobell was allowed to walk away—no interrogation, no suspicion attached. He spent the entire war a spy for the Union, protected in large part by the fact he was a black man. Thus, he worked at different places—as a laborer helping to build earthworks, even as a vendor visiting Southern encampments. Said Pinkerton one time: "He had only to assume the role of a light-hearted darky, and no one would suspect his real role." Helpful in Scobell's spying career, too, was the fact that his equally "invisible" wife stayed in Richmond, the Confederate capital, as a cook—presumably feeding valuable information, knowingly or unknowingly, to her spy husband. With war's end though, no medals, no hoopla—the pair simply disappeared from the pages of history.

RED SHIRT, WHITE SHIRT

In the Union camp hard by the Rappahannock River few of the men in blue gave much thought to the new black man Dabney, hired to serve at headquarters both as cook and *body servant*, in the terminology of the day. This in early 1863, after Fredericksburg and before Chancellorsville, and at "Fighting Joe" Hooker's headquarters, it says in an old account.

And few thought it so very odd when the free black from a farm across the river offered to share his knowledge of the local terrain. Nor did it seem so unusual, either, when he showed a lively interest in the Union Army's signals system. And why should anyone be too astounded when Dabney picked up on the various signals and remembered them quite easily, as well?

The earth did not fall off its foundations when one day his wife—having arrived in camp with him—announced that she would like to go back across the river because, it was explained, she had opportunity to work as a servant over there for a "secesh woman." Neither Hooker nor his staff made any real objection.

Life went on with Dabney still home, at Union headquarters, and his wife gone over there, across the river.

Perhaps, though, her job wasn't quite what it first seemed, since soon it turned out that she really was a laundress at a Confederate Army headquarters.

If, in truth, such a situation really had been permitted, a husband at one headquarters and his wife at that of the opposing army, it does seem surprising to us today that such an arrangement would have been allowed by either headquarters, had either set of officers really known.

But . . . on with the story! At Hooker's headquarters, people began to realize that the servant and cookman Dabney seemed to know amazing things about Confederate plans and movements. Yet he never left the Union encampment—too busy being a cook and body servant. Hooker had his reliable scouts and other intelligence sources, but as time went on, few of them could match the stream of accurate information that Dabney seemed to pick up on a daily basis.

How did he do it? Well, he agreed one day to explain the mystery to one of the Union officers. He took the officer to a nearby spot with a view across the river to the outskirts of Fredericksburg. He told his listener to take note of a cabin close to the river on that opposite side—to look at its clothesline!

Here's what he allegedly said: "Well, that clothesline tells me in a half an hour just what goes on at Lee's headquarters. You see my wife over there; she washes for the officers, cooks, and waits around, and as soon as she hears about any movement or anything going on she comes down and moves the clothes on that line so I can understand in a minute." In sum, Dabney's tutelage in Union signals had come home to roost! He and his wife had worked out a system of their own that wasn't from the manual, exactly . . . but, like a baseball manager's signalling to his pitcher, it worked very effectively.

"That there gray shirt," explained Dabney to his dumbfounded listener, "is Longstreet; and when she takes it off it means he's gone down about Richmond."

There were other shirts, too. "That white shirt means [A.P.] Hill; and when she moves it down to the west end of the line, Hill's corps has moved upstream. That red one is Stonewall Jackson. He's down on the right now, and if he moves, she'll move that red shirt."

Dabney was able to point out a clothesline signal being sent even as they gazed across the river. See the two blankets pinned together at the bottom, he asked his companion. "Why that's her way of making a fish trap; and when she pins the clothes together that way, it means that Lee is only trying to draw us into his fish-trap."

Who knows? Perhaps something like that was in Lee's mind not long after, when he engaged Hooker at Chancellorsville (May 1-2) and sent his "Red Shirt" (Jackson) on a 14-mile loop to strike Hooker's forces at their western flank . . . except that in carrying out the maneuver, Stonewall Jackson was mortally wounded by his own men. He died shortly after, and A.P. Hill (Dabney's "White Shirt") was one of the last names he mentioned.

More Than A Few Ghosts

Yours to believe or not, quite a few ghostly stories came out of the Civil War era . . . such as the repeated sightings over the years of a phantom train plying the rails of upstate New York, its headlight stabbing through the night. Abe Lincoln's funeral train, it is alleged.

Or Lincoln's very own story—lengthy, detailed statement, in fact—that he dreamed of a person lying dead in a casket, surrounded by mourners, in the East Room of the White House. In his dream, Lincoln approached a soldier guarding the catafalque bearing the body that was lying in state. The dead man's face was hidden, covered up.

"Who is dead in the White House?" the dream-Lincoln demanded to know. "The President," came the horrifying reply. "He was killed by an assassin.."

A haunting dream indeed! "I slept no more that night," said Lincoln later, "and although it was only a dream, I have been strangely annoyed by it ever since."

It was shortly afterwards that Lincoln was killed by an assassin, John Wilkes Booth, and himself lay in state in the same East Room of the White House.

It of course would have been quite natural for Lincoln, a constant target of hate mail, vilification and death threats, to fear assassination on some inner level. Outwardly he usually did appear calm and unafraid, but he would have been less than human not to have worries, and they easily could have manifested themselves in a nightmarish dream. Mary Todd Lincoln, however, saw it differently. Hysterical in the aftermath of his fatal shooting, she quickly claimed, "His dream was prophetic."

For that matter, another somber moment in the Lincoln White House came with the death of their young son Willie in the winter of 1862 from a severe fever. The boy's mother went to bed and screamed until exhaustion overtook her and she fell asleep. Lincoln, in the meantime, went to his secretary John Nicolay's office, the "Lincoln Sitting Room" of today, and sobbed and wept.

During the funeral five days later, it is said, a fierce wind springing up under black skies rolled up tin roofs all over Washington, toppled chimneys and upset church steeples.

Years later, half a century afterwards, to be more exact, President William Howard Taft was quite annoyed one day when told that a kitchen worker was quitting and other servants might do the same because of a White House ghost. Maids and housemen had been frightened by sightings of a gossamer figure, even the cold touch of an invisible hand, it was alleged. Nonsense! exploded Taft. But . . . he did ask whose ghost. And he was told that it was the pathetic Willie Lincoln, who had died in the second floor Prince of Wales Room—the same chamber where his slain father's body would be embalmed three years later.

Taft still didn't think much of such mewlings—he told his staff never to discuss such happenings again.

Even so, ghost stories persisted at the White House, while many other odd and ghostly tales related to the Civil War also have emerged from widely scattered sites over the years.

At Virginia Military Institute, for instance, home of the young cadets who fought the Battle of New Market against heavy odds, they say that Civil War sculptor Sir Moses Ezekiel's statue of *Virginia Mourning Her Dead* has been known to moan in grief on some evenings . . . even to show tears on her finely chiseled face.

Not far away from VMI's home in Lexington, Virginia, stands a 20-room mansion with 13 fireplaces (one with no accompanying chimney) called "Selma." The story is that a young Confederate soldier was chased into the Shenandoah Valley home one day by a Union cavalryman and killed in the dining room, in front of its fireplace. A bloodstain remained there for years.

So, it seems, did his ghost. Visitors often asked the owners of the house about the mysterious stranger they had encountered, while servants repeatedly told of a "soldier gentleman" they had seen. According to L.B. Taylor, Jr., author of a series of books about Virginia ghosts, no one other than the immediate family was in the house at those odd moments. "Although ownership of the mansion passed through several hands over the years, the apparitional soldier stayed on." According to Taylor, too, Phyllis Atwater of Charlottesville, Virginia, who said she was "very sensitive" to psychic phenomena, conducted a "release ceremony" at Selma in which she counseled the soldierly ghost to leave the house and find his final peace. He did.

Another site of "haunted" visitation, writes Taylor, is the Lee family's ancestral home of Stratford Hall in Westmoreland County, east of Fredericksburg, Virginia. This was the magnificent home built by L. Thomas Lee in the 1730s, later to be home to

"Lighthorse Harry" Lee, father of Robert E. Lee, and, briefly, for young Robert, too. The ghosts allegedly seen in and about Stratford Hall and its various outbuildings are associated with earlier family members, rather than Civil War figures, but there also have been reports of a ghostly boy and dog seen at the brick home in Alexandria, Virginia, where Robert spent most of his boyhood.

More grim are the visions at sites associated with Mary Surratt, the boarding-house owner convicted of taking part in the assassination plot against Abraham Lincoln . . . and hanged in the yard at Washington Arsenal Prison, (the first woman ever executed for murder in the United States, notes writer Taylor). The old prison site is now Fort Leslie J. McNair, and here a ghostly middle-aged woman dressed in black has been seen "floating through the hallways," by one officer's account. Here, too, strange voices and touchings by unseen hands.

Similar sightings were reported years earlier at the H Street site in Washington where Mary Surratt once operated her boarding house.

Do people respond to such stories of the macabre? Indeed!

So many people wanted to see the reappearing bloodstains on the farm porch near Port Royal, Virginia, where the fatally wounded John Wilkes Booth died that the owners "finally had to remove the boards and refloor the porch," reports Taylor.

Likewise, when Mary Surratt's specter was reported at the H Street house in Washington, "crowds gathered outside the house daily." Her daughter sold the house, "but the purchaser was driven away within six weeks because 'his nervous system was reputedly shattered by what he had seen and heard.' " *The Boston Post* followed the story and said other proprietors came and went in "swift succession, swearing that in the dead of night Mrs. Surratt walked the hallways clad in her robe of death." Then, too, Mrs. Lincoln once said that her two dead sons, Willie and Eddie, appeared at the foot of her bed every night! Yours to believe . . . or not.

"Shot For You"

Truly now, how bad was it? It all may seem so distant, that period of history so remote . . . and surely warfare in that distant day and age was archaic, mere child's play by today's grim standards. So, truly, what was it like? When those old-timers fired a gun or a cannon, a fellow could duck, right?

Well, on occasion, perhaps a fellow could see it coming at that. James Longstreet, Confederate general of considerable note both then and now, once recalled the time at Antietam Creek (Sharpsburg, Maryland, that is) when he, Robert E. Lee and fellow general D.H. Hill started up a ridge to reconnoiter, and Hill insisted on staying on his horse while the other two more wisely dismounted.

Perhaps jokingly—but prophetically, as it turned out— Longstreet warned Hill he would draw Union fire and added, "give us a little interval so that we may not be in the line of fire when they open up on you."

Minutes later, now at the top of the crest with his companions, Longstreet saw a particular puff of smoke from the cannons on the Federal left. The gunner had to be a mile distant, but Longstreet told Hill, still on his horse, "There is a shot for you."

Sure enough, seconds later, the cannon shot "came whisking through the air" toward the very spot where the three men waited. It came and it sheared off the front legs of General Hill's horse . . . without, however, harming the rider.

It was rare, however, that a battlefield victim "saw it coming" or could duck away. In the same battle, the same day, in a suicidal charge like Pickett's at Gettysburg, a massed, overwhelming wedge of bluecoats advanced on the center of Lee's line— advanced, more specifically, on Confederate General John Gordon of Georgia and his men, with bayonets at the ready. "As I saw this solid mass of men moving upon me with determined step and front of steel," said Gordon later, "every conceivable plan of meeting and repelling was rapidly considered. To oppose man against man and strength against strength was impossible, for there were four lines of blue to my one of gray."

Gordon's first thought was to open fire the moment the Union men came into range, but he just as quickly realized that would not be enough. "I could not hope to kill and disable a sufficient number of the enemy to reduce his strength to an equality of mine."

At the same time, he knew from all visible signs that his Union counterpart ("superbly mounted") would have ordered the bluecoats to advance with unloaded guns, a familiar battlefield tactic intended to keep a few men from stopping to aim and fire. A scattered few doing so in the front ranks obviously would stop others behind . . . and disturb the solid wall of men assembled to advance en masse. As Gordon could see, it was the Union's intent "to break through Lee's center by the crushing weight and momentum of his solid column."

The only thought that appealed to Gordon in the few minutes he had to form a battle plan—and stop the Union tide—was one he had never tried but could trust to have terrible effect. "It was to hold my fire until the advancing Federals were almost upon my lines, and then turn loose a sheet of flame and lead into their faces. I did not believe that any troops on earth, with empty guns in their hands, could withstand so sudden a shock and withering a fire."

And so it was. With difficulty to be sure, Gordon restrained his own men from firing, even when they could see the eagles on the buttons of the blue uniforms, until finally "it would not do to wait another second," and Gordon shouted with all conceivable lung power, "Fire!"

At that, "My rifles flamed and roared in the Federals' faces like a blinding blaze of lightning accompanied by the quick and deadly thunderbolt."

No Union man in that front line could have ducked, surely. None who survived would ever say, if alive today, that the fire-power of the 1860s was any less frightening than that of today.

"The entire front line," related Gordon in his later account, "with few exceptions, went down in the consuming blast." Gordon, himself, considered the effect of his tactic "appalling."

The Union commander, he noted, went down, too, but the

victim in this case was only the horse, "the rider unhurt."

The sudden and massive volley saved Lee's center for the moment; the blue ranks had to fall back as the Rebels continued to fire into the Union mass.

But the unhorsed Union commander was not yet through for the day. "Beyond the range of my rifles he reformed his men into three lines, and on foot led them to the second charge, still with unloaded guns."

But again repulsed. After that, yet again, four successive charges in all, "in the fruitless effort to break through my lines with the bayonet."

At last the Union men loaded their own weapons, drew up in close ranks and within easy range opened a "galling" fire of their own. From that point the battle between "these hostile American lines" waxed "furious and deadly" for some time after. "The list of the slain was lengthened with each passing moment . . . "

Indeed, Antietam went down in history as the bloodiest single day of the Civil War, with nearly 26,000 men on both sides counted as casualties. The 5,000 or so of them killed outright obviously didn't, couldn't, duck the fire.

No Whizz, Bang Heard

Far from "ducking" the shot and shell of the Civil War, the war's fighting men often just couldn't get away from all the shooting . . . of all shapes and sizes. One who could later tell you was Prussian-born Heros von Borcke, a staff aide to Confederate cavalry General "Jeb" Stuart. He was placed in a doctor's home in Sharpsburg, Maryland (Battle of Antietam Creek), the morning of September 16, 1862, with about ten couriers while Stuart rode on a reconnaissance mission up the nearby Potomac River. Von Borcke's job was to look over the incoming reports and "forward any important information" to Generals Lee, Longstreet or "Stonewall" Jackson, who was just then approaching from freshly seized Harpers Ferry.

The Union artillery began to find the range about 11 o'clock in the morning, with a nearby church steeple an obvious reference point. Outside the doctor's house, the streets of the small village had been full of wagon trains, artillery, ambulances, galloping riders, but now no one indoors or out could be counted as safe. Indeed, as von Borcke sat there, a shell "fell with a terrific crash through the top of the building . . . "

About noon, the shelling "became really appalling, and the explosion of innumerable projectiles stunned the ear."

Von Borcke remained on a sofa on the first floor to be available as Stuart's headquarters contact. He was sitting there, writing in his journal, "when a shell, piercing the wall of the room a few feet above my head, covered me with debris, and, exploding, scattered furniture in every direction." Simultaneously, "another missile, entering the upper part of the house and passing directly through, burst in the courtyard, killing one of our horses and rendering the others frantic with terror."

Von Borcke and his couriers hurriedly left the house at last, but the Prussian had a difficult time calming his horse enough to climb into the saddle for a fast retreat. The streets now were filled with dead and wounded men, overturned wagons and ambulances, and in the village "cannonballs whizzed incessantly through the air, and pieces of bursting shells, splinters of wood, and scattered fragments of brick were whirled about in a dense cloud of powder smoke that enveloped all things."

Von Borcke escaped personal harm after leaving the village in "an exciting ride", but his horse had been pinked on a hind leg by a shell fragment.

Others engaged in the Battles of Antietam and its preliminary at South Mountain often never knew what hit them. Death, maiming, or recoverable injury struck with no warning whatsoever.

George Smith, a minister from Georgia, was at South Mountain with the Phillips Legion, a regiment commanded by Colonel William Phillips. Smith and his fellows soon encountered the bluecoats while charging into the woods. "I saw a poor fellow fall and heard him say, 'Lord Jesus, receive my spirit.' I went to him and said, 'My friend, that's a good prayer; I hope you feel it.' He answered, 'Stranger, I am not afraid to die; I made my peace with God over thirty years ago.'"

If Smith found that response surprising, he didn't have long to ponder it. The bluecoats suddenly were on all sides of the Georgians, and they, in fact, were in retreat. "Just then I felt a strange dizziness, and fell, my arm dropping lifeless by my side." Worse, "blood was gurgling from my throat."

He thought he was mortally wounded—and was close to correct, since the ball had "entered my neck, and, ranging downward, came out near my spine, paralyzing my arm." The men with Smith were not overly encouraging. " 'Yes, parson,' they said, 'it's all up with you.' " (He did live to tell the tale, though.)

Likewise, Union Sergeant A.F. Hill witnessed—and soon enough felt—the random danger of the battlefield. Marching with George Meade's division, Hill and his men came under Rebel artillery fire. At the command to lie down, Hill instead took a seat on a stump—just then "a large ragged fragment of a shell whizzed savagely past the top of my head and struck the ground a few paces in [the] rear with a fierce *splat*. It must have struck my head had I been a moment later in sitting down."

Moments later, another shell—"Whizz, bang!"—burst ten or 15 feet above Hill and his comrades, but with no apparent ill effect. The next day, though, Hill ran into more Rebel fire—this time, "a regiment of rebels who had lain concealed among the tall corn arose and poured on us the most withering volley we had ever felt." And then another and another. "The slaughter was fearful. I never saw men fall so fast. I was obliged to step over them at every step."

Minutes later, Hill saw a pair of Rebs helping a wounded comrade from the field, their backs turned to him. "I was going to fire, but . . . I could not. I sought another mark; and seeing a rebel in the act of loading his gun just at the edge of the cornfield, I fired at him."

No mention of the outcome, but the battle continued to rage in any case. Minutes later Sergeant Hill had organized his men, and all were firing at a line of Confederates, Hill trying to bring down the opposing side's enemy color-bearer. " . . . I aimed every shot at the point over which the flag waved. At every fire I looked eagerly to see it fall."

Someone apparently was looking at Hill. "I had fired a dozen rounds at the rebel flag when I suddenly became conscious of a most singular and unpleasant feeling in my left leg. I was in the act of ramming down a ball at the time, and I would have finished, but my left foot, of its own accord, raised from the ground, a benumbing sensation ran through my leg, and I felt the hot blood streaming down my thigh. The truth flashed upon me—I was wounded."

That's how it often happened—out of the blue; not even a whizz, bang. That was the end of the war for Hill, who was carried from the front by his comrades, then trundled over a rough, *rough* cornfield in a wagon and soon was told the bad news. The bone in his upper thigh was "all smashed," the leg would have to come off. He protested, but the doctors were firm.

He had been left with other wounded outside a small school-house serving as a field hospital. "It was evening when my turn came. I had lain during the whole afternoon . . . listening to the horrible screams which came from within and occasionally, to kill time, gazing upon a heap of men's arms and legs which lay piled up against the side of the house. The sound of battle could still be heard."

Then he was carried inside, and again he asked if his leg absolutely had to be taken off. The doctor "coolly thrust his finger into the wound and felt the pieces of shattered bone. 'That bone,' said he, 'is shivered all to pieces, and if you value your life—'

" 'Can my life be saved only by—?'

" 'Yes, and even then I doubt—I—' He hesitated.

" 'You think it a doubtful case, even then?'

" 'Yes.'

"I said no more. Chloroform was administered I sank into unconsciousness, and when I awoke,—it was all over." Over . . . except that Hill was another one who did survive to tell the tale, in a book published nearly 30 years later. He had been fortunate after all.

WOMEN OF THE TIMES

A few women of the times . . . not all like **Bridget Fury**, born in Cincinnati under the name Delia Swift, but long since removed to New Orleans as a prostitute, pickpocket, mugger, and even murderess. She moved on to becoming a madam after being freed from prison by the Federal authorities occupying the city in 1862. Born in 1837, she would have been in her late twenties during most of the Civil War. She had her own street gang at one time. After her release from prison under a general Union pardon, she again had to serve behind prison walls, this time for robbery. It is believed she died at age 35 or 36, unsung by decent folk but thoroughly notorious in the South for her life of crime.

—**Rose O'Neal Greenhow** revelled in rubbing elbows with *ante-bellum* Washington society, meeting high and mighty figures such as President James Buchanan and South Carolina's famous John C. Calhoun. She would be a remarkable heroine of the war, too—as a spy for the Confederate cause. It was her information, quite likely, that alerted Southern forces to the approach of Union General Irvin McDowell at the time of First Bull Run in 1861, a significant Confederate victory.

Rose Greenhow did not travel among the high and mighty of *wartime* Washington for very long. Once her spying activities came to light, she first was placed under house arrest, then was held in the Old Capitol Prison. Amazingly, she still sent out her information, and at last she was forced to leave town—deported South. Then, seemingly and safely placed among her compatriots of the Confederacy, the Maryland-born widow traveled to England and France in 1863 to win friends and influence Europeans on behalf of the South. She also published an account of her detention in Washington under the Lincoln administration called *My Imprisonment and the First Year of Abolition Rule at Washington*.

In 1864, she returned to her native land and met a tragic end off the coast of North Carolina. Her small boat was swamped as she tried to reach the shore during a storm that roiled the waters. Weighted down by a money belt filled with gold for her beloved Confederacy, she was drowned on the spot.

—Private **Franklin Thompson** of Company F, 2nd Michigan Infantry, born in Canada in 1841, would go down in history as the only *female* member of the post-war Union veterans' organization, the Grand Army of the Republic. Startling, yes, but fitting, since Private "Franklin" was really a young woman in soldier's uniform, real name Sarah Emma Edmonds. It seems she had worked her father's farm in boy's clothes as a child, had run off from an "arranged" marriage, had sold Bibles in the United States under the name Franklin Thompson and subsequently joined the Union army, at first serving as a field nurse.

She then operated as a spy, passing through enemy lines in Virginia in both male and female guises, as both black and white. When she eventually contracted malaria, she deserted for fear of being exposed as a woman while ill. As a woman once more, she became a civilian nurse for a religious organization. After the war, she married—and shocked her old comrades of the 2nd Michigan by appearing at a reunion as herself, a woman. She joined the Grand Army; she also petitioned Congress, successfully, to forgive her desertion by official action. Most amazing of all, perhaps, at the Battle of Antietam, she now reported, she had buried a Union soldier who was a woman! Incidentally, in 1934, another woman's remains were found in a common grave for nine soldiers killed at Shiloh, all Union.

—**Louisa May Alcott**, yet to write *Little Women*, spent time during the Civil War working as a nurse at a Georgetown hospital—the basis for her *Hospital Sketches* of 1863. Her first novel, *Moods*, would appear the next year, with her best known work, *Little Women*, emerging soon after the war in 1868.

—It was the idea of **Margaret Anna Parker Knobeloch**, and it won informal approval from the Union's Secretary of War, Edwin Stanton, usually an implacable enemy of anything Confederate. Please allow her, proposed this Northern-born, Southern-raised woman, to provide aid for Confederate prisoners held near her home in Philadelphia, the money to be provided by Southerners then living in Europe. Married to a German, John Knobeloch, who had returned home to avoid the Northern draft, Margaret could make the necessary funding arrangements through their European contacts. Stanton allowed her work to go forward in exactly that manner, from 1862 through the end of the war. Margaret did her Good Samaritan work among the prisoners held at hospitals in Philadelphia, where she had been born, and at Fort Delaware nearby.

—This woman's dream began during the Civil War but would not reach fruition until a tragic anticlimax, the assassination of Abraham Lincoln. As an apprentice to the famous sculptor Clark Mills, **Vinnie Ream**, not yet 20, was determined some day to render Lincoln in stone. He, in fact, agreed to sit for the young woman in late 1864. After he was killed a few months later (April 14, 1865), Vinnie Ream was among the artists who competed for the honor of producing a Congressionally commissioned life-size, full-length statue of the martyred president. As the first woman ever given a Congressional sculpturing commission, she won the $10,000 contract. Her work, completed in 1870, went into the Statuary Hall at the U.S. Capitol, where it still may be seen today.

—**Harriet Tubman**'s first name, her name before she escaped slavery in 1849, was Araminta. Once safe in the North, she could have stayed inactive, but no . . . even before the Civil War began, she repeatedly risked recapture to travel south and help guide other runaway slaves to freedom—possibly as many as 300, among them her own parents. When war erupted, she again could have remained inactive, her self-appointed duty largely done. But no, again risking her own freedom, and even life, she joined Union forces on the South Carolina coast as a cook, nurse and laundress—and perhaps as a spy, too, well able because of her black skin and knowledge of the slave life to operate behind the Confederate lines unsuspected for what she really was—an enemy of all that smacked of slavery.

—A female doctor of the 19th century, a suffragette, a divorcee, and a winner of the Medal of Honor was **Mary E. Edwards**, 30 years old when the Civil War began. How could all that be? Well, it seems that she graduated from a New York medical school in 1855, but soon found it difficult to build a practice as a recently divorced woman. Along came the Civil War, and a post at the Patent Office Hospital in Washington as an army surgeon.

But that was not enough for this young woman. She soon had arranged a field post as an assistant surgeon in an Ohio regiment, the 52nd. She was captured while tending to civilians outside her unit's encampment and was held prisoner in Richmond for four months. Exchanged, she returned to her army duties, but no longer "in the field." A few months after the war's end, she was awarded the Medal of Honor for her wartime performance and she became an active suffragette and reformer, travelling and lecturing, often in male clothing. She didn't get along with her fellow reformers, and she later was fired from a government job for insubordination. She wound up making appearances in carnival sideshows. In 1917, Mary Edwards was told to return her Medal of Honor, in accord with new government policy stating that it could only be given for bravery in combat, rather than for meritorious service. She ignored the request! And, when she died at 87, she still had her medal.

WOMAN AT THE LEAD

When all is said and done in respect to the Battle of Brandy Station, Virginia, often noted as the largest cavalry engagement in *American* history, one more thing might be said . . . of the hulking *German* horseman who fought on one side, and of the dashing *Frenchman* who rode in yon opposite side.

Both officers had earned their epaulets in the armies of Europe. They were among the thousands of foreign-born immigrants (or passing visitors) who took sides for either Union or Confederacy. They were, at the same time, among the handful of "furriners" who rose to high rank, created legend . . . or both.

For instance, the Confederacy's brave and esteemed General Patrick Cleburne, a product of County Cork, Ireland. Here was an immigrant who arrived on these shores as a young man, who became one of the South's most astute and beloved generals—before he fell in battle at Franklin, Tennessee.

At Brandy Station, much earlier, the German fighting for the

Confederates was Major Johann August Heinrich Heros von Borcke, a staff officer and aide to "Jeb" Stuart of cavalry fame. Easily noticed, Borcke once was described by a Northern journalist as a "giant, mounted on a tremendous horse, and brandishing wildly over his head a sword as long and big as a fence rail."

The dashing Frenchman riding opposite the Prussian-born giant at Brandy Station was named, as fact would have it, Alfred *Napoleon* Alexander Duffie. A graduate of the St. Cyr military academy and a veteran of the Crimean War, "Nattie," as friends and comrades called him, was at Brandy Station in command of a Union division.

It is not our purpose here to ascertain if the two met in the field or knew much of one another, but rather to rush on . . . to cite also, among others, Prussian-born Carl Schurz. An immigrant and a Lincoln political disciple appointed general, he was a division commander at both Second Bull Run in 1862 and at Gettysburg. He was in the lines opposite the Irish-born Cleburne at Chattanooga, as well.

Another German-born general with political "clout" was the less fortunate Franz Sigel, who sported an impressive-looking array of battle stars, only to ruin it all by emerging the loser in the Battle of New Market, despite the superior force he had wheeled up against the Rebels and their VMI cadets.

Rushing on further, Hungarian-born Julius Stahel began his adult life by rising from private to lieutenant in the Austrian army. He turned European revolutionary and then fled to America as a journalist and educator. Here he became, in time, a Union general, a veteran of both Bull Run battles, and winner of the Medal of Honor.

Perhaps the most romantic of all the immigrant figures who appeared in the ranks of the Civil War soldiery for either side, however, was a Russian named *Turchin*. And, no, not the Ivan Vasilosvitch *Turchininoff* who graduated from the Imperial Military School of St. Petersburg, who served on the staff of future Czar Alexander II. Nor even the same John Basil *Turchin* (his name now altered for the sake of the American tongue), recent immigrant and Union colonel made notorious by allowing—

indeed, encouraging—his men to sack and pillage the town of Athens, Alabama.

No, not that one, but rather his Russian-born wife! *Mrs*. Turchininoff—Turchin, that is—who allegedly took command of her husband's regiment for several days while he was ill, who may have led that same regiment in battle (minor though it was) one day in Tennessee. And who rushed to Washington, it also is averred, gained entrance to the White House and persuaded Abe Lincoln to void the court-martial verdict against her husband for the rape of Athens—and even to promote him to brigadier general!

ROAD TO GETTYSBURG

Seen and heard on the road to Gettysburg—At the Potomac River, on June 23, 1863, Colonel Abner Perrin of the 14th South Carolina Infantry Regiment: "I do not suppose that any army ever marched into an enemies' [sic] country with greater confidence in its ability . . . and with more reasonable grounds for that confidence." Likewise, British Lieutenant Colonel Arthur Freemantle, a friendly, self-appointed observer traveling with Robert E. Lee's northbound columns, was moved to call the troops marching before him "a remarkably fine body of men . . . [who] looked quite seasoned and ready for any work."

The next day, over on the Maryland side of the Potomac, a famous Confederate threesome was gathered at Robert E. Lee's tent for a conference—Lee himself, A. P. Hill and James Longstreet, his two corps commanders. In came a youngster named Leighton Parks, an acquaintance from Lee's invasion of Maryland the year before. The small boy appeared this time with a bucket of raspberries for Lee, who picked him up, kissed him and invited him to stay for lunch. The child then took turns on the great commander's knee, on Longstreet's knee and on a horse ordered forward by A. P. Hill.

Soon after, Lee's march northward resumed.

Seen and heard on the road to Gettysburg as the Maryland

countryside fell behind—British observer Freemantle on the Pennsylvania Dutch: "They are the most unpatriotic people I ever saw, and openly state that they don't care which side wins, provided they are left alone. They abuse Lincoln tremendously."

Confederate division commander Dorsey Pender, in a letter to his wife on June 28: "I never saw troops march as ours do; they will go 15 or 20 miles a day without leaving a straggler and hoop and yell on all occasions."

Also seen and heard . . . *Cincinnati Gazette* reporter Whitelaw Reid wrote that the Union army "had done surprisingly little damage to property along their route." Breaking off the fruit-laden boughs of cherry trees seemingly was the army's worst offense. But Yankee stragglers and drunks were another proposition altogether! Approaching Gettysburg on July 1, first day of the watershed battle, Raid found "drunken loafers in uniform" in every farmhouse. "They swarmed about the stables, stealing horses at every opportunity and compelling farmers to keep up a constant watch." Further, "In the fence corners groups of them lay, too drunk to get on at all."

Back with the invading Confederate force, British observer Freemantle, on the other hand, was impressed by the lack of Rebel stragglers and the order from on high forbidding indiscriminate foraging in the enemy country. Even so, "in such a large army as this there must be many instances of bad characters, who are always ready to plunder and pillage whenever they can do so without being caught." Stragglers left behind no doubt would do their harm, thought Freemantle. "It is impossible to prevent this," he later wrote, "but every thing that can be done is done to protect private property and non-combatants, and I can say, from my own observation, with wonderful success."

At Chambersburg, Pennsylvania, he also noted, some Texans were ordered to break up a few barrels of whiskey "liberated" in or near the town. The order was a "pretty good trial for their discipline . . . [but] they did their duty like good soldiers."

Freemantle, like Pender, was impressed by the good marching order of the Rebel soldiery. As the Confederates closest to the Brit drew near Gettysburg on July 1, they heard firing ahead and began to see the wounded carried back from up front, stripped "nearly naked" and displaying "very bad wounds." Even so, the men moving forward did not flinch.

"This spectacle, so revolting to a person unaccustomed to such sights, produced no impression whatever upon the advancing troops, who certainly go under fire with the most perfect nonchalance," wrote Freemantle. "They show no enthusiasm or excitement, but the most complete indifference. This is the effect of two years' almost uninterrupted fighting."

Also on July 1, Northern reporter Reid reached the village of Taneytown, Maryland, just 18 miles from Gettysburg. Here, he was clear at last of the stragglers and drunks seen earlier. Here, all was abustle. "Army trains blocked up the streets; a group of quartermasters and commissaries were bustling about the principal corner; across on the hills and along the road to the left, far as the eye could reach, rose the glitter from the swaying points of bayonets as with steady tramp the columns of our Second and Third Corps were marching northward."

Robert E. Lee, meanwhile, had learned on June 29 of George Meade's ascension to command of the Union army that was catching up to Lee's own Confederate force. The distinguished Rebel commander saw that events were leading him to a small town to the east, just above the Maryland-Pennsylvania line. "Tomorrow, gentlemen," he told a group of officers taking a walk with him, "we will not move to Harrisburg, as we expected, but will go over to Gettysburg and see what General Meade is after."

As for Meade's possible actions: "General Meade will commit no blunder in my front, and if I make one he will make haste to take advantage of it."

For that matter, how did either of the two commanders drawing close to Gettysburg strike the unacquainted observer? Freemantle first met Lee the morning of June 30 . . . and was most impressed. "General Lee is almost without exception, the handsomest man of his age I ever saw. He is 56 years old, tall, broadshouldered, very well made, well set-up—a thorough soldier in appearance; and his manners are most courteous and full of dignity. He is a perfect gentleman in every respect."

The Southern commander didn't smoke, drink, chew tobacco or swear. He usually wore a "high black hat," along with his lengthy grey uniform jacket, blue trousers and Wellington boots. Neat in dress, "in the most arduous marches he always looks smart and clean."

Whitelaw Reid, meanwhile, found Union commander Meade early on July 1 at a headquarters half a mile east of Taneytown (named for U. S. Chief Justice Roger Brooke Taney, who wrote the majority opinion in the famous Dred Scott case). "In a plain little wall tent, just like the rest, pen in hand, seated on a camp-stool and bending over a map is the new 'General Commanding' of the Army of the Potomac," wrote Reid later. Meade, the correspondent also noted, was a slender, dark-haired bearded man of middle age, neither handsome nor graceful, "who impresses you rather as a thoughtful student than a dashing soldier."

While Reid was at Meade's headquarters, another reporter, Lorenzo Crounze of *The New York Times*, galloped up with news of a fight developing to the west, near Gettysburg. "Mount and spur for Gettysburg is, of course, the word," wrote Reid later.

Robert E. Lee, a bit earlier, had heard the distant thunder of artillery. His advance elements obviously had found the enemy, but how many . . . how serious was the meeting? Lee hurried to Cashtown, just west of Gettysburg, to confer with his Third Corps commander, A. P. Hill, who was pale looking, ill. He didn't know much yet, and Lee rushed on, blindly, toward the sound of the guns, until he reached Dorsey Pender's division, three miles outside of Gettysburg. From there, open country lying before him, he could see the action ahead through his binoculars. And action it was. The battle had been joined.

LOVE STORY

Harry and Bob—pals in college, and now each a soldier. And Bess. Bess Marl, the love of Harry's life.

The love, also, of Bob's life!

Bess, you know, lived on a farm outside Gettysburg, where the two young men went to school. Before the war . . .

Bob used to pay calls on pretty young Bess, but he didn't always tell everybody back at the school. They might kid him just too much. *We used to keep such things quiet at college.*

Harry was smitten, too. He kept up with the young woman's family. He knew that her father and brothers all joined the Union Army once the war broke out. And so did he.

As did Bob. Join the army, that is. The Confederate Army, in his case.

With the menfolk all scattered to pieces, the young woman and her mother stayed at the farm outside Gettysburg.

Until the day, early July of 1863, that the war suddenly turned and came right at them—a tornado coming down to touch on the ground. And their farm in its path.

There came the moment that July 1 when a young Confederate officer on horseback emerged from a thicket outside Gettysburg, dismounted and climbed to the top of a rise to scan the terrain ahead with his field glasses. It was Bob.

And there came another moment when a low voice behind said: "Surrender or die!"

But laughter in his voice, according to the Gettysburg College *Mercury* of April 1899. It was a young Union officer speaking. Harry!

Starting, Bob at first had whirled and reached for his revolver, but then he saw who it was. And they joyously embraced. Two old pals from college days. "For a while the grim business on which they were engaged was forgotten, and they fairly overwhelmed each other with questions," recalled the *Mercury* of last century.

Harry suddenly mentioned her—Bess. That was when Bob confessed he used to visit Bess quite frequently. Now Harry started.

"Don't you remember?" queried Bob.

"No, I don't." A bit stiffly, now.

"Well, perhaps I didn't tell you where I went; we used to keep such things quiet at college, but that is where I made the calls you and the other fellows used to jolly me so much about."

But Bob had a question. "How is she?"

For two or more years, Bess and family had lived within Union perimeters, and Harry of course was a Union officer, was on *that* side of the Civil War's dividing line. Bob was not.

And now Bob *was* close to her home, a scout for Robert E. Lee's invading army. He was so close and he was burning to know about her. Bess.

Harry provided a reply—and a question of his own. "Her father and brothers are all enlisted in the Northern army, and she and her mother, as they remained on the place, are right in your line of attack. But Bob, how come you are so interested?"

The truth was out. Bob's face turned red, and Harry's then darkened with anger. Both Bob Lancy and Harry Sinclair loved Bess Marl.

They acknowledged the fact with some difficulty, Harry after a while urging Bob to shield her while the farm remained within Confederate lines, and Bob agreeing that they, someday, would let Bess decide between them. "Then the two men pledged each other to shield and protect the girl for whom they would both have given their lives." They shook hands on it, with Bob warning they might not meet again. And so, goodbye. *And protect.*

Late afternoon now, and two women are seen on the plain below the onlooking sky, tiny figures in the scheme of the ages, hurriedly packing their goods into a wagon with the help of a servant. Bess and her mother. Fleeing their home because it was in the line of battle, caught between forces, and likely to be blown to pieces the next day.

Down the road they trundled . . . as from the adjoining woods came a Reb horseman.

As elsewhere among the trees watched a concerned onlooker.

Horseman and wagon-riders drew closer and closer to one another, until at last full realization. Bob recognized them. And they, Bob. "Why Miss Bess," said he, "I am in luck."

And she, now that they were met once again?

After informing them the road ahead was clear, Bob acknowledged he must ride off to his duties of war. *And yet . . .* "Not before he had looked deep into Bess Marl's eyes," we are told. And hers did frankly meet his, we are informed as well, "then dropped as he inquired where he might see them [Bess and her mother], if he lived."

Lived? With that frightening statement, "Miss Marl had looked up quickly and then had bent to arrange something in the wagon and he saw her lips trembling; then with a lingering hand clasp he was gone."

Bob was gone, but not Harry. In the woods nearby he had been the silent spectator. He surely did not mean to spy. He, himself, had been "about to ride up to the wagon," the *Mercury* divined, but Bob had appeared too soon, too quickly.

Now, in what pain did Harry ride away?

We'll never know.

All we know is that after the grim battle the next day—well, *during* battle, it seems—they, Bob and Harry, "clashed in hand to hand combat." Sabers "flashed." A stray shot coursed through the air. A young man went down. One of Bess Marl's two young men.

His old friend and college chum was by his side at the last. Tell her, said the stricken one of the two suitors, "Tell—Bess—I—knew she—loved you and so I didn't—."

Didn't what?—Approach at the same moment?

We'll never quite know what else he might have told his old college pal. Mumbled something also about his mother. Pointed to his coat pocket and said, "Give—Mother—."

And no more. Harry. *Oh, Harry!*

Coincidences At Gettysburg

The incredible things that do happen! As happened, for instance, at Gettysburg. Decisive conflict, great sprawling battle for more than 165,000 men, for hundreds of awed, terrified civilians, with more artillery shells hurled from one side to the other than those sent arcing their deadly way through *ALL* of Napoleon's battles. Microcosm battle, too, microcosm of the American Civil War in its entirety, and with like chance, ironic encounters and other oddities.

Here, at Gettysburg, for instance, Robert E. Lee's invading Army of Northern Virginia had achieved an initial victory in the first day of the three-day battle. Far to the west, Ulysses S. Grant at the same time was still drawing tight the noose he had placed around Vicksburg. At Gettysburg early the afternoon of that July 1, a wounded officer from Georgia lay near death in a Gettysburg home turned into a field hospital. Just before he died, he was heard to say: "There now, there now, Vicksburg has fallen, General Lee is retreating and the South is whipped."

So it was . . . *three days later*, yes. Both the Gettysburg and Vicksburg battles lost by July 4, and the decline of Confederate fortunes now inevitable.

On the way to Gettysburg, meanwhile, on June 30, a New York cavalryman, Abraham Folger, had been captured by Lieutenant Colonel William H. Paine's 2nd North Carolina Cavalry. Passing a tannery while being escorted to the rear—the Confederate rear—Folger saw a discarded carbine lying on the ground. He seized it and immediately shot his captor's horse. The stricken animal inadvertently threw its rider, Colonel Paine, into one of the tanning vats.

Turning the carbine on the officer's orderly, Folger ordered him to help Paine out of the vat, then marched them both to his own lines, not far away. The Confederate officer had gone completely under the foul tanning liquid. "His gray uniform with its white velvet facing, his white gauntlet gloves, face and hair, had all become completely stained so that he presented a most laughable sight," wrote Folger later.

For Folger, in fact, double and triple laughs. The carbine that subdued both Rebel prisoners had held only one round—the one he used to kill the unfortunate horse. His two prisoners could have run or turned on him with impunity, if only they had known. More amazing, though, Folger had been captured once before during the Civil War—by the same Colonel Paine's 2nd North Carolina Cavalry! It had been the winter before, recalled Folger later, "and you can just believe that I was glad to return the compliment with interest."

Coincidence, coincidence! Or sometimes more than that? On June 28, advancing elements of Lee's army stayed overnight in tiny Wrightsville, Pennsylvania, not far from Gettysburg. One house occupied so briefly by the Southerners belonged to Mr. and Mrs. Samuel Smith. Their son Silas, carrying a pocket Bible, had gone off to war with the Union army months before. He had been wounded and captured. He died of his wounds in a Confederate hospital, far, far from home.

When the Rebels left Wrightsville and the Smiths returned to their home on Locust Street, across from a church, there was their son's pocket Bible on a table, his name and address still written on the flyleaf. Someone had left it, but who?

The Southern troops quartered in Wrightsville had been led, incidentally, by John B. Gordon of Georgia, destined himself for a thought-provoking coincidence in connection with Gettysburg. It came in fact, during the heat of battle on July 1 as Brigadier General Gordon, in command of a brigade under Jubal Early, fought Union troops for control of a hill north of Gettysburg. The Union troops were led by a brigadier also, Francis C. Barlow of New York, and when he fell gravely wounded, his men had to leave him behind as they retreated before the fired-up Rebels.

Gordon came along on his horse, saw his stricken counterpart and dismounted to ask if he could anything for him. Both men thought Barlow surely must die from his terrible wound, and Gordon made arrangements, at Barlow's request, for the latter's wife, a Union nurse, to pass through the lines to be by her husband's side in his final hours.

Gordon went on his way, assuming that Barlow would die. But he didn't . . . he survived to fight another day, to prosper later as an attorney and rise to the post of Attorney General of New York. He heard, in the meantime, that a General Gordon had died in battle the year after Gettysburg.

But no, John Gordon also had survived the war, to become Governor of Georgia and a U. S. Senator, and so, at a political dinner in Washington, D.C., years after the Civil War, each was startled and gratified to meet a man he had thought dead all those years . . . to meet each other!

Nor were those two the only soldiers at Gettysburg either destined for high achievement in later life . . . or, in some cases, descended from historically significant luminaries. In the latter category were a great-grandson of Patrick Henry, the 53rd Virginia Infantry's Colonel W. R. Aylett (wounded); a grandson of former President John Tyler, the same 53rd Virginia's color-bearer, Robert Tyler Jones (badly wounded); Harriet Beecher Stowe's son Frederick, a Union staff officer; African explorer-missionary Dr. David Livingstone's son Robert, a Union soldier (wounded, captured, died in prison camp).

As for those with future portent, Chaplain (Father) William Corby of the Irish Brigade (New York, Massachusetts and Pennsylvania) later would be president of Notre Dame University; Captain Emil Frey of the 82nd Illinois Infantry, a Swiss-born immigrant, later would be President of Switzerland (captured at Gettysburg, however, and held 18 months at Libby Prison in Richmond). Lewis T. Powell, private in the 2nd Florida Infantry, later, under the name Lewis Paine, would join John Wilkes Booth's conspiracy and hang for the assassination of Abraham Lincoln (at Gettysburg, Powell was wounded and captured; he soon would escape and change his name.) Finally, there was one George Nixon, whose grandson would be father of future U. S. President Richard M. Nixon. Forebear George was a private with Ohio's 73rd Infantry. Fortunately for descendant Richard, George's nine children already had been born—but they were left fatherless, since the 43-year-old George was mortally wounded in the second day of battle at Gettysburg.

Many of the wounded, Union or Confederate, were taken to a field hospital a mile east of Gettysburg. There they began the road to recovery—or, often, death. It was at this giant hospital that Union soldier Frank Stokes one day saw two nurses and a "ward-master" carrying a recumbent Confederate soldier on a stretcher to the "dead house" to await burial. "After they passed me a few steps, the supposed dead man partly raised himself up on the stretcher and asked what they intended to do with him." With a "hearty laugh," the hospital workers turned and carried their patient back to the wards.

In a similar incident, Private Luther White of the 20th Massachusetts was himself trundled to the very edge of an open grave. The men carrying him on an "army couch" dropped it with such a jolt, the supposedly deceased young man awoke, raised his head and said, "Boys, what are you doing?" He, too, was spared a premature burial.

Also at Gettysburg was a badly wounded officer from Georgia who had been captured. He and his companions were to be escorted to prison camps in the north, but the Union surgeons said this man, named Henry D. McDaniel, could not possibly survive the rigors of such a trip. His friends came to say goodbye, but McDaniel said he would not stay behind. Either put me on a litter and take me with you, or I'll start walking until I drop dead, he said.

The doctors then gave way, and the difficult march began. Steadily, the patient in the litter grew weaker. The group stopped at a small Pennsylvania town for a rest. The townspeople gathered to stare and look curiously. McDaniel appeared all but gone. A friend, a Colonel Nesbit, drew close to see if he indeed might really be dead, but McDaniel's eyes suddenly flew open and he motioned Nesbit to come close. When Nesbit did, the wounded man grabbed his friend's coat and pulled him still closer, to impart what might be his final words.

"Nesbit," he whispered. "Nesbit, old fellow. Did you ever see such an ungodly pair of ankles as that Dutch woman on that porch has got?"

Needless to say, McDaniel was not yet ready to die. He, in fact, recovered, returned to the South and some time later was reincarnated as the Governor of Georgia.

OLD WHITE OAK

The old white oak, writes Gettysburg historian Gregory A. Coco, stood alone and solitary in its open field for probably 150 years. The field in turn was a part of the Bliss Farm at Gettysburg, once the home of Adelina and Williams Bliss.

No buildings from the Civil War era remain there today, thanks largely to one of the many thousands of incidents that, altogether, comprised the three days of deadly battle at Gettysburg, July 1 through July 3 of 1863, between two armies, 165,000 men in all.

With Confederate sharpshooters picking at his men from buildings on the Bliss Farm, Union General Alexander Hays finally, on the third day of battle, decided he must order the barn and house of his Yankee countryman burned down, to deny the Reb marksmen their sanctuary. The man who volunteered to carry out the mission had to zigzag right up to the buildings where the enemy was sheltered and set them afire.

That volunteer was Sergeant Charles A. Hitchcock of the 111th New York Infantry, reports National Park Service Ranger Historian Coco in his book *On the Bloodstained Field II*, and Hitchcock suffered a serious wound in the arm in the process. Nonetheless, he accomplished the task—house and barn soon were brightly ablaze.

The white oak, in the meantime, reared its lovely head in an empty field not far away, and it, too, was a haven for Rebel sharpshooters harassing the Union lines. And on the third day of battle again, wrote Lieutenant Tom Galwey, 8th Ohio Infantry, he was confounded by Reb marksmen shooting at his company from beneath the solitary tree, not 30 yards in front of the Union men.

To the surprise of the Yankees, however, there came a pause at one point as one of the Rebs hidden behind the old oak cried out "Don't fire, Yanks!"

Not knowing what to expect, the Ohioans complied, curious to see what would happen next.

"A man with his gun slung across his shoulder came out from the tree," recalled Galwey. Some of the Union men, angry and grieving over comrades already struck down by the Confederate shooters, took quick aim at this bold enemy, "but the others checked them, to see what would follow."

The Yankees could see that their Reb enemy carried a canteen in his hand as he made his way about halfway to the Union line. He stopped then, kneeled and gently gave a wounded man a drink from the canteen—a wounded Yank!

"Of course, we cheered the Reb," wrote Galwey. Indeed, the Union men by now had risen to their feet, and the Rebs behind their Good Samaritan had stopped firing, too, and they, too, were standing in full view—everybody easy targets now for their opposites. But it was a scenario that would not, could not, last.

"As soon as the sharpshooter had finished his generous work, he turned and went back to the tree, and then at the top of his voice shouted, 'Down Yanks, we're going to fire.' And down we lay again."

Their war, their battle, at the foot of the old white oak, resumed and the next day, Lee's army now in retreat, "a heap of Confederates was found under that tree," said Galwey. "Whether the hero of the day before was one of the ghastly dead will probably never be known."

Indeed, only the oak ever could have told, and the oak did last and maintain its lonely vigil for another century and even more . . . until, on June 20, 1987, a severe wind storm blew down the old tree, its full story never to be told.

Black Faces In The Crowd

Robert Morrow went to West Point, too—as a body servant to Cadet James J. Pettigrew of North Carolina. Pettigrew went on to become a Confederate general and to suffer a mortal wound while leading a division in Pickett's Charge at Gettysburg. Morrow, on the other hand, had sought refuge in Union-held New Bern, North Carolina, early in the war.

There he became a teacher in schools formed to educate the newly freed blacks in the state's Federally held territory. He was a favorite of Horace James, a Northern minister and former Union Army chaplain appointed superintendent of Negro Affairs in North Carolina. Morrow was a Union soldier himself—a sergeant in the newly formed 1st North Carolina Heavy Artillery, one of the all-black military units manned by escaping slaves—and freed blacks—who wanted to fight for the Union. He had been "for many years a body servant of the rebel General Pettigrew, whom he deserted for liberty and Union," wrote James in 1864. Morrow was "an enthusiastic and excellent teacher," added James.

Sadly, though, Morrow contracted yellow fever while recruiting additional black troops on Roanoke Island and died suddenly in his bed one night. "It matters little to him that he left the world without warning," wrote minister James also, "for he daily walked with God."

* * *

The obituaries of 1915 told this man's rare story—born a slave in South Carolina and later a member of Congress from South Carolina. And in-between, organizer of a spectacular escape from slavery for himself and 16 fellow blacks, with five women and three children among them.

Early in the Civil War, Robert Small was a pilot aboard the Confederate Army supply steamer *Planter*, often plying the waters of Charleston harbor. On the night of May 13, 1862, the vessel's captain went ashore, and Small made his move—taking over the *Planter* and steaming, hell-bent, for the Union warships blockading the harbor. After saluting the Confederate forts on his way toward the open sea, Small delivered himself and his escaping party to the Federal naval authorities, who then benefitted from his knowledge of the area's waters and the Charleston defenses. He spent the rest of the war as a Union pilot and after the war, during Reconstruction, served as a South Carolina lawmaker and member of the House of Representatives in Washington. In his early 20s at the time of his escape, he lived to the age of 76 before his death in 1915.

* * *

No name in particular, they came forth in droves, to greet, to follow, to help, to entreat the Union conquerors—especially the highly visible William Tecumseh Sherman in his march, not only to the sea, but afterwards, northwards, from Savannah north into North Carolina with the intention of meeting Grant's great host at the gates of Richmond.

The march originally had begun in Atlanta, as Sherman's subordinate Major General Henry W. Slocum later recalled: "We were dependent upon the country for our supplies of food and forage, and every one not connected with the army was a source of weakness to us." And so, "on several occasions . . . we had been compelled to drive thousands of colored people back, not from lack of sympathy with them, but simply as a matter of safety to the army. The refugee-train following in the rear of the army was one of the most singular features of the march."

Somehow, by underground communication all their own, slaves and former slaves, escapees, blacks of all stations in life—Southern life—for miles and miles in advance knew the Union column was on its way. "It was natural," wrote Slocum, "that these poor creatures, seeking a place of safety, should flee to the army, and endeavor to keep in sight of it. Every day, as we marched on we could see, on each side of our line of march, crowds of these people coming to us through roads and across the fields, bringing with them all their earthly goods, and many goods which were not theirs. Horses, mules, cows, dogs, old family carriages, carts, and whatever they thought might be of use to them were seized upon and brought to us."

Allowing the black refugees to follow behind the blue-clad line, the Union troops found "at times they were almost equal in numbers to the army they were following." And so, the two columns moved on . . . the soldiers in front, their liberated followers close behind. "Old stages, family carriages, carts and lumber wagons filled with bedding, cooking-utensils and 'traps' of all kinds, with men, women, and children loaded with bundles, made up the balance of the refugee-train which followed in our rear." And where they all wound up, each and every one, only their scattered descendants of today may know.

* * *

Not so fortunate was a runaway slave named Jake from A. M. Reed's Mulberry Grove plantation below Jacksonville, Florida. When a group of Reed's slaves organized a mass escape in hopes of fleeing to nearby Union forces, one of them was shot in the legs and the exodus was halted in its tracks. Two of the men did manage to flee, however, and slaveowner Reed himself made note of the event in a diary: "About 12 p.m. found my negroes preparing to leave. In the melee, Jake and Dave escaped carrying off my boat, the *Laura Shaw*."

The two escapees reached friendly Northern shelter in the form of a gunboat, and just two days later the Yankees steamed up to Reed's wharf with the runaway Jake, "to get his family and things," wrote Reed in an added diary entry. Unfortunately, after the mass escape attempt Reed had acted promptly to begin moving his slaves into the "interior," far from Yankee gunboats and soldiers. Jake's wife Etta was among them.

A bitter Jake could only leave again with his newfound friends, going with them to Federally-held Jacksonville. When the Yankees then temporarily pulled out of Jacksonville that fall of 1862, Jake was among the 276 blacks who went with them for protection. After a second occupation and evacuation by the Federals, Jacksonville fell to them still again in March 1863 . . . to the all-black First South Carolina Volunteers (many of its soldiers runaways from North Florida), without a shot being fired.

According to History Professor Daniel L. Schafer of the University of North Florida, most of the 500 civilians living in Jacksonville at the time were whites "who regarded this third occupation by their former slaves to be the 'last crowning humiliation' in their wartime experience." As one result, even the "ladies of the town" insulted and cursed the black soldiers, it seems.

Among others, Jake was back, and he apparently wasted no time in searching for planter-banker A. M. Reed, openly "threatening to take vengeance on him." According to Reed's daughter Hattie, Jake hoped "to meet Pa face to face to teach him what it is to part man and wife." Frightened now, Reed wouldn't stay alone at night at his plantation. Hattie reported, "We are moving away as many things as possible."

The "bold soldier boy," as she sneeringly called Jake, was known to have put a gun to the head of one man who had helped thwart the mass escape of Reed's slaves months before, says historian Schafer in the book *Civil War Times in St. Augustine*. Now, poor embittered Jake went too far—after threatening to burn down Reed's home, "he was arrested and confined for the duration of the Union occupation." As for his unfortunate wife Etta, she had been sold to new owners "somewhere in Georgia."

GETTYSBURG FACTS, STATS

Where more than 1,300 memorials and commemorative markers now stand in one central area, the Union fielded 246 infantry regiments for the famous Battle of Gettysburg, along with 38 cavalry regiments and 68 artillery batteries. Drawn up in opposition, on the Confederate side, were 167 infantry regiments (plus two small batteries); 28 cavalry regiments (and again a battalion) and 67 artillery batteries.

The Union men came from units representing 18 states, including Maryland, in addition to the ranks of the Nation's Regular Army. The Confederate units hailed from 12 states, again including Maryland, its people divided in their loyalties.

Accessible to the visitor of today is a Federally owned and maintained National Park of 3,874 acres, including the 22-acre National Cemetery that Abe Lincoln dedicated with a short speech only a few months after the battle took place. The Gettysburg Address, of course.

Also heavily trodden, blooded, too, during the three-day battle of July 1863 are another 12,000 adjoining acres. Next door to the military park and cemetery is the Eisenhower National Historic Site, the farm to which "Ike" (also of military and battle fame) retired after his 20th-century presidency.

Thirty miles of paved roads wind through the park, among the 1,300-plus markers and memorials, past dozens of Civil War cannon and 45 historic structures pre-dating the battle. At one end, also maintained by the National Park Service as a "living history" project, is John Slyder's "Granite Farm" of Civil War vintage.

After Lincoln's dedicatory remarks in November of 1863, the new national cemetery was available for the re-burial of Union men who had fallen in the battle itself. Nearly 3,600 bodies from the battlefields were re-interred in sections set aside by states (with space for the Regular Army men and 979 "unknowns" as well). By far the most "populous" state section in the cemetery holding those early burials was New York's, with 867 bodies re-buried. The smallest such grouping was that of Abe Lincoln's home state, curiously enough—Illinois, with only six bodies dug up and re-interred.

From its Confederate Avenue to the many Confederate monuments scattered about, the battlefield park includes tributes to the Confederacy, too. "Alabamians!" says one of the Confederate memorials, "Your names are inscribed on fame's immortal scroll."

Union General Samuel W. Crawford, who had begun the war as an army surgeon posted at Fort Sumter, contributed to the great memorial park by purchasing the very terrain where his men of the Pennsylvania Reserves had fought in defense of the Round Top. He held and preserved that ground until it could become a part of the magnificent park that developed adjacent to the original national cemetery.

It was a Pennsylvania outfit, incidentally, the 56th Infantry Regiment, that fired the first volley against Robert E. Lee's invaders from the South in the opening engagement of the battle, July 1, 1863. So extensive was the aftermath over the next three days that Union men later retrieved nearly 25,000 firearms left on the battleground, plus more than 10,000 abandoned bayonets and 350 sabers.

Still another "stat" explains why the 900-man 151st Pennsylvania Infantry was called the "Schoolteacher Regiment"—113 of those 900 really were schoolteachers in more ordinary times.

Pickett's ill-fated charge on the third day virtually ended the Battle of Gettysburg, with absolutely dismaying, sad loss of life and widespread bodily mayhem even among the living. One wounded general, Lewis Armistead, a brigade commander under Pickett, did not die of his injuries, however. His death was attributed to just plain exhaustion.

Lee Family Saga

Still more from the Lee family saga—lying abed from his battle wounds was William Henry Fitzhugh Lee, second son of Robert E. Lee. In two years of wartime service, "Rooney" Lee, a Harvard graduate in his mid-twenties, had accumulated an impressive list of battles stars—he had led the 9th Virginia Cavalry during "Jeb" Stuart's famous "ride around McClellan" on the Virginia Peninsula between the York and James rivers. Rooney had served in the Seven Days battles of 1862 that were a part of the Peninsula campaign; he was at Second Bull Run, Antietam, and Fredericksburg, followed by Chancellorsville. He then, in the spring of 1863, was wounded at the great cavalry battle known as Brandy Station and was forced out of action for a time.

One day not long after, Union gunboats stole up the Pamunkey River, an offshoot of the York near West Point, Virginia. Rooney Lee was convalescing at his wife Charlotte's family home, Hickory Hill, in Hanover Country. To the northwest, his famous father was on his way to destiny at a place called Gettysburg.

Disembarking at young Lee's own White House plantation on the Pamunkey River June 25 were 1,000 Union cavalrymen, who quickly mounted up and rode for the Virginia Central Railroad bridge across the South Anna River, 30 miles from White House. Their raid resulted in destruction of the bridge and the capture of 360 horses and mules, plus 100 "Johnny Rebs," with only eight Union casualties—overall, a success. The real goal, though, turned out to be Rooney Lee, who was surprised and captured at Charlotte Wickham Lee's nearby Hickory Hill home.

Rooney was carried off on his mattress before the eyes of his remonstrating mother and his frail, pregnant wife. The Federal raiders also took his father-in-law's carriage and horses—used to convey the prized prisoner back to their own lines. He was taken to Fort Monroe, Virginia, a hostage held as counter to Confederate threats to execute two Union officers.

His capture was a blow to his arthritis-stricken mother and to his wife Charlotte. It was decided that both women should seek the quiet solace of a spa—Hot Springs, Virginia—but with the elder Mrs. Lee confined to crutches and any travel subject to the vicissitudes of war, the journey to the western part of Virginia wouldn't be easy. The solution arrived at was a slow train, with the women traveling in a freight car outfitted like a bedroom. The train traveled so slowly the ladies could leave the big sliding door open and enjoy the scenery passing them by.

At Hot Springs, however, Charlotte's health didn't improve, and so they moved on to nearby Warm Springs. There, Mrs. Lee Senior wrote, they settled into "a delightful cottage with a portico all around, covered with beautiful vines & roses & looking upon a meadow full of haycocks & a clear stream running thro it & very near the bath . . . mountains all around."

They had taken the cottage for a month, and soon Robert E. Lee's wife was happy to hear that her prisoner-son Rooney was on his feet and beginning to use crutches as he continued to recover from his wounds. She wrote his sister Mildred that she hoped his prospects for exchange could be considered real, since Charlotte's health was "very delicate."

By October of 1863—long after General Lee's defeat at Gettysburg in July and with his son still held as a prisoner—the Lee ladies had returned to Richmond. There, Mrs. Lee Senior and her two daughters, Agnes and Mildred, moved into a small house on Leigh Street—too small, it is said, to accommodate Charlotte as well.

Rooney's wife found quarters some distance away, and General Lee soon wrote that he was "sorry" the Leigh Street abode wasn't large enough to include Charlotte. "It takes from me half the pleasure of your accommodation," he wrote to his wife Mary Custis Lee, "as I wish to think of you all together; and in her feeble condition and separation from her Fitzhugh [Rooney, that is], none can sympathize or attend to her as yourself."

One comfort for the family during this period was the presence of eldest son George Washington Custis Lee, an 1854 West Point graduate serving as an aide-de-camp to Confederate President (and fellow West Pointer) Jefferson Davis. Like many other deskbound soldiers, however, Custis was unhappy at being kept away from the battlefield by his posting in the capital—diarist Mary Chesnut wrote that he earlier "offered himself to the Yankees in place of his brother, as he was a single man with no wife and children to be hurt by his imprisonment or made miserable by his danger." The Yankees, though, "preferred Rooney."

Came the Christmas season, and Rooney was still in captivity. Some onlookers, such as diarist Mary Chesnut, complained that Charlotte had been foolish to take Rooney so close to Union lines for his recuperation, rather than to the comparative safety of Richmond. Still, all were saddened on her behalf to know she had lost the child she had been carrying.

General Lee, meanwhile, was able to visit at the Leigh Street house for a short time, but Mary Lee was shocked by his appearance—his hair and beard had turned white. She also worried over the severe pain he occasionally suffered in his left side.

By now it was clear that the Lee family had lost the magnificent Arlington House. Under a Federal law passed by Congress the year before, the government imposed real estate taxes on property in "insurrectionary districts". It could—and would—confiscate said properties when the said taxes went unpaid. The added catch was that the taxes had to be paid in person, by the property owner or owners.

In the case of Robert and Mary Lee, that was impossible. General Lee obviously couldn't pass through the Federal lines outside Washington to pay the tax for his wife, rightful owner of the estate. Nor was she physically able to try passing through those lines herself, although she did consider the attempt. Instead a cousin went on her behalf and tried to pay the real estate tax levied on the Arlington property. But Federal officers rejected the cousin, and the government then "legally" confiscated Arlington House, its grounds now destined to be a mass burial ground for good.

General Lee was able to repeat his Richmond visits almost until Christmas Day of 1863, but he returned to his troops for Christmas Day itself. Rooney was still a prisoner, not to be released until an exchange finally was arranged in March of 1864. On the day after Christmas 1863, Charlotte Wickham Lee, not yet 23, died.

THREE GENERALS NAMED WINFIELD

Two generals named Winfield Scott simultaneously took to the field—on opposite sides, mind you—for at least two of the Civil War's major campaigns . . . and neither one was "Ole Fuss and Feathers" himself.

The real Winfield Scott, Mexican War hero, General-in-Chief of the U.S. Army and the country's military idol for the past two decades, was in his mid-seventies and too corpulent to mount his horse when the Civil War broke out. Not yet disposed to step aside entirely, he realized he was not physically able to lead in the field; thus, it probably was Winfield Scott's idea to offer field command of the Union armies to his chief-of-staff and fellow Virginian—Robert E. Lee.

After Lee said no and remained loyal to their seceding native state, Scott remained on duty and directed Union forces from Washington until shortly after the embarrassing Union defeat at First Bull Run, on the very doorstep of the capital. With "Little Mac," George McClellan, then brought to the fore and reporting directly to President Lincoln, Scott saw his duty and retired—with full pay and rank.

Out in the field, meanwhile, two far younger men, both born in the 1820s and both named for the hero of the War of 1812 (even before his feats of the Mexican War of the 1840s), were leading their troops against each other's forces. One of them, in fact,

Confederate Winfield Scott Featherston, was at First Bull Run with his 17th Mississippi in the summer of 1861.

By spring of the following year, both Featherston and his Union counterpart, Winfield Scott Hancock, were commanding troops in the Peninsula campaign, George McClellan's abortive drive against Richmond, and both brigadiers commanded brigades at the Battle of Williamsburg, where Hancock earned his first plaudits of the war by leading a vital flank attack against the Rebels.

Both men appeared at Fredericksburg in late 1862, with Hancock now leading a division, but after that, their wartime careers took them on widely divergent paths.

Confederate general Featherston soon moved into the western theater—to appear at Champion Hill in Mississippi and in the Vicksburg campaign, in which he served as a brigade commander under William "Old Blizzards" Loring, the one-armed Mexican War veteran who led his troops into battle with the cry, "Give them blizzards, boys!"

Featherston also took part in the defense of Atlanta under Joseph E. Johnston's overall command. The Winfield Scott namesake next served under John Bell Hood as the latter moved into Tennessee for his sequential disasters at Franklin and Nashville. Not yet bowed, Featherston was with Johnston again in the final days in North Carolina, surrendering finally at Greensboro.

The war's other Winfield Scott—Hancock, that is—carved out an illustrious career after commanding a Union division at Fredericksburg, a debacle for the North. As 2nd Corps commander, Hancock appeared at Chancellorsville and at Gettysburg in 1863. He then served as a major general under Ulysses S. Grant during Grant's final drive on Richmond and Petersburg in 1864; Hancock led his troops at the high-casualty battles of The Wilderness, Spotsylvania and Cold Harbor.

His contribution at Spotsylvania was vital to Grant's victory there, but his corps took significant losses at Cold Harbor, and then, during the siege of Petersburg, Hancock was embarrassed at the minor clash known as Reams Station, where Confederate generals A.P. Hill and Wade Hampton exacted 2,400 casualties among the 8,000 in Hancock's command.

Both of the "Winfield Scotts" serving in the field during the Civil War suffered combat wounds—the Confederate Featherston at Glendale during the Seven Days campaign outside Richmond in 1862, and Union officer Hancock at Gettysburg. Both also had political interests—Featherston, a Tennessee native and an attorney in Mississippi before the war, had served two terms in the U.S. House in the 1840s and 1850s. After the war, he served in the Mississippi legislature. He lived until 1891.

Alter ego Hancock, meanwhile, aired his political ambitions 15 years after the Civil War in a major way—he was the Democratic Party's nominee for President in 1880, but he lost the general election that fall to another former Union officer, James A. Garfield. Hancock remained in the army for the next six years . . . until his death in 1886.

Ironically, the original Winfield Scott also had dallied in politics—in 1852, the hero of the Mexican War had run for President as the Whig Party's nominee, only to be defeated by Franklin Pierce, a very junior and undistinguished officer under Scott's command in Mexico 15 years earlier. (One Jefferson Davis incidentally, served as Pierce's Secretary of War.)

The venerable General-in-Chief Scott survived his retirement through the Civil War years, living until 1866. While chafing at his inactive seat on the sidelines, Scott nonetheless could take pride in seeing his Anaconda Plan pretty much followed by the Union to ultimate, albeit fearfully costly, triumph. That was Scott's strategy which called for Union control of the Mississippi Valley, thus splitting the Confederacy in two, coupled with a suffocating naval blockade of the South's Atlantic ports. Scott lived long enough to write his memoirs and to send a copy to Grant, also once a junior office with Scott in Mexico., The book was inscribed in touching terms by "Ole Fuss and Feathers." His personal note to Grant was, "From the oldest general to the greatest general."

CAT PARTIES ENDED

A tale painful to relate, but necessary to complete the record in any case, is that of the unnamed cat that paid a visit one day to Captain Isaac Coles of Virginia while he was sitting on his bunk and conversing with a compatriot from Kentucky. Their quarters, located at Hilton Head, South Carolina, consisted of a long structure with rows of bunks on each side and plank tables set up in the middle aisle for meals. The two men, in fact were discussing meals—food!—and the long time, 40 or 50 days at least, since they had had a decent meal.

It was fall of 1864. Rations had been short and unappealing in their Yankee-operated prison camp. And, yes, Coles and his partner indeed were Confederates. Prisoners, too.

When along came the general's cat—presumably his cat, at any rate, since the next day he apparently issued orders to lock up any and all other pets in sight or hearing distance. *General John Foster*.

It all started out innocently enough. Captain Coles and friend merely were talking of how to exist on their prison camp's "pitiful" rations. They were speaking rather pathetically of "our reduced state and of our longings to satisfy the very humble cravings of the inner man."

Coles later wrote in good humor of his wartime adventures—his account appearing in *War Recollections of Confederate Veterans of Pittsylvania County* (Virginia)—but on this particular occasion, "We were nearly desperate," he recalled, and, "anything would have been joyfully tried that looked like meat." Their stomachs were "gnawing and begging" and by no means to be ignored, when, he said, "like an answer to prayer," along came this "big, fat cat" into the barracks-like building, "daintily tripping in, straight up to us, fawning at our feet."

And ah, sad to say, the rest would be history—cat history. For the starving prisoners reacted—not with rancor or vehemence, mind you, but nonetheless . . . *immediately*! "My boyish antagonism to the feline kind vanished, and I hailed her as Manna from heaven, or quail, or what you will—it certainly looked like

Providence to me as surely providing for us as for His other children in the wilderness."

The two men glanced one to other—"He, too, had a look of inspiration—and so from common impulse we acted."

Perhaps "the fair visitoress" never quite knew exactly what hit her; we can hope that her end was mercifully quick. And certainly, she never knew the indignities that came next. "How joyously we skinned and dressed her! We surmised she was General Foster's pet. We hoped so!"

No time was wasted.

"We parboiled and stewed her up, no pepper nor salt. She was deliciously fat, she must have been a notoriously fine mouser."

The entire culinary event unfolded without a hitch. "She required no grease, we baked our corn meal and could scarcely contain ourselves until the feast was ready. And it was a king's dish indeed, a whole pan full, two whole yawning stomach fulls and to spare! We invited several to dine with us . . . "

Not a scrap was left, and afterwards Coles and his partners were quite ready to declare "the cat as an article of food was misunderstood, that it was wholesome and delicious."

The only regret was that when General Foster ordered "all dogs and cats locked up next day," there went any hopes for "another cat party."

THE FIGHTING McCOOKS

And then there were the amazing McCooks of Ohio—one family, seventeen of its menfolk serving the Union, all but one as Army men, five as generals. Patriarch of the clan was Daniel McCook, born 1798 in Pennsylvania and residing, actually, in Illinois. In his sixties by the time of the Civil War, he saw ten sons, a brother and five nephews step forward to serve the Union cause. Three of his sons were killed—as was Daniel McCook himself.

Considered too old for duty in the field, eager volunteer Daniel McCook had been allowed to serve as a paymaster of volunteers far behind normal Union lines, but even homebound troops were called out to oppose John Hunt Morgan's raid into Ohio in midsummer of 1863. In the running clashes that ensued, the eldest of all the "Fighting McCooks" was mortally wounded near Buffington Island, Ohio.

His son Daniel Jr., a law partner to William Tecumseh Sherman in civilian life, became a brigade commander . . . one of three Ohio brothers to reach general's rank. He fought at Chickamauga and Chattanooga, among other battles, then, in the Atlanta campaign, suffered a fatal wound of his own as his brigade led a charge at Kennesaw Mountain . . . a costly charge ordered by General Sherman. This Dan McCook received his brigadier's star on July 16, 1864, and died the next day.

His two brothers also reaching general's rank were Alexander and Robert, both also veterans of the fighting in the war's western theater.

Alexander survived the war, served in the U.S. Army until 1895 and retired as a major general, although his Civil War reputation was tarnished by the Union defeat at Chickamauga, where he and his command had joined overall Union commander William S. Rosecrans in retreat from the battlefield.

Robert L. McCook, meanwhile, Alexander's brother, was not fortunate enough to survive the fighting—and he died a controversial death. Laid low by illness, he nonetheless was on a scouting foray in a horse-drawn ambulance when, accosted by a band of Southern irregulars near Decherd, Tennessee, he was shot while trying to outrun them. Fatally injured, he died the next day . . . but many of his Northern countrymen felt his death was outright murder rather than an act of war.

Others among the Fighting McCooks of Ohio included cousin Edward, fourth Union general in the clan and still another veteran of service with Sherman and U.S. Grant in the war's west. Also an attorney before the war, Edward McCook took part in George Stoneman's raid into the Atlanta area, his command taking significant casualties before returning to Union lines. He also joined in James Wilson's 1864 raid into Georgia and Alabama that resulted in the capture of Selma.

A war survivor, Edward McCook later served as governor of the Colorado Territory and as an envoy to the future state of Hawaii. He built a postwar fortune in business ventures that included "telephone companies in Europe," says Stewart Sifakis in his *Who Was Who in the Civil War*.

Meanwhile, there also was cousin Anson—a brigadier general as well. As an officer in the 2nd Ohio, he traveled east to fight at First Bull Run (a battle proving fatal to another cousin in the same regiment, probably Private David McCook, hospital guard). He returned to the western theater to serve quite honorably at Perryville, Murfreesboro, Tullahoma, Chattanooga and Atlanta. Late in the war, he commanded a newly-formed regiment back east in Virginia's Shenandoah Valley. A war survivor also, he returned to the practice of law and served as a Republican Congressman.

The only known sailor among all the McCooks of Ohio was Roderick, born in 1839 and an Annapolis graduate. He served as a line officer in the Atlantic Blockading Squadron and commanded a battery in the naval assault of 1862 against New Bern, North Carolina. Near war's end, he also took part in the Union's amphibious operations against Fort Fisher at the mouth of the Cape Fear River in North Carolina. Illness then forced him to accept a postwar naval career on lighthouse duty.

Sidling Down To Richmond

"I feel as certain of crushing Lee as I do of dying," Ulysses S. Grant is said to have declared in those dark days of 1864 when his strategy of bludgeoning Robert E. Lee into submission was taking terrible toll of Grant's own forces.

Not only were the casualties cause for vilification in the North, behind Grant's back, but in Lee he faced a legend pumped larger than life even by the Northern press. And yet the dogged, newly emplaced commander of the Union armies was undismayed.

As a fellow West Point graduate and veteran of the Mexican War, Grant felt it was to his advantage to have known Lee, the man and U.S. Army Officer, before they were fated to become enemies locked in titanic struggle.

"The natural disposition of most people," wrote Grant later, "is to clothe a commander of a large army whom they do not know with almost superhuman abilities. A large part of the National army, for instance, and most of the press of the country clothed General Lee with just such qualities, but I had known him personally, and knew that he was mortal; and it was just as well that I felt this."

Refusing to bow to Lee the legend, Grant slipped and sidled in one lateral move after another in the spring of 1864, from one costly battle to another . . . from the Wilderness to Spotsylvania, to Cold Harbor and finally to Petersburg. "I propose to fight it out on this line if it takes all summer," he said at one point. He settled, in the end, for his siege of Petersburg, the vital rail hub just below Richmond, a siege that lasted until early 1865—followed quickly by Lee's surrender at Appomattox.

If Grant thought Lee was "mortal," he also viewed the Confederate strategist as "a large, austere man, and I judge difficult of approach to his subordinates." In the "sidling" campaign of 1864 marked by staggering Union casualties, Grant felt his "austere" opponent enjoyed certain advantages, actually.

The Union might have had superior numbers, but Lee was defending a familiar countryside—"every stream, every road, every obstacle to the movement of troops and every natural defense was familiar to him and his army." Lee also had the support of local citizens, who furnished "accurate reports of our every move." Lee, further, had "a railroad at his back" and needed no rear guard.

So towering was Lee's reputation when Grant came from the West to take over the war effort, noted Grant also, "It was not an uncommon thing for my staff officers to hear from Eastern officers, 'Well, Grant has never met Bobby Lee yet.'"

But then Grant did, and even the ordinary soldier of the South could see the difference.

"Surprise and disappointment were the prevailing emotions
. . ." recalled one Confederate veteran of Grant's "sidling" campaign in 1864, "when we discovered after the contest in the
Wilderness, that General Grant was not going to retire behind the
river and permit General Lee to carry on a campaign against
Washington the usual way, but was moving to the Spotsylvania
position instead."

Usually, added Sergeant Major George Cary Eggleston of
Lampkin's Virginia Battery, the Union fought a battle, retired,
obtained a new commander, then had to deal with a fresh Confederate offensive. Not so with Grant, who simply shifted position
and spoiled to fight again.

By the time of Cold Harbor, "we had begun to understand
what our new adversary meant . . . [that] the era of experimental
campaigns against us was over; that Grant was not going to
retreat; that he was not to be removed from command because he
had failed to break Lee's resistance; and that the policy of pound-
ing had begun, and would continue until our strength would be
utterly worn away."

In short, added onlooker-participant Eggleston, "He
intended to continue the plodding work till the task should be
accomplished, wasting very little time or strength in efforts to
make a brilliant display of generalship in a contest of strategic wits
with Lee."

Eggleston had it exactly right. In what some consider the
first display of modern or total war, Grant employed overwhelming resources to wear down Lee, press home his final campaign
and, within the year, win the war for the North. Or, as Lincoln
would say, for an undivided Union.

Later, though, whatever he thought of Lee as man or legend,
it largely would be Grant's intervention that would derail a move
to try Lee for treason.

Friendly Boost Given

Few reporters could ever claim a helpful source, a friend in court, like the contact that Harry E. Wing developed *inside* the Lincoln Administration.

Wing, a law school graduate, had served as a color corporal with the 27th Connecticut from September 1862 until the end of that year, when a wound suffered at Fredericksburg drummed him out of the Union Army. He previously had reported for the *New Haven Palladium*, and now, taking up residence in Washington, he began reporting capital affairs, first for the *Norwich Bulletin* (also in Connecticut) and then for *The New York Tribune*.

He wanted action, however, and he persuaded the *Tribune* to assign him as a courier from the paper's reporters accompanying the Federal Army of the Potomac. That job led quickly to new status as a real reporter, but he still was the "new boy" of the crowd at the time of the great Battle of the Wilderness in the spring of 1864. As low man on the seniority list, he would carry the pooled dispatches back to the nearest telegraph station, but that journey would take him through the war-torn territory of northern Virginia, which was subject to the unpredictable meanderings of John S. Mosby's guerrilla band.

Indeed, Wing was chased by Rebs of some kind, then held up by Confederate cavalrymen before he reached a Union camp boasting a telegraph unit. It was restricted for military use, but Wing managed to inform Secretary of War Edwin Stanton that he had the first news from the first day of battle at the Wilderness.

Stanton of course wanted to see the story, but Wing kept insisting it should go out to his newspaper as well. Never one to sit on his temper, Stanton then ordered Wing's arrest, and at its next stage, the tempest reached Abraham Lincoln in the White House.

Far more agreeable, he not only overruled Stanton, but he sent a train for reporter Wing. The two met at 2 a.m. in the White House, with Wing providing a full verbal report of all that he had seen and heard during the crucial day of battle. Lincoln was moved to kiss the journalist when he also conveyed a personal message from U. S. Grant (just beginning his ultimately successful "sidling" campaign of 1864 against Robert E. Lee) that there was no reason to turn back, despite the heavy Union casualties.

Lincoln now told Wing to allow the Associated Press to share in the story, the only account of the battle to reach official Washington so far. Still Wing's friend in court, Abe Lincoln next day furnished the reporter with an escort allowing him to retrieve a horse he had hidden in a thicket while escaping from Confederate raiders. Wing remained a war correspondent until Appomattox, then became co-publisher of the *Litchfield* (Connecticut) *Enquirer* and, later in life, a minister.

"Down, You Fool!"

For Supreme Court Justice Oliver Wendell Holmes, Jr., it was an annual pilgrimage over a period of many years—his visit every September 13 to Arlington National Cemetery across the Potomac from his work place, the Nation's highest court. The date was a birthday, and the man he came to memorialize, with flowers in hand, was his divisional commander at one point during the Civil War, Major General John Sedgwick.

Appointed to his bench seat in 1902, serving until retirement in 1932, and dying in 1935, Holmes today is recalled as a creature of the 20th century. We tend to forget that he was born in 1841, that he was in his 20s during the Civil War—and he indeed did serve!

Not only did he serve, but he fought at Balls Bluff, Antietam, Fredericksburg, and Chancellorsville; he was wounded three times, and in fact at Antietam was left for dead. His father, the famous New England author-poet, then published the personal story ("My Hunt After 'The Captain'") of searching out his badly wounded son after receiving word that he had been shot in the neck. It seems that young Captain Holmes was taken into a home in Hagerstown, Maryland, for his immediate care and treatment. Several days passed before his father, a doctor, finally tracked him down, on a train bound for Philadelphia . . . and, obviously, much recovered.

Fairly famous in those days were their greetings, one to another:

"How are you, Boy?"

"How are you, Dad?"

In his article for the *Atlantic* (December 1862 issue), the elder Holmes was moved to point out how careful people of their time and social status were to hide strong personal emotion. "Such are the proprieties of life, as they are observed among us Anglo-Saxons of the nineteenth century, decently disguising those natural impulses . . . ", wrote the Boston Brahmin.

His son, the young captain, in short time was back in the field and eventually promoted to lieutenant colonel. At the Battle of Chancellorsville in the spring of 1863, he was wounded one more time—a nick in his heel that kept him from remaining with his 20th Massachusetts Regiment. Still recuperating, he was assigned duty as aide to Union General Horatio Wright, who in the spring of 1864 was in command of the 6th Corps as Ulysses S. Grant moved into position to squeeze both Petersburg and nearby Richmond in an inescapable vice.

While Grant was busy in that regard, however, and Sherman was marching on Atlanta in July, Confederate Lieutenant General Jubal Early made his sudden dash, with 12,000 troops, from the Shenandoah Valley into Maryland and drew up before Fort Stevens, a back door to Washington itself.

Since the Nation's capital was lightly defended at best, Wright's 6th Corps hustled back from the Union lines outside Petersburg, traveling up the Potomac River by steamboat and disembarking to a personal welcome by Abraham Lincoln himself. With Wright and his 6th Corps, naturally enough, was the young Colonel Holmes. And when Lincoln then visited Fort Stevens to see the front lines for himself, there was young Holmes again, assigned to escort the President. And when Lincoln impulsively stood up suddenly, his signatory top hat such an obvious target, shots rang out and the Confederate rounds whizzed close by. The future Supreme Court Justice wasted no time and minced no words as he pulled Lincoln down, while blurting, "Get down, you fool!"

Holmes in later life rarely volunteered the story of his brush with Lincoln, which may have saved the President's life but also was deeply embarrassing to the young officer. Holmes eventually did tell the story to both Supreme Court Justice Felix Frankfurter and to Professor Harold J. Laski of the London School of Economics and Political Science, if not a few others.

As events turned out, too, Lincoln himself had eased the Colonel's possibly lasting pain . . . and made things aright when, leaving Fort Stevens, he turned and said, a bit wryly, "Goodbye, Colonel Holmes, I'm glad to see you know how to talk to a civilian."

Sadly, the same General John Sedgwick whom Holmes faithfully remembered for years after the war is most famous today for a wry comment of his own. It happened at Chancellorsville, May 1863. Warned of Confederate sharpshooters nearby, he said, "They couldn't hit an elephant at this range." The words hardly were out of his mouth when he was struck down by a sharpshooter's round.

Perhaps as a result, Holmes was more than commonly sensitive to the effectiveness of unseen snipers when he pushed Lincoln out of harm's way. Possible?

BRAVE MEN SPARED

The fiery, hot-tempered Confederate cavalry leader Nathan Bedford Forrest began his unbending ways early in life—as "man of the house" while still a boy he had to grow up in a hurry. And he did, skipping school, supporting the family as a farmhand, then as a livestock dealer and finally as slave trader and cotton planter of moderate wealth.

An incident when he was only 10 served notice of what was to come. A neighbor's bull kept breaking loose and rampaging through the Forrest family's precious stand of corn, despite repeated pleas and complaints. Finally, young Forrest told the neighbor he could expect to have his bull shot if it wandered one more time.

The neighbor let it be known that anyone shooting his bull would be shot himself.

The bull indeed broke loose one more time and again found its way into the Forrest cornfield. The lad took up his rifle and shot the beast on the spot. The neighbor then appeared with a rifle in his hand and violence in his heart. He started over the fence in between them but the 10-year-old shot again. The round whistled through the neighbor's clothing. He took due notice, turned and ran for home.

The same Forrest, as a full grown man, was so mean and ornery, as is well known among Civil War buffs, he once threatened his own commander, General Braxton Bragg. Amazingly, with no military schooling whatsoever, he rose from enlistment as a private in the future 7th Tennessee Cavalry to general's rank, with a reputation as a genius at cavalry warfare tactics. His reputation for ferocity in battle accordingly was great—and deservedly so. Still, one Southern woman had it slightly wrong the day he and his unit galloped through town with Union men closely pursuing. "Why don't you turn and fight, you cowardly rascal?" she shouted. "If old Forrest were here, he'd make you fight!"

This same officer may or may not have ordered the massacre of black Union troops at Fort Pillow—a controversy never quite settled and of course fed by his apparent post-war role as a founder and possibly the first Grand Wizard of the original Ku Klux Klan.

At least once, though, Forrest showed unexpected softness of the heart. Two Union soldiers, Germans from Wisconsin, had been taken prisoner near Forrest's headquarters outside of Memphis, Tennessee. Since food rations were short and exchanges of prisoners were difficult to arrange, explained *Harper*'s magazine in 1871, "orders had been issued to take no prisoners, but execute them on the spot."

The firing squad assembled, and things looked bleak for the two Union men as Forrest himself strode into sight to command the grim proceedings. Still, to the surprise of the onlookers, Forrest included, the two young Germans merely lit up their pipes and stood chit-chatting with each other, seemingly unconcerned.

Forrest barked his orders. The firing squad formed up and stood to attention. And still the two captives did not flinch or break down. They kept on smoking.

Forrest continued his drill, "Shoulder arms," he shouted. "Ready. Aim . . . "

The Rebels took aim, waiting for the final command to fire.

But no. Forrest then barked, "Ground arms" and, "Right about face."

There would be no execution after all! "Git up and git!" he told the two Yankees. And to his onlookers, the rarely perturbed Forrest merely explained: "Brave men are too scarce to be shot down like dogs."

CHRISTMAS

Christmas of 1861, that first Christmas of the war . . . what was happening? In Washington, the Lincolns had guests for Christmas dinner at the White House. He and his Cabinet also met at some length on this Christmas Day—in the White House, as was the custom.

In the field this first Christmas, Union and Confederate shooting—skirmishing, they call it—took place near Frederick, Maryland. Union ships stopped and seized a Reb blockade-runner off Cape Fear, a minor Union expedition was in motion in Missouri . . . no great results to report.

It was a Wednesday, and just days before, there had been consternation in the Lincoln White House over Mary Todd Lincoln's spendthrift ways. She already had exceeded her Congressional appropriation for interior refurbishment . . . and she was in tears over the embarrassing issue. Husband Abraham was upset too, saying, none too prettily, "it would stink in the nostrils of the American people" to know he approved expenses "overrunning an appropriation of $20,000 for *flub dubs* for this damned old house, when the soldiers cannot have blankets."

The Presidential home, in any case, did look much better for the holidays, and despite the tragedies of war there was momentary joy and warmth for the Lincolns in being all together . . . one last time. Eldest son Robert was down from Harvard; his young brothers Willie and Tad were on hand, as well. Two months later, in February of 1862, Willie, only 11, would be dead, a victim of fever. After that shock, Mary Todd Lincoln, already subject to emotional swings, never would be the same again.

—Christmas Day of 1862, second Christmas of the war, came to a nation more war-weary by far. The Lincolns marked their holiday by visiting the wounded in Washington hospitals. Fighting, no major battles, but real fighting, took place at widely scattered sites—William T. Sherman was moving down the Mississippi from Memphis to Vicksburg, and there was fighting near Brentwood and on the Edmonson Pike in Tennessee, and at Ripley, Mississippi, and near Warrenton, Virginia, and at Green's Chapel and Bear Willow in Kentucky. Few could be happy with the state of the divided nation this day.

—On Christmas Day of 1863, a Friday, little change in the inclinations of the belligerents would have been apparent to the unacquainted spectator looking down from on high. Except, perhaps, for more naval action. In South Carolina's Sono River, Federal gunboats dueled with Confederate shore batteries, with severe damage to the Union's *Marblehead*, while a similar exchange took place between the USS *Pawnee* and shore guns at St. John's Island near Charleston. Ashore, Union troops destroyed Rebel salt works at Bear Inlet, North Carolina, and fought the Johnny Reb at Fort Brooke, Florida.

—By Christmas Day of 1864, a Sunday (since 1864 was a Leap Year), the obvious end was now in sight . . . *obvious*, except that the Union suffered ignominious defeat in its attempt to land 6,500 troops, supported by nearly 60 warships, at Fort Fisher, North Carolina.

The entire assemblage had to sail back to Hampton Roads in Virginia . . . to round after round of recriminations among the Federal commanders. The amphibious assault would be repeated three weeks later, January 13, 1865, with far greater success.

Elsewhere on Christmas Day, John Bell Hood's shattered Army of Tennessee was hurrying, as well as it could, out of Tennessee, with skirmishing at Richland Creek, Anthony's Hill and White's Station. Petersburg, Virginia, still was under tight siege by the Union forces commanded by U.S. Grant; and in the western theater Sterling Price's Rebel forces were in retreat from Missouri. The Confederacy was shrinking in size and spirit day by day. What would the next Christmas Day hold for all?

—Christmas Day of 1865, joy? On this Monday, the heart-rending war was over at least, had been over for several months, a nightmare halted, but its stark images to linger and haunt for generations. By now, the Confederacy had fallen; Jefferson Davis was a prisoner; Henry Wirz, commandant of the notorious Andersonville Confederate Prison in Georgia, had been hanged; Abraham Lincoln had been killed, assassinated; Tennessee-born Andrew Johnson instead was President. Four alleged conspirators in the Lincoln assassination, including a woman, Mary Surratt, had been hanged. And, *interesting postscript*, the Thirteenth Amendment to the U.S. Constitution had gained final ratification, with Alabama, North Carolina, Georgia and Oregon all voting for it since December 1. The Thirteenth Amendment? Abolished slavery.

WHAT DOES A SLAVE?

What exactly does a slave do? A Civil War era slave in the South, that is? Far from field hand or typical household servant, but a slave nonetheless, was one *Laurence*, personal valet to James Chesnut of Mulberry Plantation, Camden, South Carolina, one-time U.S. Senator, briefly Confederate Senator, general-rank Confederate officer and aide to President Jefferson Davis. Chesnut, Laurence and Mrs. Chesnut—the famous Civil War diarist Mary Boykin Chesnut—lived for a time right across the street in Richmond, Virginia, from the Davises, Jefferson and Varina.

Laurence appears often in Mary Chesnut's wartime musings. For instance, early, early—during the shelling of Fort Sumter in Charleston Harbor. The cannon boomed night and day. War had come. Slavery was such a keen issue! What thought the slaves themselves? Mary Chesnut did wonder.

But she saw no change in their manner. "Laurence sits at

our door, as sleepy and as respectful and as profoundly indifferent (as all the blacks in general)." No reaction to the shelling, and as for the whites . . . well, "people talk before them [the slaves] as if they were chairs and tables. And they make no sign. Are they stolidly stupid or wiser than we are, silent and strong, biding their time?"

A few weeks later, Mary's husband had to pass through the newly-named Confederate capital of Richmond. Here, all was confusion—crowded city, unbearable heat, overflowing hotels. The former Senator had to share his hotel bed with a Confederate Congressman from Louisiana, while also sharing the room with still others.

Chesnut, traveling with four slaves, had left his horse overnight in Petersburg, just below Richmond. The dependable Laurence stayed with the animal until she could be transported to Richmond the next morning. "My hands were so full with the four negroes, all green except Laurence," wrote Chesnut to his wife, "that I had no time to take a meal from the time I left Kingsville [South Carolina] until I got here."

That was in June of 1861, and by mid-July the two Chesnuts, husband and wife, had openly discussed the issue of Laurence's true loyalties. Laurence was in charge of his master's personal items, some of them valuable—his watch, for instance, and "two or three hundred gold pieces [that] lie in the tray of his trunk." Laurence was supposed to take those things to Mary Chesnut if anything happened to her husband, then an officer in the field.

She wondered if this expectation would hold true. "Maybe he will pack off to the Yankees—and freedom—with all that."

"Fiddlesticks!" said her husband. "He is not going to leave me for anybody else. After all, what can he ever be better than he is now—a gentleman's *gentleman*?" To which she replied, "He is within the sound of the enemies' guns, and when he gets to the other army, he is *free*."

But Laurence did not run off to freedom. By August of the same year it was recorded that "[he] does all our shopping." Mrs. Chesnut was worried about the gold, however, and so she had sewn it into a money belt with her diamonds for safekeeping during an emergency.

Laurence's reaction? "Laurence wears the bronze mask." Whenever she left her trunk open, "Laurence brings me the keys and tells me, 'You oughten to do so, Miss Mary.'" And when her husband left money in his pockets, "Laurence says that's why he can't let anyone but himself brush Mars Jeems' clothes."

By October of the same year, the Chesnuts had discovered that Laurence made "an excellent tailor," and, former Alabama Senator Clement Clay's wife Virginia, "never tired of laughing at the picture he made seated cross-legged on Mr. Chesnut's trunk darning."

And he did have a mind of his own, as the saying goes. Chesnut's second cousin, Mary Stevens Garnett, once said, "I thought Cousin James was the laziest man alive until I knew his man Laurence." To this, Mary Chesnut added that Laurence would "not move an inch or lift a finger for anyone but his master." One time, a friend, British-born Ellen Middleton, "politely sent him on an errand—and he was very polite about it too."

Except that hours later she espied him sitting on the front yard fence. And she asked if he had gone on her errand.

"No, Ma'am," he said, "I am waiting for Mars Jeems."

His master, "Mars Jeems," meanwhile had taken to calling Laurence "Adolphe", after the dominating valet in *Uncle Tom's Cabin*. But Chesnut defended Laurence as "simply perfect as a servant for him." And he was indeed most dependable, as he himself would assure Mary Chesnut during the winter of 1862 and 1863, when Richmond was feeling the deprivations of war . . . but a certain amount of entertaining was called for nonetheless. "You give me the money, I'll find everything you want," he told her. There was "no such word as 'fail' with him."

This was a time when turkeys cost $30, "but Laurence kept us plentifully supplied."

Once, too, Mary Chesnut wanted to entertain Varina Davis and a mutual friend. Laurence had produced a basket of cherries . . . but wouldn't it be nice if they had some ice, too!

"Respectfully Laurence said—and also firmly, 'Give me money and you shall have ice.'"

Somehow he knew of an icehouse on the other side of town,

across the James River, and, "In a wonderfully short time we had mint juleps and cherry cobblers."

But there also came a time when Laurence slipped up, with embarrassing consequences. He had gone to one of Richmond's "negro balls," as Mary Chesnut called them. He had forgotten his mandatory pass as he changed his coat for the affair. When a fight broke out at the ball, the police came. Those present were ordered to show their passes—Laurence "was taken up as having none."

A household maid and cook named Molly delighted in telling Mary Chesnut the next day why Laurence was missing. Molly and Laurence often argued, it seems. And so Molly appeared before their mistress in tears from laughing. "Come and look," she evidently said. "Here is the fine gentleman, tied between two black niggers and marched off to jail."

Apparently she and Mary Chesnut were looking at Laurence from a window. "Laurence disregarded her and called to me at the top of his voice. 'Please Ma'am—ask Mars Jeems to come take me out of this. I ain't done nothing.'"

"Mars Jeems" soon did go to his rescue, a never-forgotten moment in the Chesnut household. "He was terribly chopfallen when he came home, walking behind Mr. C. He is always so *respectable* and well behaved and stands on his dignity."

Laurence didn't hesitate to offer his protection when the dread Yankees were close to a lightly garrisoned Richmond in 1863, but it must also be reported that on January 4, 1864, he was drunk. Further, he and Molly "had a grand row."

In the next month, further mortification for Laurence. Drunk again. At breakfast, told to move a chair, he lifted it high over his head and it "smashed" the chandelier above. Chesnut was so furious that he told Mary to send Laurence away . . . all the way back to their plantation home in South Carolina. So, there he went, "gone back ignominiously," but surely not for long! "He will soon be back, and when he comes he will say, 'Shoo! I knew Mars Jeems could not do without me.' And indeed he cannot."

He did return, of course, but the Chesnuts had to excuse a former landlady's report that both Molly and Laurence were apt to be a bit noisy when the Chesnuts were away from home. "They went about the house, quiet as mice when we were at home," it seems. "Laurence sat at the door and sprung to his feet if we passed. When we were out they sung, laughed, shouted, danced . . ."

Laurence nonetheless was back in the family's good graces by the time the Chesnuts entertained the Jefferson Davises at dinner in Columbia, South Carolina. That was in October of 1864, the Confederate dream slipping away fast.

"Our world, the only world we cared for," wrote Mary Chesnut, now was being "literally kicked to pieces." Everything would change. She spent the last weeks of the Civil War in search of safe places to stay . . . out of the Yankee path. One of those unhappy stops, ironically, was at Lincolnton, North Carolina, where the unfortunate Laurence ran into an angry buzz saw of a landlady to the Mary Chesnut entourage.

"Refugees in Lubberland," she called this section of her memoir diary, and Lincolnton's chief attraction was that it was "a thoroughly out-of-all-routes place."

Still, it was, by Chesnut standards, also thoroughly miserable. "Here I am brokenhearted—an exile," wrote Mary Chesnut later. "Such a place [where she had rented rooms]. For a feather bed, a pine table, and two chairs I pay 30 dollars a day. Such sheets!—but I have some of my own."

They had arrived—Mary Chestnut, a house servant named Ellen (taking Molly's place for a time) and Laurence—and "before I was well out of the hack," Laurence had encountered "the woman of the house." She, for her part, simply *attacked* the startled black man. She said "she would not have him at any price." She said "his clothes were too fine for a nigger—'his airs indeed'—and poor Laurence was as humble—and silent."

He did plead, "Miss Mary, send me back to Mars Jeems." And then, when "Miss Mary" looked for a pencil to write a note to her husband (who had remained in South Carolina with his command), it was Laurence, unfortunately, who brought forth a gold pencil case.

That set off the landlady again, "Go away", she apparently shouted. "I wants no niggers here with pencils—and airs."

Laurence "fled before the storm"—but not before saying that "Mars Jeems" wouldn't want his wife staying there if he knew "how you was treated."

A friend and fellow refugee told Mary Chesnut not to pay attention to people like the Lincolnton landlady. "They will never comprehend the height from which we have fallen," said Susan Middleton.

Chesnut and her maidservant Ellen, meanwhile, were more happily quartered at another rental space in Lincolnton. But only temporarily.

In the end, of course, just like the stereotype, the Chesnuts returned after the hostilities were over to a ruined plantation that once was home to a few hundred slaves and their large white family, the Chesnuts. The slaves were free now; some left and some stayed on. James and Mary Chesnut were left financially strapped for a while; they never did regain the great wealth they had known before the war.

Mary Chesnut's last diary reference to Laurence the slave comes in a letter from James Chesnut, dated March 15, 1865, still before Appomattox. James informed Mary that he was sending a Confederate officer and Laurence to Lincolnton to bring her down to Chester Court House, South Carolina, where he had found three vacant rooms with access to half a kitchen for them all. They would go home to the Mulberry family plantation outside Camden later.

There came a time, in the difficult postwar period, when the family's cash income stemmed from maid Molly's efforts at selling eggs and butter. Molly was it? Yes, soon after the war she swore she would never leave "Missis" (Mary Chesnut). Ellen, too, would stay. Her husband Claiborne one day "asked enormous wages for her," but Mary Chesnut told him, "You and your child [Ellen's, too] are living in one of our houses, free of rent. Ellen can go or stay as she pleases."

And Mary told Ellen, "I have no money, Ellen."

But Ellen said, "Claiborne is an old fool always meddling and making—I don't care for money, I gits money's worth."

More Staggering Stats

What *were* the odds, anyway? You know, if you had had to go in, whether inspired by zeal for one cause or the other, or by less voluntary stimulus such as conscription? If there were 10,000 and even more combat actions, *fights*, what were the chances of the average soldier or sailor getting by without being hurt—mortally or otherwise? After all, if 8 percent of the Union's 583 generals, or 65, were killed, mortally wounded, or fatally diseased, what chance stood the lower, presumably more exposed ranks? And in the Confederacy, if an even greater 18 percent of that side's 425 general officers, or 92 in all, had to succumb to one lethal threat or another, again, what were the average enlisted man's odds against wounding or death?

Well, statisticians can always play games and sources can be unreliable in situations such as the American Civil War. With all its actions, its confusion of records, its wanton destruction here and there, its sometime loose organization to begin with . . . and all the time that has passed since, one cannot always be sure of some "facts." Still, E.B. Long in his day by day *Almanac* of the Civil War can be considered an astute student of such matters, one well able to have separated the wheat from the chaff, as *he* cites the statistics saying that in the Union Army chances were that one in every 65 men would be killed in action, that one of 56 would die of wounds, that—here's the real shocker!—one of every 13.5 men would die of disease! Further, an even greater one in ten would be wounded in action, while one in 15 would be captured or cited as missing. Gloomily here, too, a rampant one of every seven men captured would not survive his prisoner status in the hands of the Confederacy.

As the figures may indicate, and Long makes note, "Disease in the Civil War claimed a far deadlier toll than the battlefield." The sicknesses to avoid most were those affecting the bowels—diarrhea and dysentery combined to kill at least 44,558 Union soldiers. The next leading killer was fever of various kinds, under various names and, obviously, not always scientifically diagnosed (or expertly treated, for that matter). Mark down 40,656 deaths to fevers, and that's now more than 85,000 casualties from those two areas of illness alone, far more than America lost in the 12-year Vietnam War of the 20th century.

Another 20,000 or so Union deaths can be attributed to pneumonia, with still others to be blamed upon sicknesses such as smallpox, measles, consumption (tuberculosis). As for Confederate stats in this area, the fact is that those totals don't exist. But Long cites Bell Irvin Wiley's *Life of Johnny Reb* as authoritative and reliable enough in concluding that "for every soldier killed in battle or of mortal wounds, there were three deaths from disease." Once again, the bowels were the average soldier's most vulnerable area, but measles, typhoid (which was one of the Northern fevers, too), and smallpox also were prevalent killers.

When you add it all up—combat, disease, accident, what-have-you—the final Civil War casualty figures are, as is well known, truly staggering. In the North, total Army deaths, all causes, were 360,222, of which less than a third—110,100 to be exact—were combat-blamable. The Federal Navy, for its part, was an active partner that emerged from this terrible war with only, if such a word may be used, 1,084 dead in combat and another 3,000 stuck down by disease or accident.

The comparative Confederate figures are, again, not so easily or reliably obtained, but Long says, "Probably the best and most accepted estimate is 94,000 Confederates killed in battle or mortally wounded, while 164,000 died of disease. Total deaths thus came to 258,000."

It may seem odd, but the side that won the war, the North, wound up with many more dead and wounded—107,000 more. But then, the North entered the fray with many more men.

Often hidden in the thickets of such figures are the ways that men died. Not all fell in some neat bookkeeper's row before a fusillade of bullets . . . not at all.

No, war's actual toll, its pain and suffering, can be more graphic, really. The details sting even now. The U.S. Navy's losses, low as they were by comparison with the Army's, include men, 342 of them, scalded to death, usually when boilers on their ships were blown open, and the men, 308 of them, who were drowned, usually when a ship broken open in combat or otherwise damaged spilled them into the sea or river.

The Army's losses, for that matter, include executions—267 by their own, Union side, and 64 by the Confederate enemy. Another 520 Federal soldiers were simply murdered, while nearly 5,000 were drowned, 391 took their own lives, 31,000 succumbed as prisoners of war, and 313 died of sunstroke.

And how might all these horrendous figures compare with those compiled in America's other wars?

First, consider that, as Long puts it, "Total deaths in the Civil War for both sides may be placed at least at 623,026, with a minimum of 471,427 wounded, for a total casualty figure of 1,094,453."

By comparison, American counted 13,283 dead in the Mexican War, 2,446 in the Spanish-American War, 117,000 in World War I, 407,000 in World War II, 54,246 in Korea, and 58,000 in Vietnam. In short, the Civil War outranked them all individually, and falls "only" 30,000 short of the total dead in all these wars put together.

Ends

OLD ABE THE SOLDIER BIRD

Somehow, says the legend, he always found his own army, the blue, and even his own regiment, Wisconsin's 8th, when he returned from one of his hunting forays with a chicken, rabbit or lamb in his clutches.

Allegedly, too, he had ranged for miles across the war-torn countryside to come up with his prey, and sometimes he was gone for as long as two or three days. When not so engaged, he liked to go to the nearest stream in the mornings for a splashy bath.

The real fact is that he usually was kept on a leash of 16 feet . . . but he sometimes broke loose. But quite true, from their first meeting at Madison, the state capital, he stuck by his Wisconsin regiment throughout the war, on the march or in battle—37 battles, and various skirmishes, they say. He was there for the siege of Vicksburg, for the taking of Corinth, and for a march of Sherman's at Red River. The hotter the battle, the more likely and the more frequent his piercing scream.

Once you heard his shrill cry, incidentally, you never forgot. *Hail Columbia*! That apt symbol, the 8th Wisconsin's mascot . . . named "Old Abe." That is, the "Eagle Regiment" and its "Old Abe the Soldier Bird." That is, the 8th Wisconsin's bald eagle that went to war with his Wisconsin boys, followed them through their fights and their marches, ignored those Reb taunts of "Yankee Buzzard" or "Owl, Owl" and came home again with only a *somewhat* cropped set of tail feathers (from a bullet, yes).

In the interim, he had gone through St. Louis with the boys, who turned down one man's $500 offer for the bird, and another's pledge to swap his farm for the still-young but handsome eagle. He had supped on many an unwary chicken, including the time he and his handler were invited to visit a curious farmer's barnyard . . . with violent result when he espied a nearby fowl.

They say he not only loved his boys but their music. A favorite tune was "Yankee Doodle." He watched carefully over drill and parade, and on the march or in camp knew when to soar and when to perch. It was considered quite an honor to be a regimental eagle-bearer. He became so well-known that luminaries such as Grant or Sherman routinely doffed their hat in salute when passing his mobile roost.

You could say he was also popular with the enemy, since Confederate General Sterling Price once ordered his men to capture the symbolic bird. They weren't successful—Old Abe the Soldier Bird stayed with his regiment until he returned to Wisconsin in 1864.

That was his original home—a Chippewa Indian, they say, had found him as a wee chick, or eaglet, then sold him for a bushel of corn to a white man who carried him into Eau Claire just as its men were gathering to march off to war. "An eagle!" the men had shouted. "Let him enlist!"

Eau Claire's Company C then took him to Madison mounted on a perch with bunting in the colors of the Stars and Stripes. State officials gave him a new perch and the 8th Wisconsin took him on as a mascot, as inspiration for its name, Eagle Regiment.

Old Abe was so much a part of his soldiering outfit that he even went home on furlough . . . with his boys, of course. On one such visit, he took part in a fund-raising affair sponsored by the Ladies Aid Society of Chippewa Falls. That evening, Old Abe and fellow members of the regiment's Company C sat by as a minister from Eau Claire delivered a patriotic sermon.

On the way back to their duty station, it also is reported in the Wisconsin Historical Society's handsome book *Old Abe The War Eagle* by Richard H. Zeitlin, the eagle and his last eagle-bearer of the war period, a German immigrant named Burkhardt, encountered a train conductor who said the soldier would have to buy a ticket for the eagle—"who, after all, occupied a seat." When Old Abe's bearer objected, the conductor said, "Pay for that thing or I'll put you out!" The Union soldier then stammered in his best English, adds Zeitlin, "that Old Abe was a free American eagle and, therefore, should ride for free."

Even that didn't impress the resolute conductor, but he finally backed down when Burkhardt's compatriots and other passengers in the car turned a bit stormy in his defense. And Old Abe traveled for free.

About four years old by now, the bald eagle returned to duty with his head and tail feathers turned white—a mark of full and proud maturity for the species.

With the end of the war near in 1864, the question did arise as to Old Abe's peacetime future. The men of his regiment debated the choices before them—send him to Washington as a gift to the Federal government, present him to the state of Wisconsin, or send him back to Eau Claire with its Company C? "The entire regiment participated in the decision-making process," reports Zeitlin, "voting unanimously to present Old Abe to the state authorities in Madison."

Thus it would be. Victor Wolf, Company C's commander, officially passed along Old Abe, who then took up residence on the grounds of the State Capitol while his compatriots of the Eagle Regiment went back to war for almost another year.

Officially classified a "war relic" after the hostilities finally ended in 1865, Old Abe became more than a local curiosity. "As the years passed, Old Abe's fame grew," notes Zeitlin. In the meantime, he lived in a two-room "apartment" in the basement of the Capitol. "He had access to a specially constructed bath tub, was fed fresh rabbits and had several sawhorses to roost upon. The 'Eagle Department' never lacked for visitors."

He escaped a couple of times, but was recaptured. He did some traveling in the postwar years as well, appearing at various patriotic exhibitions and at the Philadelphia Centennial in 1876. Old Abe lived on until 1881, when, his lungs damaged by smoke from a fire in a nearby storeroom, he died in the arms of his last attendant.

Debate immediately arose over what next—a dignified burial or a trip to the taxidermist's bench? As Zeitlin says, "Taxidermy won out over burial." Although the result, sadly, "did not look especially life-like," Old Abe was displayed in the Capitol's Grand Old Army Memorial Hall (and once was "visited" by Teddy Roosevelt). A fire in 1904 destroyed the building, together with the eagle's remains.

Still, Old Abe did not entirely fade away. A six-foot likeness in bronze sits atop the Wisconsin memorial at the Vicksburg Wartime Military Park. Many other Old Abe likenesses appear in

Wisconsin itself, even in the Atlanta (Georgia) Cyclorama, and as the logo for at least one large manufacturing company. Further, reports author Zeitlin, Old Abe's likeness is on the shoulder patch of the U.S. Army's 101st Airborne Division—"The Screaming Eagles."

BLEAK HOLIDAY

Confederate Representative Warren Akin of Georgia arrived in Richmond on November 27, 1864, to take his seat in the second session of the Second Confederate Congress. Arriving three weeks late, due to the birth of a daughter at home, he entertained high hopes of returning to Georgia for Christmas.

The war wasn't going well, prices in the Confederate capital were greatly inflated and his legislator's salary might not match his expenses, he soon noted in letters to his wife, Mary. But there was the Christmas recess to anticipate. Recently introduced Senate legislation called for adjournment on December 20, a recess to last until January 10. That would give Akin three weeks for the difficult journey home and return to Richmond.

True, he also wrote on December 11, "We are getting on slowly with the business of Congress . . . " In any case, the Georgia lawyer, farmer and slaveholder instructed his wife that he would telegraph immediately once the Christmas recess won Congressional approval.

She should then send their slave Bob to meet him partway home with a wagon. "The rail roads will often fail to make connections, and I may be behind time," Akin warned. He had ridden in a boxcar partway to Richmond the month before.

Three days later, on December 14, he wrote with bad news—the resolution as passed by the full Senate would allow only an eight-day Christmas recess, not enough time for Akin to spend any time at home, it seemed.

There was one hope, however. Possibly his House chamber would amend the Senate's resolution to allow a longer Christmas break. "You know not how anxious I am to go home," this father of seven children wrote to his wife.

On December 16, Akin wrote that the House still was debating a bill to try to stabilize Confederate currency. "We are getting on very slowly." Then the bad news: "I am sorry I cant [sic] go home Christmas, but must bear it as well as I can. The Senate agreed to a recess of only eight days, and the House refused that, so the matter, I presume, is at rest."

Two days later, Akin mentioned that the food at his boardinghouse was fairly plain, far from hotel standards but ample. Akin (and two Virginia state legislators) were staying with the George Washington Gretter family, whose home at Fifth and Leigh streets was a "pleasant walk" of about a quarter-mile to Capitol Square.

The war news was worse than ever as the last Christmas of the Civil War approached. Akin cited the recent (November 30) debacle of John Bell Hood's Army of Tennessee at Franklin, with six Confederate generals among the dead. "The loss of Generals at Franklin in Hood's army was awful . . . and I have no doubt when we hear the truth, our loss in officers of the line and men was awful . . . "

Even worse, about two weeks later, would be the disaster at Nashville that shattered Hood's army. The battle began December 15, but in Richmond, three days later, Akin had heard only "a rumor . . . that Hood had another fight and has been terribly beaten."

The Georgia Congressman was afraid the rumor was true, and if so, Hood's "whole army is lost, I fear." Indeed, Hood would cross into Mississippi on Christmas Day, he soon to resign his command, his army no longer an effective force.

By December 21, meanwhile, Akin again was writing home, this time with Christmas only four days away. "There will be no recess at Christmas, and I do not expect to get home until Congress adjourns, and I fear that will be March or April, and may be May."

As always seems the case, anywhere, anytime, the legislative pace was slow. One important issue to the Confederacy in its final months was the proposal to open the ranks to blacks, a notion dismissed early in the war. By now, however, the South was desperate, and the prospect of additional manpower was a serious matter. The Second (and last) Congress would authorize President

Jefferson Davis to ask the member states for 300,000 black soldiers—slaves into soldiers—but not until mid-March 1865, too late to induct more than a few, much less deploy them.

Sitting at his desk in the House, on December 22, Akin again wrote his wife: "O how glad I would be to eat dinner with you and my dear children Christmas . . . " The next day, he lamented the course of the war and the suffering throughout the Confederacy, rather than dwelling again on the yuletide, except to say at one point, "One more day and then it will be Christmas. O how glad I would be if I could go home tomorrow."

He also reported that a turkey in Richmond by now cost $125!

But then the House decided there would be a brief Christmas recess after all, an adjournment for two business days.

It was the day after Christmas before Akin wrote his wife again. He reported that he had spent the day with "Anderson's Brigade"—probably Georgia's General George T. Anderson. "Rode out . . . [on horseback] and felt the effects of it last night." Akin, a good Methodist and occasional lay preacher, wrote that he preached a bit, and, "I was very tired and did not get back until dark."

Akin did offer one observation of his Richmond surroundings. "The defenses are very strong, indeed, and I think the Yankees will be greatly slaughtered if they ever attack our men in their works."

He had been invited, he said, to two eggnog parties, "but have not gone to any." Instead, he tried to visit Vice President Alexander H. Stephens, also of Georgia. But, alas, Stephens was not home, and Akin returned to his lonely room and resumed writing a letter to his wife. He expressed regret that the House was not discharging its duties this day after Christmas, noting that members for some time had been determined "for going home and frolicking."

Akin remained in Richmond for the next several weeks, troubled not only by the Confederacy's declining hope of survival but also by his family's difficulties. His wife, their seven children and six or seven slaves had been forced from their home in Bartow

County, and then from a temporary abode at Oxford, southeast of Atlanta, to escape Union forces. They were now "in exile" at Elberton in Akin's native Elbert County.

The legislator finally rejoined his twice-displaced family on March 5 after a "long and tedious journey through the country." Congress still was in session when he left Richmond, and we don't know the reason such a dutiful member left his post after much sacrifice earlier. It may be that his sense of duty to family finally prevailed. It may be, too, that he saw the proverbial writing on the wall—the surrender at Appomattox was barely a month away when Akin returned to Georgia.

Although his home and law office in Cassville had been burned by Union troops, Akin took his family back to Bartow County and picked up his legal practice after the war. He lived until a week before another Christmas, that of 1877. His widow lived until 1907. They were survived by two daughters and four sons.

The seventh child, another son, Elbert, had died in a pony-riding accident. Warren Akin learned that sad fact a few days later, on his way home from Richmond in the bleak year of 1865.

Unlucky John Bell Hood

Unlucky in love and war—in life itself, really—was John Bell Hood, who built a fine combat record at lower command level early in the war, who continued in brave and dedicated service even after losing a leg and suffering a crippled arm but wound up the culprit historically (and somewhat unfairly) tabbed with the loss of Atlanta to William Tecumseh Sherman.

Hood, later, in post-war years, found himself assailed in the public prints by Sherman all over again for certain mistakes and alleged shortcomings. And this after Hood had had to endure the very public censure of his own former commander, the controversial Joseph E. Johnston (arguably, for his dilatory deployments, the real culprit of the Confederacy's loss of Atlanta).

Hood, an 1853 graduate of West Point, started off the war

well enough—initially commander of the Texas Brigade, he fought well at Gaines' Mill outside of Richmond, at Second Bull Run and at Antietam, all in 1862. Soon wearing two stars, he was known far and wide as a "fighting general."

Unmarried, still relatively young, this Kentucky native might have been a fine "catch" for many a Confederate belle caught up in the romance of The Cause. Unfortunately, Hood chose to woo a very sophisticated young woman from South Carolina who was in Richmond with her father, head of the Confederate conscription hierarchy. Sally Buchanan Preston (called "Buck") was known as a charming but wily "tease," and Hood was destined only to dance the dance of the moth about her bright flame . . . until more gripping events swept him up and away.

He would suffer in other ways, too, from the same doggedness seen in his hopeless pursuit of Sally "Buck" Preston—with unhappy personality clashes often resulting. At Antietam in September of 1862 he blindly persisted in a contretemps with a fellow Confederate general, Nathan George Evans (like Buck Preston, from South Carolina), over a number of ambulance wagons Hood's men had captured the previous month at Second Bull Run.

Hood, it seems, had wanted his sick and wounded men to have use of the wagons, but Evans told Hood to turn them over to the South Carolina troops. "Whereas I would cheerfully have obeyed directions to deliver them to General Robert E. Lee's Quartermaster for the use of the Army," wrote Hood after the war, "I did not consider it just that I should be required to yield them to another brigade of the division, which was in no manner entitled to them."

Hood refused the order, whereupon he was "placed in arrest" and told to expect court-martial proceedings. Lee, in the meantime, was moving into Maryland with the Army of Northern Virginia, the Battle of Antietam soon to take place. And now Hood persisted in his dispute to the point of dangerous insubordination. "I was still under arrest, with orders to move in the rear of my two brigades," recalled Hood, a popular commander in those days. At South Mountain, near Antietam Creek, shells began to burst near Hood's column. He could hear the men, as they angled up the ascent, calling out—"Give us Hood!"

At the base of the ridge, Hood came upon Lee, who told him, "General, here I am just upon the eve of entering into battle and with one of my best officers under arrest. If you will merely say that you regret this occurrence, I will release you and restore you to command of your division."

But the stubborn Hood would not back down, even before the venerated Robert E. Lee. He repeated his long-held assertion that the release of his wagons would be unjust, unless they were given up to use by Lee's entire army.

Lee repeated his request, and Hood still would not retreat from his position. An exasperated Lee finally had to concede. "Well," he said, "I will suspend your arrest till the impending battle is decided."

With that, Hood hastily remounted his horse and galloped off to lead his division, credited ever since with stopping the Union attack on the Confederate left near Dunkard Church and West Woods during the Battle of Antietam Creek.

Almost a year after Antietam, Hood was badly wounded at Gettysburg, his left arm crippled. Hardly recovered from that wound, he bravely traveled to the western theater of war with his commander, James Longstreet, just in time to appear in the field at Chickamauga, September 18 to 20, 1863—and lose his right leg to another severe wound. Hood insisted upon resuming duty, although he had to be helped in mounting his horse, needed a safety belt to him keep in the saddle and hereinafter always traveled with an orderly in charge of the general's crutch.

It was after the amputation of his leg that Hood was reassigned to his onetime commander (outside Richmond), General Johnston. The touchy Johnston, one of only five full generals in the Confederacy, was widely known for his dispute with President Jefferson Davis, who had ranked him fourth among those five.

Hood was reunited with Johnston in the face of Sherman's advance into Georgia, a campaign marked by successive Southern defeats and withdrawals, until finally the two were backed up close to Atlanta. At this point came the order for Hood to replace Johnston as commander of the Army of Tennessee and do what he could to stop Sherman. And at this point, there was little that Hood really could do, but some analysts have faulted the Kentuckian for his apparent confusion in some of his actions as the new head of an entire army.

Worse, far worse, would come after Hood escaped Sherman's siege lines around Atlanta September 1 of 1864 and left the city to its fiery fate. Hood next crossed northern Alabama and struck into Tennessee, his avowed purpose to cut Sherman's supply lines from the rear.

Now, all on his own as a full army commander, Hood found himself approaching Franklin, Tennessee. When West Point classmate John Schofield's Federals escaped Hood's planned entrapment at nearby Spring Hill, Hood blamed his subordinate Benjamin Cheatham for failing to cut off Schofield, a feat easily accomplished by seizing the turnpike leading westward to Nashville. So enraged was Hood that he rescinded an earlier recommendation for Cheatham's promotion. When Cheatham then appeared before Hood to volunteer his error in the matter of the turnpike and apologize, Hood rescinded again—now allowing the endorsement of promotion to stand. Hood then persisted in assaulting Schofield with the most massive infantry charge of the whole war. But the Union troops held for five hours . . . Hood in the end had to back off, after losing 6,252 men, among them six generals killed outright, to the Union's 2,326 casualties.

The curtain rang down for Hood at Nashville two weeks later, December 15, as his former West Point instructor, the Virginian George Thomas, dealt Hood's Army of Tennessee a final, shattering blow in two days of grim battle. It was Christmas Day as Hood retreated into Mississippi, soon to relinquish command at his own request.

After the war, Hood refought many of his battles all over again in a famous "Reply" to Joe Johnston's final depiction of Hood's failings, the "Reply" becoming centerpiece of Hood's personal memoirs. Sherman then launched a flank attack on the ill-fated Confederate hero in which Sherman listed various steps his one-time enemy Hood *should* have taken in response to the Union campaigns in Georgia and Tennessee.

Sally "Buck" Preston, meanwhile, had retreated from Richmond back to South Carolina before war's end—Hood apparently found marital bliss with another woman. Their marriage, their lives, ended in 1879, sadly, in a state of financial duress . . . in a yellow fever epidemic in New Orleans. Hood was only 48.

"ON WISCONSIN . . . ON!"

Few regiments have ever had a hero like this one, the "boy adjutant" of the 24th Wisconsin Volunteer Infantry, only 17 when he and his companions marched off to war in 1862. Nor have many heroes ever had a son as an expert—and moving—chronicler of their deeds. But this one surely did!

Three battles are the story here. At Stone's River the first three days of 1863 his regiment lost nearly 40 percent of its men—every mounted officer was felled, except for the youthful adjutant. The Wisconsinites began one day's action in a well prepared line of rifle entrenchments, with artillery in supporting position. So fierce and swirling was the action that the Wisconsin regiment had to change frontal position 14 times. By nightfall, the regiment's men were back in their rifle pits again—but facing opposite the direction they had started out in that morning. The enemy still was in front, and the young adjutant was congratulated by Phil Sheridan, who noted: "You haven't lost a foot of ground."

The youth's finest hour was yet to come. He missed the Battle of Chickamauga due to a bout of typhoid fever—and one has to wonder if he really had his strength back by the time of Missionary Ridge on November 25, 1863. Overlooking Chattanooga, Tennessee, in brooding style that late fall, the mountain-like rise presented a corrugated ground strewn with boulders, etched by gullies and ravines, covered with difficult underbrush. Braxton Bragg's Confederates awaited attack from the besieged city below; they waited in defensive lines beginning with rifle pits at the base and continuing up the steep, tough slopes to the crest.

Attack was the order of the day, and none too palatable for

the Union troops under U.S. Grant's overall command and, in the case of the 24th Wisconsin, under the command of Grant's able subordinate Phil Sheridan.

He it was who must take the rifle pits at the foot of the mountain, and that indeed was done . . . with bayonet. The rifle pits cleared, the next and far more imposing task was the steep, pitted rise itself, repeatedly swept by shot and shell. But would, or could, the conquerors of the rifle pits now start up the steep slope into the very teeth of the withering fire from the entrenched enemy?

Years later, the young Wisconsin adjutant's famous son would write *his* account of what happened next:

> No one seems to know just what orders may have been given, but suddenly the flag of the 24th Wisconsin started forward. With it was the color sergeant, the color guard of two corporals, and the adjutant. Up they went, step by step. The enemy's fire was intense. Down went the color bearer. One of the corporals seized the colors as they fell, but was bayoneted before he could move. A shell took off the head of the other corporal, but the adjutant grasped the flag and kept on. He seemed to be surrounded by nothing but gray coats. A Confederate colonel thrust viciously at his throat, but even as he lunged a bullet struck and the deflected blade just ripped a shoulder strap. No movements yet from the Union lines. And then, above the roar of battle, sounded the adjutant's voice: "On, Wisconsin!"
>
> They come then; they come with a rush and a roar, a blue tide of courage, a whole division of them. Shouting, cursing, struggling foot by foot, heads bent as in a gale! Gasping breath from tortured lungs! Those last few feet before the log breastworks seem interminable! They falter! Officers are down! Sergeants now lead! And then, suddenly, on the crest—the flag! Once again that cry: "On, Wisconsin!" Silhouetted against the sky, the adjutant stands on the parapet waving the colors where the whole regiment can see him! Through the ragged blue line, from one end of the division to the other, comes an ugly roar, like the growl of a wounded bear! They race those last few steps, eyes blazing, lips snarling and bayonets plunging! And Missionary Ridge is won.

The adjutant then fell to the ground, "exhausted, his body retching, racked with pain." He was covered with blood and mud, "his smoke-blackened face barely recognizable, his clothes torn to tatters."

Sheridan, no virgin to combat, was obviously stunned by his young officer's feat. "Sheridan, the division commander, utters not a word—he just stares at him—and then takes him in his arms. And his deep voice seems to break a little as he says: 'Take care of him. He has just won the Medal of Honor.'"

It wasn't long before the hero of Missionary Ridge distinguished himself all over again. At 19, incidentally, he was a colonel, the youngest such officer in the entire Union Army, wrote his son later. And it was as one of 11 Union colonels leading 11 regiments that he took his 24th Wisconsin up the again-steep slopes of Kennesaw Mountain, Georgia, in 1864.

One by one, all 11 colonels went down, the youngest colonel of them all struck a crippling blow and left looking dead. A shot had passed through one arm and coursed into the chest area as well—but there stopped, thankfully, short of mortal damage by a wadded obstruction.   Halting the bullet just outside the walls of the heart had been his wallet, and in it, letters from home, a Bible . . . a farewell message.

The farewell message was the result of a meeting the night before of all 11 regimental colonels—and their concerted conclusion that their task of storming the Kennesaw would be suicidal. Each then wrote a farewell message.

The former "boy adjutant" from Wisconsin, now a full-fledged regimental commander, faced one more harsh test before the war would be over for him. He did first recuperate from the wounds suffered at Kennesaw; he then found himself at Franklin, Tennessee, a debacle for the South but a tough fight for anyone who was there. And here, once again, the youthful Wisconsinite proved himself both hero and leader. His successor as regimental adjutant, Captain Edwin Parsons, later wrote what happened after the Rebels suddenly struck the Federal line in front of the 24th Regiment, the Rebels who struck hard, and fast . . . and broke through!

> Not an instant could be lost. The whole army was imperilled unless the breach could be closed. I saw the Colonel

swing into his saddle and heard his yell, "Up, Wisconsin!" There was no time to form lines. We just rushed pell mell to meet the enemy in a desperate hand to hand melee. I saw the Colonel sabering his way toward the leading Confederate flag. His horse was shot from under him, a bullet ripped open his right shoulder, but on foot he fought his way forward trying to bring down those Stars and Bars. A Confederate Major now had the flag and shot the Colonel through the breast. I thought he was done for but he staggered up and drove his sword through his adversary's body, but even as the Confederate fell he shot our Colonel down for good with a bullet through the knee. The other regiments of the reserve were now up and we drove the enemy back and healed the breach. When I returned to the Carter House, where they had brought the Colonel, I saw four dead Generals lying on the porch side by side.

Franklin, Tennessee, the day that six generals died, all Confederate. But more than a few Union casualties, too. And our "boy colonel," what of him? Woefully stricken, obviously enough . . . but, wrote his son later, he recovered and "rejoined the regiment in time to bring it home at the end of the war."

At Franklin, he had served beyond simple heroics, if heroics can be called simple; he had served beyond the one-dimensional in the effect his acumen and leadership had wrought upon the battle itself. In the words of Union General David S. Stanley: "It is rare in history that one can say a certain unit saved the day. But this was the case at Franklin when the 24th Wisconsin, with no orders from higher up, by its spontaneous action, repelled the enemy and rectified our lines. In this it was bravely led by its young Colonel, Arthur MacArthur."

And so, with the end of the war, the 24th "marched triumphantly through the streets of Milwaukee before the cheering crowds," wrote Arthur's son nearly 100 years later. "But there was many a sob and tear in that great gathering. The regiment had lost more than two-thirds of its officers and men. They were mustered out on June 10, 1865, and Arthur MacArthur was again a civilian."

So wrote a proud son who, himself, was destined to be first in his class at West Point, to earn seven Silver Stars for heroism in World War I, to be awarded the Medal of Honor for his defense of the Philippines in World War II. So wrote Arthur's son, Douglas MacArthur.

LONGEST SIEGE

As the guns began their deadly drumbeat, only boys and old men were on hand to fight back . . . at first. In a few days, 90,000 troops were wheeled up against 10,000 defenders assembled here. And yet . . . yet, "No lovelier day ever dawned than June 9, 1864," one of the surviving women later recalled of the first salvos.

Like all Petersburg, and even like the enemy at its gate, she was unprepared for the longest siege of any American city, for the ten months of shelling, blockade, economic deprivation, starvation balls, death in the trenches, lack of food, disappearance of dogs, cats, even rats, inflated prices, daily bombardment, and death in the streets or backyards.

It went on, and on, until April 2-3, 1865, just days before Appomattox. Robert E. Lee, accompanied by his horse, Traveller, was here much of the time to direct the defense of Petersburg.

The siege today is not so well known as the Battle of the Crater, that Union-triggered explosion beneath Confederate trenches just outside the city that resulted in a Union debacle.

Actor Joseph Cotton, a Petersburg native whose grandfather's farmland was a battlefield, narrating the story for a tourism film, said, "This battle for Petersburg would be the life-and-death struggle for the entire Confederacy."

He knew so personally because, as he explained, "I was born and grew up in Petersburg, and my brother Whitford still lives here. As boys, we heard a lot of stories about life here in the siege. There are people all over town whose family histories are bound up with Petersburg's time of trial."

Cotten recited those memories in a short film, *The Echoes Still Remain*, premiered in 1978 by Petersburg's tourism experts of the 20th century and shown at the city's Siege Museum, established in an *ante-bellum* commodities exchange and bank building.

By his narrative, too: "It would be a very personal struggle for survival as well. For now Grant's big guns began to fire directly on the city. They went on for hours that first day [June 9]—and that was only the beginning of almost daily shelling during the next 10 months. By the middle of the summer, both armies had dug in for a prolonged siege." To those trapped in Petersburg, he said, the countryside for miles around looked like "one enormous camp."

The Crater, as he said, was the "most spectacular battle of the siege", but he noted also, "All the careful engineering that enabled the Union forces to tunnel under the Confederate line and blow a huge hole in it brought no advantage to either army, and both sides suffered heavy losses."

The really devastating event for Petersburg—now no longer the major Southern trade and industrial center, mill town, port and rail hub that it once was—was the siege. The siege, and the daily bombardment by the Union forces outside the walls. Others in addition to the late actor have spoken of it.

"As soon as the enemy brought up their siege guns, or heavy

artillery, which was only a few days after taking their positions, they opened on the city with shell without giving the slightest notice, or without giving opportunity for the removal of non-combatants, the sick, the wounded, or the women and children out of range of fire," wrote John H. Claiborne, a Confederate doctor here at the time. "To persons unfamiliar with the infernal noise made by the screaming, the ricocheting, and the bursting of the shells, it is impossible to describe the terror and the demoralization which was immediately created."

Indeed, can't we ask, has any city in America endured more? Besieged and supply-starved, pounded by artillery day after day. Skirmishes here, fights there. Vastly outnumbered by the enemy in not-so-distant trenches. The brave, dwindling army; its beloved, bearded commander, Moses-like. The women, too. The children . . . the citizens of the city, all 10 months trapped. In the 20th century, it has been a city forgotten, neglected, run-down. But to U.S. Grant and Robert E. Lee in the 19th century, in the midst of the American Civil War, Petersburg was a prize to be sought—or held—at nearly any cost, for it then fed the Confederate capital of Richmond from a hub of far-spoking railroad supply lines.

Grant had come, at end of his "sidling" campaign, in June and, denied entry, sat down and encamped outside, with all his many troops to the Confederacy's tattered and tired few. By the time his siege ended there were 125,000 Federals assembled, to Lee's 57,000 or so.

The siege dictated a lifestyle for both sides. Deprivation, of course, was the order of the day for those inside the siege circle. That and a siege *mood*, you might say. Perhaps akin to gallows humor. The social life, for instance. The dances. "While we were in the trenches and matters comparatively quiet," wrote William M. Owen, a Confederate artillery officer, "we would often slip into town and get the girls together and have a dance."

If firing broke out, the tattered cavaliers "would have to scamper," but they'd be back in a hour or so. And then, this sort of conversation:

"You have kept the dance for me, Miss ___? Only a small affair; one man killed, that's all."

"Oh, is that all!" she would reply. "Come, they are forming the set."

They tell also of Confederate artillery genius Colonel E. Porter Alexander, an innovator who produced bullet-proof wooden shields for his Rebel artillerymen's guns. Wrote Owen also: "He [Alexander] introduced a system of awards for the men who could collect the largest amount of leaden bullets and fragments of shell fired by the enemy, and [he] would have the men chasing projectiles and fragments even before the former exploded."

Predictably, Alexander himself was seriously wounded one day collecting bullets in view of the enemy. On the Union side, a house of frustration also, General Benjamin Butler, another innovator, seriously proposed a super fire engine that would "squirt water on earthworks and wash them all down," according to Union Colonel Theodore Lyman.

"By 1864, General Grant knew that to conquer the South he must immobilize this strategic little city," Cotten gently reminds in his film.

"The closeness of the battlefield made the siege a strangely intimate experience," he says also. "Especially for the families whose men were part of the defense force. Almost daily, servants carried letters and small gifts—an apple, a bouquet of flowers—between the battlefield and the homes of the city."

The shortages extended to firewood, clothing, shoes. But food was the worst problem, as Grant's forces cut one rail line after another of the five radiating from the city.

"Many people actually starved to death during the siege," said Petersburg's director of tourism, John R. Elliott, in 1978. "The amazing thing is what Americans did to an American city."

Cotten also reported: "Eventually the pigeons disappeared from the street. Then the cats and dogs and even the rats. The suspicion grew that most of them had found their way into somebody's stew pot. It happened in the best of families."

Soon to come were "starvation" parties and dances, with hosts and guests ignoring the lack of any refreshments. Wrote Army surgeon Claiborne later on: "Ball followed ball, and the soldier met and danced with his lady love at night, and on the morrow danced the dance of death in the deadly trench."

In all, 42,000 Union men and 28,000 Confederates died or suffered wounds before the siege was lifted.

The end was determined, really, when Grant captured 3,000 Confederates and seized the last remaining rail line into Petersburg on April 1, 1865. After the Rebel lines collapsed April 2, Lee withdrew, and Grant came forward then. The Union troops entered the tired and tattered city April 3.

"We sat all day in the front room," wrote one Southern survivor, "watching the splendidly equipped host as it marched by on its way to capture Lee. Our hearts sank within us!"

The triumphant Union forces issued a small but real newspaper on the day of their takeover here: *Grant's Petersburg Progress*.

Headlines—

"Petersburg Ours!"

"We Are Here"

"Hallelujah!"

And the lead paragraph in the account that followed, the unsigned author's sense of timing somewhat off—

"For nearly six [sic] months the Army of the United States has kept watch and ward over the city of Petersburg. Since last June the roar of shells and the whistle of bullets have disturbed the silence of the woods in the vicinity, and today the old flag waves from the Court House. The United States armies and U.S. Grant have foreclosed and entered in possession and Petersburg is ours."

That pretty well tells it all. Richmond fell the same day as Petersburg. In six more days, at Appomattox, Lee's army, the heart of the Confederacy itself, collapsed. In those six days also, Abe Lincoln himself had visited the stubborn Southern city that held up resolution of the war for so many months.

Petersburg's own *Daily Express* got back on its feet and published on April 13 with this temperate advice for its readers.

"Our cause, whatever may have been the varied opinion of its justice or demerits, is now lost—hopelessly, irretrievably lost—and it is no less the part of duty than of wisdom to submit quietly and willingly to the 'powers that be,' acknowledge the supremacy of the flag that waves over us and strive, under the blessing of God, to secure all the happiness and prosperity that the symbol of the United States can confer." So be it . . . except that on the next day, April 14, Lincoln was assassinated, and all the equations of April 13 suddenly and forever were skewed.

Each To His Own Pathway

Brothers-in-arms were James McQueen McIntosh and John Baillie McIntosh. James, born in Florida in 1828, was the West Pointer of the two. Graduating at bottom of his class in 1849, he first served with the U.S. Army's infantry and then, on frontier duty, with the U.S. Cavalry—until the Civil War broke out.

Brother John, born in 1829, also had seen military service—in the Navy during the Mexican War. He was strictly a civilian—a businessman in New Jersey—when the Civil War swept them both up.

Each of the two brothers would reach a general's rank before it was all over, too.

James served in the western theater, while John, also in the cavalry branch, served in the east. John, in fact, collected quite a few major-battle stars. He was at Seven Days near Richmond, at South Mountain and Antietam in Maryland, at Chancellorsville in Virginia again, at Gettysburg in Pennsylvania; then it was back to Virginia for Petersburg, Shenandoah Valley and Third Winchester.

He didn't come through the war entirely unscathed. After Gettysburg (1863), he was injured when his horse fell—a quiet command of the cavalry in the Washington defenses helped him to recuperate. Then, at Winchester in September 1864, he lost a leg.

His brother's one major battle had been much earlier—at Pea Ridge, Arkansas, on March 7, 1862.

James McIntosh, the West Pointer of the two, fell there, shot in the heart, while leading the mounted troops of Ben McCulloch's Division. Ben McCulloch of course was fighting Union troops in Arkansas. James, the brother of a Union general, had been a *Confederate* general.

John, it is said, was moved to join up—on the Union side—

when his brother James joined the Confederacy. At least we can say, they never met in combat.

Squint To His Eye

He was a jolly prankster, this Hancock, and one could wonder if he had anything more than still another trick in mind one day. As his fellow prisoners held at Richmond knew all too well, he was likely to cut up, to mimic, to "put on" remarkable facial expressions at the slightest provocation or excuse.

He had been a Union scout under Grant, but in 1864 he was captured and accused of being a spy. For his next incarnation as a prisoner, he had ample reason to use his diverting talents to relieve the cheerless prison life with merry song and dance. One evening, though, even as he sang for fellow prisoners, he suddenly stopped, threw up his hands, staggered, and then fell like a bag of sand to the floor.

He didn't stir, and a remarkably few, if any, of the onlookers thought it was a joke. The guards solemnly were told, and then the post surgeon. The man *looked* dead. But the post surgeon of course would determine *that*!

As Hancock couldn't have known in advance (could he?), the post surgeon was quite out of sorts, having just returned from a lengthy outing on horseback. He was tired and anxious to go to his quarters for the night. Thus, he might not have looked too closely before his hasty pronouncement: "Dead!"

In just 20 minutes, the recumbent Hancock was placed in a wagon to be sent to the hospital for preparation for burial.

The driver set off dutifully, but found upon his arrival that he was quite alone—nobody, that is to say, *no body*, remained in the wagon. Frantic, he retraced his path to see if the corpse had bounced out of the wagon. But . . . no luck there either. He asked a few people if they had noticed a body by the roadside. Not really.

Hancock, in fact, was entirely alive and still in Richmond. Indeed, where otherwise could he go? If he plunged into the countryside beyond, he could run into a Rebel patrol.

Had the Union scout planned his escape? Surely not with a doctor's unexpected acquiescence. Yet he had money hidden away in his clothing. And now he simply walked through the streets of Richmond to a good hotel, checked in and plunged into a nice clean bed for the night.

The next day he bought fresh clothes and wandered freely, speaking to various persons he met in his bold travels. To some he said he was in the Confederate capital as a businessman securing a government contract; to others he imparted the news that he was a Confederate secret agent.

After dinner, however, he was arrested on Richmond's Main Street. Provost troops, the equivalent of today's military police, spotted him as the man exactly fitting their fugitive's description. But only for a moment, since on closer examination it appeared their prisoner was cross-eyed and his mouth pulled to one side.

With his accosters confused, Hancock then drew on the good offices of his hotel clerk. Incredibly (it may seem), the clerk was passing by at the moment—he spoke up for Hancock, who then was allowed to go free.

So far so good, but not for long. In four days, the escapee was out of money—broke. At the post office he was arrested once more. He resorted again to his contortions. His mouth pulled, his left eye squinted and he pretended to be deaf. He was taken in this time anyway and returned to his former abode—once more a prisoner.

But now neither the guards there nor his fellow prisoners could say with any real certainty that he was the man who had escaped . . . that he was Hancock. They were so confused by his remarkable squint.

Every story, or course, has its end, and Hancock's was fast approaching.

"For seven long days the scout kept his mouth twisted around and his eye on the squint, and then he got tired of it and resumed his accustomed phiz," says the 19th-century book *Stories of the Civil War*, adapted by Albert F. Blaisdell. The minute he let go the squint, everyone recognized him as Hancock.

Back in custody, accused of spying, he all too soon would have been executed—as others in the same circumstance often were. It was his good fortune that Appomattox was close to hand, even though, during his spurt of freedom, Richmond had not quite yet fallen. "The close of the war gave him his liberty with the rest, but 10 days longer would have seen him shot as a spy," says Blaisdell's book.

UGLY BLOWS EXCHANGED

Scuffleburg was the meeting place. Hidden away in a hollow of the Blue Ridge Mountains in Virginia, it was "a place peculiarly adapted to the meeting of partisan rangers to transact business pertaining to their system of warfare." So wrote one of those rangers, one of *Mosby*'s Rangers, J. Marshall Crawford.

The despised Yankees, he added, "imagined it a second Gibraltar, filled with all kinds of infernal machines and implements of warfare, and believed that none of them who got there ever returned." And so: "The foot of no Yankee soldier ever trod its magnificent thoroughfares, or reposed his wearied form under the stately oaks and chestnuts . . . while the mountain breeze refreshed his burning cheek with the perfume of the wild honeysuckle, and the air was musical with the songs of birds . . . "

Whether no Yankee ever intruded in truth, Scuffleburg remained a meeting place, a rendezvous point typical of Mosby, the University of Virginia graduate, lawyer and onetime cavalryman under "Jeb" Stuart who conducted harassing raids against the Union occupiers of northern Virginia. Typically, Mosby and his partisan-like troop struck, then dispersed, only to meet again by prior arrangement at hideaways like Scuffleburg.

So successful was this master of the hit-and-run attack that his hunting ground, with all its hidden lairs, became known as "Mosby's Confederacy." As the war wound down, however, it became more and more ugly for the often-romanticized Mosby and his proud rangers. Life was no lark, and the air no longer was "musical with the song of birds." Instead, in those last months, death was on the wing.

West of the Blue Ridge in the fall of 1864, Union cavalry commander Phil Sheridan was the latest target of Mosby's harassment. The "Grey Ghost's" officially titled 43rd Virginia Battalion "had been having a generally bang-up time throughout October, sniping at [railroad] workers, derailing locomotives, lobbing howitzer shells into Union camps, and helping themselves to enemy paymasters' strongboxes," writes Roy Morris, Jr. in his biography, *Sheridan: The Life and Wars of Phil Sheridan*. In one such raid, they grabbed $173,000, and in another they grabbed off a nice hostage, a brigadier general named Alfred Duffie.

Instead of trading purely military blows, however, the Union and Confederate antagonists often were exchanging executions.

"Several members of the Fifth Michigan Cavalry, surprised that fall by Mosby's men while looting a farmhouse, were shot or hanged," writes Morris; "hams were tied to the victims' legs, along with a card promising other foragers a similar fate." In another "hardcase" incident, a Union straggler evidently was surprised while skinning a stolen sheep. He was killed and a hoof was jammed into his mouth. A note left with the body said: "I reckon you got enough sheep now."

This all came at a time when Sheridan was torching his way northward through the Shenandoah Valley, laying waste to fields, barns, food stores, a time for years after to be called "the Burning." Then, too, Ulysses S. Grant had ordered that Mosby's troopers should be treated as partisans, rather than soldiers serving their cause honorably. There had been fatal misunderstandings and deliberate executions, back and forth, for weeks.

"A self perpetuating cycle of atrocities, reprisals, and counter-reprisals," Morris calls it, and rightly so.

An incident in late September had inflamed feelings on both sides. When a Union lieutenant's horse bolted into a knot of Rebels, the Union man was shot and killed. His compatriots thought he was shot while trying to surrender, so they then took six newly captured rangers (one a 17-year-old who was not a member of Mosby's group) and executed all six in Front Royal, Virginia.

Mosby "bitterly vowed retribution."

Meanwhile, in another incident, John Meigs, son of the Federal Quartermaster General, Montgomery C. Meigs, was killed in another questionable episode. Outside of Harrisonburg, Virginia, one rainy day, Lieutenant Meigs and two orderlies encountered three Rebs (all six men in ponchos covering their uniforms). Shooting broke out, and Meigs was left dead.

Told that his young officer simply had been shot down execution style, a furious Sheridan "resolved to punish the unoffending residents of Dayton, the site of the shooting, on the wrongheaded assumption that the 'murderers' lived in the area and had been visiting their homes prior to the dead." He issued orders to burn down every house within a five-mile radius, but fortunately "cooler heads prevailed," and the order was canceled, a welcome respite for the pacifistic Mennonites who lived in the area. They had nothing to do with the three Rebs in question, all privates with Brigadier General Thomas Rosser's cavalry.

The story that emerged later, in fact, was that Meigs had fired on them first, from a pistol hidden under his poncho. He had wounded one Confederate, George W. Martin. The other two, Benjamin F. Shavers and F. M. Campbell, then fired back and fatally wounded Meigs. "Ironically," adds Morris, "Martin, whose own gun misfired, went into hiding for several years after the war, a one thousand dollar bounty having been placed on his head by Meigs's bereaved father, who mistakenly thought Martin had killed his son."

Still more ugly incidents had followed the unhappy Meigs affair at Dayton, which for a time was blamed on Mosby's men. A week later a Union quartermaster officer and an army doctor were "shot dead within Union lines near Newtown," also in the Shenandoah Valley. Next, the Federals hanged a freshly captured Mosby trooper on October 13. Then, in early November, Mosby acted in reprisal for the Front Royal executions of September. Erroneously blaming George Armstrong Custer for those killings, he had been collecting as his prisoners as many of Custer's men as possible. By Morris' account, he informed Robert E. Lee in late October, "It is my purpose to hang an equal number of Custer's men whenever I capture them," and Lee, "without undue gentle-manly hesitation, approved the scheme."

After seven unfortunates among 27 Yankee prisoners were selected for execution by a drawing, Mosby had them taken to Beemer's Woods west of Berryville, Virginia, close to Custer's camp. On the way, one Federal prisoner persuaded a fellow Ma-son among Mosby's men to let him go and execute another, fresh-ly captured Custer trooper instead—a switch that Mosby only learned of later and severely condemned.

In the early morning darkness, meanwhile, the unlucky Union prisoners marked for execution were brought forth—and two then escaped. The others, though, were executed, their bodies left with a note saying they had been killed "in retaliation for an equal number of Colonel Mosby's men hung by order of General Custer, at Front Royal. Measure for measure."

Mosby then sent Sheridan a note saying that he in the future would treat his prisoners with "the kindness due to their condi-tion, unless some new act of barbarity shall compel me to reluc-tantly adopt a course of policy repulsive to humanity."

There's no historical record of Sheridan's response, notes Morris, "but the absence of any Union retaliation, then or later, strongly suggests that he took the message to heart."

In the aftermath, though, Sheridan did send his subordinate Wesley Merritt on a "Burning Raid" into "Mosby's Confederacy," described as that square of country "bounded on the south by the line of the Manassas Gap Railroad . . . on the east by the Bull Run Range, on the West by the Shenandoah River, and on the north by the Potomac." In the effort to drive off Mosby and punish the local residents who put up with his guerrilla band, Sheridan ordered Merritt to "consume and destroy all forage and subsistence, burn all barns and mills . . . and drive off all stock in the region." At the same time, perhaps to avoid a new round of unorthodox casual-ties, Sheridan also told Merritt, "no dwellings are to be burned and . . . no personal violence be offered to the citizens."

Merritt did his job with terrible thoroughness, burning barns and other outbuildings, purging the land of all livestock. This time, it didn't matter that many locals were Quakers or Union sympathizers, notes Morris. By his account, Sheridan told one subordinate, "Should complaints come in from the citizens of Loudoun County, tell them that they have furnished too many meals to guerrillas to expect much sympathy."

While the countryside was devastated, Mosby was not yet knocked out of the game. By the end of 1864, his 43rd Battalion had grown to eight companies. Indeed, he was still fighting as late as the day *after* Lee's surrender to Grant at Appomattox on April 9, 1865—a final raid conducted just prior to dispersing his troops in a review ceremony at Salem (now Marshall), Virginia. The widely hailed Confederate hero returned to a law practice . . . and then surprised and angered many of his fans and colleagues by turning Republican and even supporting Grant, and then Rutherford B. Hayes, also a Union officer, for President in 1868 and 1876, respectively. Mosby served as a U. S. consul in Hong Kong and as an assistant attorney for the Federal Justice Department. He wrote two books recalling his wartime experiences. He died in 1916 at the age of 82 . . . in that Union capital, Washington, D.C.

THEY ALSO SERVED

—Not to be confused with second cousin Thomas J. Jackson, better known as "Stonewall," this Jackson also was a Confederate officer. Before the war he had been a lawyer, judge and lieutenant governor of his native Virginia. During the war, he served honorably and rose to the rank of brigadier as a cavalryman. He served as an aide on Stonewall Jackson's staff in the latter's famed Shenandoah Valley campaign. He saw action in the Seven Days campaign and in the battles of Second Bull Run and Antietam. He returned to Maryland for the Jubal Early incursion halted outside Washington, and long after cousin Stonewall's death, he returned to the Valley for resumed fighting at Winchester Fisher's Hill and Cedar Creek.

Surviving the war, he refused to surrender and sought refuge in Mexico for a time, then resumed the practice of law and became a judge again, this time in Kentucky. Not ever to be confused with second cousin Stonewall, this Jackson served quite honorably enough, thank you. William Jackson, known to his contemporaries as "Mudwall."

* * *

—This son of Indiana was a Mexican War veteran, state senator and lawyer when the Civil War broke out. Soon vaulting to the rank of brigadier, and then major general, he endured what might be described as an up-and-down military career on behalf of the Union. He won accolades for routing the Rebs at Romney, in today's West Virginia; he did well as the head of a new division under U. S. Grant at Fort Donelson, but was criticized for his slow reactions at Shiloh. Soon after, he organized a stout defense of Cincinnati. He fatally slowed raiding Confederates under Jubal Early at Monocacy, Maryland, outside Washington late in the war. He sat on the court-martial that convicted participants in the Lincoln assassination and on the one that ordered the execution of Andersonville commandant Henry Wirz. He dabbled in ventures against Mexico's Emperor Maximillian; he was governor of the New Mexico Territory, and he once served as an American diplomat in Turkey.

For none of those reasons is he best known today. Rather, the only American writer to be honored with a likeness placed in Statuary Hall in the U.S. Capitol, he was Lew Wallace, author of the phenomenally successful novel *Ben Hur: A Tale of the Christ*.

* * *

—Father and son, John A. and Ulric Dahlgren were an admiral and cavalry colonel, respectively, for the Union. Admiral Dahlgren was the ordnance expert whose 11-inch Dahlgren gun was put to effective use against Charleston by the commander of the Union Navy's South Atlantic Blockading Squadron—that is to say, Admiral Dahlgren himself. Prior to that seagoing posting, he had been chief of the Navy's Bureau of Ordnance. He probably could have felt personal pride and satisfaction at war's end . . . but for the death of his son Ulric, in both heroic and controversial circumstances, and with macabre aftermath.

A lawyer as a civilian, Ulric survived various actions unscathed until wounded at Boonesboro, Maryland, right after Gettysburg. Despite his foot injury he would not quit the battle scene until falling unconscious from loss of blood. He then lost his leg from below the knee to a surgeon's knife. He recovered to fight again . . . this time leading a 500-man detachment from Judson Kilpatrick's proposed raid on Richmond in early 1864. Equipped with a wooden leg, Dahlgren was killed March 2 in Henrico County next to the city.

The controversy came when Confederate officials claimed that papers found on his body revealed a plan to assassinate Jefferson Davis and other highly placed members of the Confederate government. The macabre came when agents of Union spy Elizabeth van Lew secretly dug up the young officer's body from its battlefield burial place and spirited it to awaiting Union hands to be carried north for re-burial in a family plot (and close official examination?).

* * *

—Another father and son pair consisted of one John Wise and son O. Jennings Wise, the first a Confederate general and the second a member of the Richmond Light Infantry Blues when Ambrose Burnside stormed Roanoke Island, North Carolina, in February 1862. The elder Wise had been governor of Virginia before the war, and soon after the hostilities erupted he served as commander of Wise's Legion in mountainous western Virginia. In command of the Confederacy's eastern North Carolina sector when Roanoke Island fell, he later served in the Seven Days' Campaign outside Richmond, fought at Drewry's Bluff, commanded Confederate elements at Petersburg and brought his men through the Battle of Sayler's Creek hurting but intact as a unit. Appomattox came just days later, but Wise, for one, never would accept the Union proffer of amnesty . . . perhaps because his son Jennings had fallen way back at Roanoke Island with mortal wound.

* * *

—His star did not shine very brightly during the Civil War, but before the hostilities broke out, there was hardly any stopping the great Western adventurer, explorer and widely ballyhooed "pathfinder," John C. Frémont. His *ante-bellum* resume was so impressive, Abraham Lincoln gave him the Army's highest rank at war's start. Indeed, the officer from the Army's Corps of Topographical Engineers had been a real pathfinder as an explorer of the Far West. Apparently acting under secret orders from President James K. Polk and not adverse to intrigue, he had been instrumental in wresting future California from Mexican claim. He underwent court-martial for his role in establishing the territory as an American state, but that didn't stop him from amassing a fortune, serving as U.S. Senator from California or even running for President in 1856 as the new-born Republican Party's first nominee for the White House (an election won by Democrat James Buchanan).

During the Civil War, however, Frémont's star dimmed after he failed to give full support to Nathaniel Lyons at Wilson's Creek in Missouri and continued his independent ways by issuing an emancipation proclamation all his own for Missouri—months ahead of Lincoln's emancipation decree. He then eluded delivery of orders sent to relieve him until a disguised emissary placed the papers in his hands. Frémont later was given a chance to prove himself against Stonewall Jackson in the Shenandoah Valley, with predictably dismal result. Assigned next to John Pope's newly formed Army of Virginia, Frémont refused to take orders from Pope and again was relieved, this time for good.

After the war, his fortune dwindling, he served as governor of the Arizona territory for ten years. His U.S. Army retirement rank was major general, the rank that Lincoln had granted him at the start of the war.

* * *

—Pegram was their name, John and Willie, sons of Virginia and brave men both. The higher ranking and oldest of the two was John, West Point graduate, cavalryman and engineer . . . major general in the Confederate Army who served with distinction in various battles and many demanding posts, in both the east and west. His wedding in Richmond in the winter weeks before Appomattox was a rare bright spot in the city's declining social life. Three weeks later, his bride, Hetty Cary, and many of the wedding guests were back in the same Richmond church—for his funeral John Pegram had been killed at a place called Hather's Run.

His brother Willie, meanwhile, had risen in rank from private to colonel and achieved a reputation as an artillerist with an array of impressive battle stars all his own. Just days before Appomattox and weeks after his brother's death, Willie Pegram was killed at Five Forks.

* * *

—The adopted son of a ranking U.S. Navy officer, this Civil War figure went to sea as a midshipman at age nine. He briefly commanded a captured prize ship at age 12, during the War of 1812. Born James, he changed his first name to David, apparently in honor of his adoptive father, Admiral David Porter. It was David *Farragut*, however, who created U.S. naval legend when, subduing the defenses of Mobile Bay, he uttered the famous cry (or something very close to the version known today), "Damn the torpedoes! Full speed ahead!" (He meant mines, actually.) While Farragut did subdue the bay's defending forts and drive off or defeat the defending Confederate ships by the end of August 1864, he also should be recalled as the Union's conqueror of New Orleans (April 24, 1862), vital to control of the Mississippi. He then helped blockade the lower Mississippi and the Gulf waters below, and supported Grant's campaign against Vicksburg higher up on the Mississippi. Coincidentally, as a child (before going to sea at age nine, that is), he had lived in New Orleans—the city he later captured for the Union.

STORY WITH A KICK

Professor John B. Minor of the august University of Virginia was worried on March 1, 1865, as Union troops filtered into

Charlottesville and the town's university precincts. He was just one member of a joint committee of university and town leaders who greeted the incoming Federal officers and asked them to prevent looting by their troops.

General George Armstrong Custer sent word by two staff officers that "no damage to the buildings would be tolerated; and that a squad would be assigned to furnish the amplest protection," wrote Professor Philip Alexander Bruce in his centennial history of the school (1819-1919).

Hardly had that assurance been conveyed, at the very edge of the University grounds, when Professor Minor "observed a couple of soldiers desert the main road, and turn in towards the rear of his pavilion [campus residence]."

Hurrying to his house on Thomas Jefferson's famous Lawn, Minor was relieved to find that his wife had intercepted the pair after they had asked the Minor servants if any silver plate were hidden on the premises. "As soon as they were told that a guard was to be stationed on the grounds, the two men remounted their horses, and rode off."

And so, they missed the mule . . . Professor Minor's balky, temperamental, difficult female mule.

She might have been a bit elderly for her kind, but she still was dear to the Minor household . . . and no bluecoat was to grab

266

her off! "Her keeper and companion, an old servant of the house, had, at the first alarm, solemnly led her off to the wooded fastness of Observatory Mountain."

That sanctuary close by the University should have been safeguard enough, but the stubborn mule didn't care for a stay in the rough, it seems. She let loose her strident bray and, so, revealed her hiding place to one and all.

The Federal officer in charge of the campus guard—"a plain illiterate man, but courteous in his deportment and kindly disposed in spirit"—suggested it would be safer to bring her back to the campus she was so used to, "as the only way to keep her out of the clutches of Federal stragglers."

Still worried, Professor Minor went the officer one better—he brought the mule back in the dark of night and, without telling his Federal guardian, installed the recalcitrant animal in his cellar.

She didn't care much for this arrangement either, "and soon showed a disposition to kick with great violence, and to make many strange and alarming noises at unexpected and ill-considered moments."

Still, she *was* in Minor's cellar, and the outside world did not hear the hullabaloo.

The next evening, the unsuspecting Federal officer, a captain from Michigan, it is believed, came to dinner at the Minors'. He was seated without incident, and prevailing among all at the table was an atmosphere of "peace and serenity, in spite of the depression of the times." With the war very nearly over, call it a moment of reconciliation. "The captain was gracious and conciliatory, and the professor courteous and agreeable."

But the mule down below, quiet until now, was not to be ignored any longer. "In the midst of their conversation, there came suddenly the sound of some extraordinary commotion that was happening beneath the floor of the dining room."

It is not recorded whether the Federal officer actually leaped to his feet in alarm but, "disturbed and suspicious," he did at least rise from the table. After all, "the uproar was so loud and so confused that it was impossible to distinguish its cause."

For a tense moment, the captain from Michigan "seemed to

be apprehensive of a personal attack from without," but Minor, convulsed with laughter, finally was able to gasp out the information that it was only the old mule hidden in the cellar below. The meal was resumed, we are told, "amid hearty laughter over the one humorous episode which lit up the dark clouds that enshrouded the hour."

Two More To Mourn

For the South, May 11, 1864, was one more unfortunate day to mark down. Phil Sheridan two days before had set out with 10,000 hard-riding Union troopers against Richmond itself, and at Yellow Tavern, six miles north of the capital city, J.E.B. Stuart, threw himself into the breach.

Himself always hard-riding, colorful, a legendary, querulous, ballad-singing man's man in an era of many another brave hero, Stuart had only 4,500 cavalrymen to begin with. He then divided the 4,500, sending James Gordon after one prong of the Federal attack and taking the remainder to block the bluebellies at Yellow Tavern.

There, a Union private named John Huff got off a lucky pistol shot. Stuart was struck in the stomach while in the saddle. Reeling from the blow, he managed to turn his horse about and ride for his own lines.

Aided by his men, he was carried to Richmond, to the home of his brother-in-law, a doctor it so happened, on Grace Street, where he would linger on for another day.

He was attended during his painful passage from life by several doctors and visited by fellow officers, by the Episcopal minister who would soon be burying him, and even by President Jefferson Davis, who knew him well.

Word had been sent to Stuart's wife Flora, who was off in the country and would have some distance to travel before reaching his side. "I would like to live to see my wife," said Stuart upon being told that his wound was a mortal one. "But God's will be done."

Jefferson Davis, in the meantime, spent about 15 minutes with the Confederacy's famous cavalryman. He took Stuart's hand and gently asked, "General, how do you feel?" and Stuart answered, "Easy, but willing to die if God and my country think I have fulfilled my destiny and done my duty."

Here was an echo of another unfortunate moment, a year earlier, when Stuart's eldest son had been mortally wounded in yet another fight. Informed that his son was dying, Stuart had sent back word that he could not go to the young man. "I must leave my child in the hands of God," he had said. "My country needs me here; I cannot come."

Now, Stuart himself was dying. As he applied ice to the wound with his own hand, he said he was resigned to his death. Close to the end, Stuart stated some last-minute bequests. He gave his horses out to his staff, stipulating that the largest horse should go to a large man among his beneficiaries. He said his sword should go to his one surviving son. For *Mrs*. Robert E. Lee, there were Stuart's own golden spurs, a symbol of his affection and respect for her husband, Stuart's commander.

Stuart asked the minister to lead in the singing of a hymn, with Stuart himself weakly joining in. He also took part in a prayer.

Earlier, his delirium had provoked memories of battle and command, old orders and even new, imaginary ones. Now, at the end, all was so much more simple and peaceful. "I am going fast now: I am resigned," he said. "God's will be done."

His wife arrived about 90 minutes after he had passed.

In the church service that followed, fellow generals were among the pall-bearers who carried his remains to the altar, while President Davis and many other luminaries of the Confederacy looked on from quiet pews. Stuart's remains then were borne to the waiting grave at Richmond's Hollywood Cemetery in a hearse decorated by black plumes and drawn by four milky-white horses.

* * *

On another unfortunate day for the South, the general's aide, Sergeant George Tucker, had to wonder why they were riding slowly, somewhat aimlessly it seemed, so close to the blue-coats who had broken through the Rebel lines at Petersburg on Sunday, April 2, 1865. A few minutes before, Robert E. Lee also had wondered about the condition (mental and physical) of his devoted subordinate, Ambrose Powell Hill.

For months, A.P. Hill, the victim of venereal disease picked up in a wayward moment of his youth, had been showing the effects of long-term illness. The West Point graduate, one of Lee's greatest lieutenants, had had to relinquish command of his army corps for a time during the great slugging matches of 1864—the Wilderness, Spotsylvania, Cold Harbor. He rode his horse in great pain, he hobbled when he walked. While just about everyone in Lee's command suffered from the hardships of deprivation and fatigue, in A.P. Hill's case, disease of the prostrate and the kidneys also was taking its toll.

When he painfully mounted his steed Champ that morning, writes James I. Robertson, Jr. in his biography *General A.P. Hill: The Story of a Confederate Warrior*, Lee had been "disturbed" by the "sudden and unexpected fire" he saw in Hill "after weeks of sickness." He sent an aide after Hill to tell him to be careful.

But he wasn't. As he and Sergeant Tucker a short while later saw a large cluster of men next to some huts abandoned by the Confederates defending Petersburg, Tucker asked whose men they were. "The enemy's," said Hill matter-of-factly.

He seemed in a daze, perhaps induced by uremic poisoning. As they rode on, skirting the danger zone, the worried Tucker interrupted again. "Please excuse me, General, but where are we going?"

Hill said they were going to General Henry Heth's headquarters. They rode on, the countryside seemingly empty again. Hill "suddenly spoke up," adds Robertson's account. "Sergeant," he said, "should anything happen to me, you must go back to General Lee and report it."

In moments they came across more Federals and turned aside toward some screening woods, both with their revolvers in hand. In the woods, though, were a half dozen more Union soldiers. "Suddenly two of them ran behind a large tree . . ." They

270

aimed their muskets at Tucker and Hill. Not 20 yards lay between the two parties. Tucker called upon the two Federals to surrender. So did Hill.

Silence.

Then, shots. Private Daniel Wolford of the 138th Pennsylvania missed. Corporate John W. Mauck, a carpenter in civilian life, did not. Struck in the heart, Hill "died instantly."

Tucker found Lee a short while later, astride his own horse on Cox Road, "handsomely dressed, sword buckled to his waist." As the sergeant made his sad report, Lee could not hide his sorrowful reaction. Indeed, an aide later said, "Never shall I forget the look on General Lee's face." With tears in his eyes, Lee said, "He is now at rest, and we who are left are the ones to suffer."

As Robertson points out also, it was only hours later that Lee's Army of Northern Virginia abandoned Petersburg and "began its death march to Appomattox."

It was chaos left behind, for Richmond also fell that day. Richmond, the capital of the Confederacy, was engulfed in fire and thousands were fleeing the doomed city, their exodus a one-way tide across the James River bridges. Against this flow some hours after A.P. Hill's death, a ramshackle army wagon carrying his body struggled to enter the city. "The family wish was to bury Hill in Hollywood Cemetery, the capital's 'Place of Heroes'," writes Robertson. But they were to be frustrated since "every road leading out of town was packed with soldiers, civilians, wagons, carriages and horses." Only the wagon carrying Hill's remains was pointed *toward* the city.

Family members, a pair of cousins, tried again about 1 a.m. on April 3. Finally succeeding in crossing the river, they found "the downtown stores were deserted and in shambles as a result of widespread looting." They needed a coffin, and after searching "from building to building," they came across "a small plain pine coffin" in a funeral home. They washed Hill's face, wrapped him in his army coat and placed him in the pine box, but with no one available to arrange burial at Hollywood and Union troops expected to march into town at any moment, the two cousins carried their burden back to the Chesterfield County estate of A.P. Hill's uncle, Henry Hill. During an illness-imposed furlough only two weeks before, Hill and his wife Dolly (the former Kitty Morgan, sister of John Hunt Morgan) had stayed there, and now this would be the slain general's burial place . . . for the time being. His body later was re-interred at Hollywood, then—and finally— beneath a monument erected in his memory in Richmond.

Prophetically, reports biographer Robertson, the 48-year-old Hill had said, while on a visit to Richmond with his Uncle Henry in March, just the month before, "that he did not wish to survive the fall of Richmond." And he didn't.

EMBARRASSING OUTING

When Mrs. Lincoln was on one of her streaks there was hardly any hiding of the fact . . . the embarrassing fact. A general's wife given special permission by the President himself to remain at a Union encampment? Mrs. Lincoln was beside herself when she heard.

"What do you mean by that, sir?" she expostulated. "Do you mean to say that she saw the President alone? Do you know that I never allow the President to see any woman alone?"

General Adam Badeau, probably didn't know, no. On the scene as aide to Ulysses S. Grant and escorting officer for Mrs. Lincoln and Julia Grant on a visit to the troops outside Petersburg just before the war's end, he was taken aback at the outburst, never suspecting that even worse was yet to come.

"I tried to pacify her and palliate my remark [about the special permission], but she was fairly boiling over with rage," he wrote later.

It was only with great difficulty that Julia Grant persuaded Mrs. Lincoln against stopping their carriage to go ask her husband if he had seen the woman in question alone. Next day, the visit to the Union encampments at City Point, [Hopewell, Virginia, today], with Grant himself showing Lincoln the sights, was to run aground on even more vicious shoals of jealousy. Then, too, would come some oddly prophetic accusations by Mrs. Lincoln against the patient Julia Grant.

The next day's fit began when Mrs. Lincoln, in her carriage again, saw that another general's wife, Mrs. Edward Ord, was mounted on a horse and riding next to Lincoln himself. That was only polite since she was the wife of the commander of the Army of the James—and the ambulance carrying the ladies was full in any case.

Mrs. Lincoln soon reacted. Again the raconteur is General Badeau, whose account some historians consider rather embellished.

"What does the woman [Mrs. Ord] mean," cried Mary Todd Lincoln, "by riding by the side of the President and ahead of me? Does she suppose that he wants her by the side of him?"

That was only the beginning, and this time Julia Grant was unable to pacify the President's wife, who in moments turned her wrath even against Julia herself. Badeau and another escorting officer were concerned "to see that nothing worse than words occurred." For one thing, they were afraid that Mrs. Lincoln would leap from her carriage "and shout to the cavalcade," so agitated was she.

It was at this point, apparently, that she angrily said to Julia Grant: "I suppose you think you'll get to the White House yourself, don't you?" Julia Grant maintained her calm, and merely replied that she was quite satisfied with her present position; it was far greater than she had ever expected to attain.

Mrs. Lincoln wouldn't let it go. *The White House, did someone say?* "Oh!" she declared, "You had better take it if you can get it. 'Tis very nice."

Four years later, Julia and Ulysses Grant indeed would occupy the White House, but one has to wonder how many seriously thought that a likely prospect before Lincoln's death. In any case, having dispensed with Julia Grant for the moment, Mary Todd now turned her blazing light once more on the unfortunate Mrs. Ord, with Julia Grant now having to defend that unlucky woman as well as herself.

Stumbling into the affray just then was Secretary of State William Seward's young nephew, a major in the Union army. He rode up to the ladies' ambulance-carriage to exchange pleasantries . . . only to say exactly the wrong thing, considering the circumstances. "The President's horse is very gallant, Mrs. Lincoln," he began. "He insists on riding by the side of Mrs. Ord."

When Mrs. Lincoln reacted by crying, "What do you mean by that, sir," related the onlooking General Badeau later, "Seward discovered that he had made a huge mistake, and his horse at once developed a peculiarity that compelled him to ride behind, to get out of the way of the storm."

Before the day's unhappy episode was over, Mrs. Ord herself innocently approached Mrs. Lincoln's carriage. By General Badeau's account, "Mrs. Lincoln positively insulted her, called her vile names in the presence of a crowd of officers, and asked what she meant by following up the President."

The publicly branded Mrs. Ord was reduced to tears before one and all, " . . . and everybody was shocked and horrified." Mrs. Lincoln railed on, "'til she was tired."

That evening, still unappeased, Mrs. Lincoln was hostess at a dinner for the ranking officers on hand, including the Grants, General Grant's staff, and General Ord. She took occasion at this gathering aboard the President's steamer in the James River to "berate" General Ord "and urged that he should be removed." An ugly scene again, obviously enough. "He was unfit for his place, she said, to say nothing of his wife. General Grant sat next and defended his officer bravely."

Julia Grant, in later life, refuted much of Badeau's gossipy report, but she and others left the impression that something unpleasant (and pathetic as well) did take place at City Point. From all reports of this and other scenes, it seems fair to say that Mrs. Lincoln's husband had his burdens, aside from the crushing weight of the Civil War itself.

Surviving To Serve Again

The remarkable thing about the battle-scarred Colonel

Hayes was not so much that one day soon he secretly would be sworn in as President while attending dinner one night at the White House of Ulysses S. Grant, but the added circumstance that on the Colonel's staff was another young officer, William McKinley, destined to serve one future day as President, too. And the fact that still another future President, James A. Garfield—four Union officers in all—hailed from the single state of Ohio.

The Nation, all unawares at the moment, did come ever so close to doing without the future services of *President* Hayes, since at South Mountain, on the eve of Antietam in September 1862, he was badly wounded above the left elbow while leading a charge by elements of his 23rd Ohio. Although the injury was severe, he rose to his feet and urged his men onward and onward . . . until he finally became so weak and faint that he fell helplessly to the ground again. There, between the battle lines, he was trapped, possibly to be captured by the enemy or, worse, left to die of his wound.

But his men dashed forward despite the Rebel fire and pulled him back to their own lines. Even so, there was the possibility that his arm would be amputated because of the tissue wreckage wrought by the musket ball that had struck him. Fortunately, Rutherford B. Hayes was able to avoid that radical step—often fatal to the wounded of the Civil War era—and after recovering, he continued to serve.

Truly a war hero by any definition, Hayes, an attorney in civilian life, began his Civil War service as a major in the Ohio Volunteers. He ended the war as a brigadier general—and a member of Congress who had eschewed the safety of the legislative corridors to remain in uniform.

Before the shooting was all over, he had survived several battles and four woundings. The first came in Virginia, in a skirmish on May 10, 1862, a minor injury inflicted by an artillery shell—his right knee, he later said, was "scratched."

After escaping the surgeon's knife at South Mountain later in 1862, he was shot in the head and shoulder—at Winchester, Virginia, in September 1864. He was able to rebound quickly enough to appear at nearby Cedar Creek a month later, there to have his horse shot out from under him and to suffer a wound in the ankle.

By that time, too, Hayes had been nominated for Congress by fellow Ohio Republicans and in the elections of 1864, he was elected to the seat. He had accepted nomination but declined to actually campaign, saying, "An officer fit for duty, who at this crisis would electioneer for a seat in Congress, ought to be scalped."

Once elected, he stuck to his brave talk and refused to serve until leaving the army in June of 1865—after the shooting had stopped—as a brigadier. His political career then led to two terms as governor of Ohio and, finally, to election as President in the U.S. Centennial year of 1876—not by popular vote, but only by a last-minute switch in electoral votes that gave him an edge of one electoral vote over his opponent, Democrat Samuel J. Tilden.

In the controversy that followed, the Hayes election was disputed until confirmed by an official commission just two days before he was scheduled to succeed U.S. Grant on March 4, 1877. The March 4th date during the 19th century was the traditional inaugural date for incoming U.S. Presidents, but in this particular and touchy year, the date fell on a Sunday. With the Sabbath considered no proper day for the inauguration of a President, it was decided to wait until Monday, March 5. But then, that would leave the Nation with no President, technically, for a day.

The final decision was to install Hayes as President twice in two days—secretly on Sunday at a White House dinner for the incoming President and publicly the next day at the usual inaugural ceremonies.

So it was that the distinguished guests proceeding from the East Room reception area in the White House to the State Dining Room the evening of Sunday, March 4, 1877, momentarily "lost" the leading luminaries of their number —Grant and Hayes. Those two, it seems, had ducked into the Red Room, where Chief Justice Morrison R. Waite quietly and quickly administered the oath of office to Rutherford B. Hayes—without benefit of the customary Bible, since that item had been overlooked by all those present.

Thus, the President who sat down to a 20-course dinner in the State Dining Room a few minutes later was not Grant, as the general public would have thought, but Hayes . . . who was sworn in all over again, with all the usual trappings, the very next day.

The new President, of course, was neither the first nor the last of the *six* Union officers, in all, who eventually would occupy the White House in the latter half of the 19th century. Grant was the first, while succeeding Hayes was fellow Ohioan James A. Garfield, who also had fought well during the Civil War and had reached the rank of major general.

Garfield's best-known Civil War feat was his return to the scene of battle at Chickamauga after his superior, General William Rosecrans, retreated in disorder. Some critics said that Garfield used that occasion to undercut his commanding officer and point to his own battlefield prowess. Be that as it may, Garfield, like Hayes, had been elected to Congress during the war but chose to remain in uniform at least until after Chickamauga, which took place in September of 1863.

Coming along a bit after Garfield, President Benjamin Harrison had been an officer with the Seventh Indiana Volunteers. His outfit took part in Sherman's Atlanta campaign, among other activities, and Harrison left the Union Army as a brigadier general in 1865. He became a U.S. Senator before reaching the presidency.

After Harrison came William McKinley—1897, the once-young officer who had joined Hayes' staff at Antietam. Originally a private in the 23rd Ohio Volunteers, he had reached the post of commissary sergeant by the time he and his unit appeared at Antietam. He won promotion there to lieutenant and assumed command of the 23rd's Company D, serving until war's end and leaving the conflict as a major who had earned his decorations. He was only 22 at the time.

Finally, Chester Arthur, the vice president who succeeded popular White House occupant Garfield, had held a desk job during the Civil War—in the quartermaster corps of his state, New York.

Grover Cleveland was yet another Civil War era President—drafted for the Union Army just as he plunged into law as his lifetime vocation, he paid another man (quite legally) to serve in his place.

As fate would have it, two of the men who survived the mean vicissitudes of combat during the Civil War, to continue their political careers and become President, died in office at the wrong end of a gun. Both Garfield and McKinley were fatally wounded by gun-wielding assassins.

Hospital Town

When Union General Godfrey Weitzel's brigade entered Richmond the morning of April 3, 1865, as the vanguard of an occupying Federal army, he rode his horse up a hill at the eastern end of the city to encounter one of the most amazing sights in the history of military medicine. For there, spread out in tableau atop towering Chimborazo Hill, row upon neat row, with straight streets and alleys in between, were the buildings and the tents of the largest military hospital ever known.

Not one, but five hospital divisions collected together, Chimborazo Hospital had the capacity to house 8,000 to 10,000 patients at a time. For nearly four years, both the sick and the wounded from battles such as Second Bull Run, the Wilderness or Spotsylvania had come to Chimborazo by the thousands for their treatment, recovery or death.

By the end of the Civil War, 76,000 patients had been through the doors of this huge medical facility, 17,000 of them wounded soldiers. And of that overall number, only a fraction more than nine percent had died.

As reported to the Association of Medical Officers of the Army and Navy of the Confederacy in 1904, Chimborazo had no equal in military history.

According to Dr. John R. Gildersleeve, president of the medical veterans' group, "It was the first military hospital in point of size in this country and in the world, the next largest in this country being the 'Lincoln' at Washington, D.C., which reported a total number of 46,000 patients; and the next largest in the world at large was the Scutari Hospital in the Crimea, which reported a total of 30,000 to 40,000 patients."

Amazing, too, was the fact that barely four years before

General Weitzel's arrival, the hospital site had been a bare, breeze-swept hill overlooking what Dr. Gildersleeve called "the tawny James on its tortuous seaward way."

With the advent of large-scale battle early in the Civil War, however, Confederate authorities realized they would need hospitals—and more hospitals. The capital of the Confederacy soon became the chief medical center of the Confederacy. Chimborazo Hill with its fresh breezes; its view; its 40 largely open acres; its water supply, and its natural drainage, was an obvious and natural choice for a major medical facility. "And early in 1862, the hospital was opened, and in one week 2,000 soldiers were admitted, and in two weeks' time there were in all 4,000."

While there were tents erected for the convalescing patients, this was not a makeshift city of tents. Instead, 150 single-story buildings 100 feet long and 30 feet wide sprang up in neat rows creating a grid of streets. With two lines of cots placed in each such ward, the long, low structures held 40 to 60 patients each. They were divided into five divisions, or "hospitals," of 30 wards each. In addition, there were 100 Sibley tents for the convalescent; a guardhouse; five soup houses; five ice houses; an administration building; a cemetery; Russian bathhouses, and a bakery that turned out 7,000 to 10,000 loaves of bread a day. And a brewery. And a nearby farm for 100 to 200 dairy cows and 300 to 400 goats providing nutritious "kid meat" for the patients. A canal trading boat, the *Chimborazo*, plied the waterways from Richmond to Lynchburg and Lexington to furnish added provisions for the hospital's clientele.

Workers in the vast complex included free blacks, whites and black slaves. Established as a Confederate Army post, Chimborazo was supervised by Dr. James B. McCaw as Commandant Surgeon. (His doctor-son, Brigadier General Walter Drew McCaw, later would become Chief Surgeon of the American Expeditionary Forces in World War I.)

As recalled by Confederate medical veteran Gildersleeve in 1904, "The hospital presented the appearance of a large town, imposing and attractive, with its alignments of buildings kept whitened with lime, streets and alleys clean, and with its situation on such an elevated point it commanded a grand, magnificent and pleasing view of the surrounding country for many miles."

This, then, was the scene that greeted Union General Weitzel as Richmond fell in the last few days of the war. With him on the ride up the hill was his brigade's medical director, Dr. Alexander Mott, who spotted the Chimborazo commandant among the awaiting Southern medical officers.

"Ain't that old Jim McCaw?" Mott cried out.

"Yes," said McCaw, as recalled later by Gildersleeve. "And don't you want a drink?"

Mott's reply was yes. "The General will take one, too, if you will ask him."

Weitzel did . . . and in perhaps unconscious tribute to the work of the Confederate doctors, he also placed them, their hospital and all its patients under his immediate protection.

So Very Personal

The war had become so *personal* by the last days before Appomattox that the Union soldiers first attacking their Confederate counterparts in the Battle of Sayler's Creek on April 6, 1865, displayed handkerchiefs as apparent invitation for their brethren in gray to surrender and dispense with any further bloodshed.

It was an eerie scene that late afternoon in the rural Virginia countryside southwest of Richmond. The Union men, for their part, had marched steadily up the incline just beyond the rain-swollen creek to attack the Rebels on the heights above. The Union men were ordered to hold their fire until the last possible moment. And, amazingly, they did. They "pressed forward," said a history of the 37th Massachusetts Volunteer Regiment later, "holding their fire till they were in plain sight of the enemy almost face to face."

The Southerners, for their part, contributed to the momentary silence by also holding fire, until the men in blue were at 100 yards or even less. They then, though, refused to heed the imploring handkerchiefs.

Battalion commander Robert Stiles, a Confederate Army major, recollected calling out to his men, "Ready!" They then "rose, all together," he later wrote, "like a piece of mechanism, kneeling on their right knees and their faces set with an expression that meant everything."

Stiles then ordered: "Aim!" And before him, "The musket barrels fell to an almost perfect horizontal line leveled about the knees of the advancing line."

As he next barked, "Fire!", the first line of Union men went down like tenpins, and the second line visibly wavered. Then another Southern volley, and this line broke, the survivors running back to the creek behind, hotly pursued by Stiles' men, who had their bayonets fixed and who poured on hot fire until actually meeting some of the Union soldiers at the bottom of the hill or in the creek in hand-to-hand fighting.

This was only a portion of the Federal center line, however, and on either flank the Federals were in fact advancing. Even here, at center, they reformed quickly, to mount a counterattack back up the hill, despite a second charge by Stiles' battalion, which then took position once more in the main Confederate line.

Now came a second assault by the Federal line overall, this time in strength overpowering and too great for the tattered, retreating Rebels to repel. Walter Watson, another Rebel officer on the scene that afternoon, reported that the opposing lines now "mingled in one promiscuous and prolonged melee with clubbed muskets and bayonet as if bent upon exterminating each other."

So personal, so close to war's end . . . so personal that Stiles later said the fight "degenerated into a butchery," a butchery of "brutal personal conflicts." He saw "men kill each other with bayonets and the butts of muskets, and even bite each other's throats and ears and noses, rolling on the ground like wild beasts."

So personal that in one corner of the battlefield, a Rebel officer seemed about to surrender to a Union officer but instead fired his pistol at the blue-clad officer and wounded him. They were so close, the Union man took hold of the Rebel, and they grappled in a rolling struggle that carried them down the slopes of a ravine. Shot a second time by an onlooking Rebel, the Union man was finally overpowered. His original assailant was taking aim again to deliver a final, killing shot when a Union infantryman, Private Samuel Eddy, took aim of his own and fatally shot the Southerner. As Eddy fired, though, still another Rebel bayonetted him in the chest so fiercely that the point emerged from Eddy's back. Private Eddy, in fact, was pinned to the ground by the blow. His assailant now tried to wrest away Eddy's rifle. Somehow, the Union private not only held onto his weapon, but he also managed to place another cartridge in the chamber and fire into the chest of the Rebel, killing him. Eddy then pushed aside the latter's body, pulled the bayonet out of his own chest . . . and walked away from the scene under his own power.

So personal was it another way, too, all at Sayler's Creek (as related in *Thirty-six Hours Before Appomattox* by National Park Service Ranger/Historian Chris Calkins), that at one point a Union corporal shot and fatally wounded a Confederate officer, then hurried to his victim's side with the words, "I am sorry I had to shoot you" and, "I am a Christian, and if you wish, I will pray for you; it is all I can do for you now." And so he did, with the stricken Confederate saying "Amen," before he died.

So very personal that when George Armstrong Custer's cavalrymen attacked a Confederate line, a ragged Rebel volley emptied many a saddle, but the Union mounts came on anyway . . . and as they jumped the Confederate defensive works, some defenders were killed, not by gunfire, but by the hooves of the leaping animals.

And they weren't all horses, either. Some, apparently seized at Amelia Courthouse a day earlier, were mules replacing lost Federal horses. One Union sergeant, Francis N. Cunningham of the 1st West Virginia Cavalry, was perfectly happy with the result. "It took my mule just about four jumps to show that he could outclass all others," said Cunningham later. "He laid back his ears and frisked over logs and flattened out like a jackrabbit."

More to the point here, "He switched his tail and sailed right over the rebs, landing near a rebel color-bearer of the 12th Virginia Infantry." What happened next was certainly an oddity of war, and also most personal fighting indeed. The color-bearer was big and brawny, it seems, but to Cunningham's hot-headed mule, no matter. The Reb "put up a game fight, but that mule had some new side and posterior uppercuts that put the reb out of the game."

So very personal was it all that George Custer's brother, Tom, a young second lieutenant, did his best to seize a Confederate set of colors. He didn't find it very easy, being shot in the face and the neck by the color-bearer and left with a cheek spotted by burned powder. Nonetheless, Tom Custer grabbed and held onto the colors while shooting his adversary quite fatally, then taking 14 prisoners. Both Lieutenant Custer and Private Eddy, in fact, were awarded the Medal of Honor for their efforts in the Battle of Sayler's Creek, in which the retreating Robert E. Lee lost 7,000 men, including six generals, all taken prisoner, to the relatively low Union casualty count of 1,180 men captured, killed or wounded. (For Tom Custer, incidentally, it would be a second Medal of Honor earned in the Civil War. Like his brother, George Armstrong Custer, he was destined to be killed by the Sioux at the Little Big Horn.)

So very personal was Sayler's Creek, just days before Lee's surrender at Appomattox, just down the road, George Custer that night shared his blanket with newly captured Confederate General Brevard Kershaw. Likewise, Union General Phil Sheridan shared his bivouac supper with his Confederate captives.

Personal note, too: Lee, on seeing some of his men streaming to his own headquarters after the battle, said: "My God! Has the Army dissolved?"

And back at City Point, outside of Richmond and Lee's recently vacated bastion of Petersburg, a visiting Abraham Lincoln was told of Sheridan's message to overall Union Commander Ulysses S. Grant that said, "If the thing is pressed, I think that Lee will surrender." Lincoln replied in that personal way all his own: "Let the thing be pressed." It was, and three days later, Lee surrendered at Appomattox.

No Opportunity For Surrender

He said it three times toward the end, and it was oh, so true. "They'll never take me alive, they've sworn to kill me if they capture me again."

After an initial burst of excitement and downright adulation for John Hunt Morgan following his remarkable escape from the Ohio State Penitentiary in late 1863, nothing had gone right for the Confederacy's famed raider. After months of confinement, he returned to a South clearly running out of steam. His political enemies, such as Braxton Bragg, had Jefferson Davis' ear in Richmond, and there were questions as to why Morgan had disobeyed orders and crossed the Ohio River into the state of Ohio, no matter how spectacular or effective the raid that ensued.

He was now based in Southwest Virginia, rugged and poor mountain country, with ill-suited troops and stronger, better-equipped and -manned Federal forces edging his way. His beloved Mattie awaited his occasional visits—and his many letters—in lovely Abingdon, Virginia.

In the last year of the Civil War, unfit men had taken the place of those many who had been killed or disabled in the many battles beforehand. Desperate recruiting measures had dragged bottom in the manpower pool. And Morgan had to use the personnel assigned to him even though he could have filled his ranks with many others. Richmond denied Morgan the better-suited, eager volunteers who wanted to transfer into his command from their own units.

He and his men, ragged as they were, did mount an expedition into eastern Kentucky by dint of a difficult mountain trek, but this final raid by John Hunt Morgan was marred by the thievery and outright robberies associated with it.

It is almost certain that when Morgan marched through Mount Sterling, Kentucky, it was his own brigade's surgeon who robbed the local bank of $72,000 . . . and disappeared, last suspected of fleeing for his native Germany. Then, too, wrote Morgan biographer Cecil Holland, "At least a half-dozen Mount Sterling stores were forcibly entered, and goods valued at several thousands of dollars—goods privately owned and in private hands—were hauled away."

Even private homes were stripped of valuables, noted Holland. "The riffraff and the criminals out of the backwash of the South who had found their way into Confederate uniforms were showing their stripe." Some soldiers reportedly took jewelry from local women at gunpoint. "A Mrs. Hamilton, riding into Mount Sterling with delicacies for the wounded, was robbed of her money and horse." Then, too, at nearby Lexington, another bank lost $10,000, more stores were broken into, more individuals were robbed.

Morgan, intent on confronting nearby Federal forces, was outraged by such behavior but unwisely put off his own investigation and discipline measures until later—a mistake that only gave his enemies in Richmond, and the North, fresh ammunition to undermine his reputation.

At the same time, Morgan did not really concentrate on the military situations ahead of him. Failing to fully assess his enemy's capabilities, he was taken by surprise near Cynthiana and, due to poor tactical planning, badly defeated. Morgan and his men then limped back to their base in Virginia.

Summer of 1864 came and went, with the Confederacy as a whole limping visibly by now. And for Morgan, the clouds left by his last raid would not blow away. Subordinate officers of his command were demanding investigation by higher authority, and there once again—as in the case of his Ohio raid in 1863—was the issue of Morgan's authority for setting out on the ill-fated Kentucky raid to begin with. Morgan promised to cooperate after his Richmond superiors decided to look into the excesses attributed to the foray. There is strong evidence that he, himself, at the outset of the raid "had issued strict orders . . . against depredations and had made his subordinate officers responsible for the good conduct of his men," wrote Holland.

Before an investigation could get underway, however, Morgan moved south from Abingdon to counter a Union move northward from Knoxville, Tennessee. Taking a train to Jonesboro, where the rail line stopped, Morgan led his 1,600 cavalry troopers into Greeneville, Tennessee, home before the war of Abe Lincoln's Vice President, Andrew Johnson. Greeneville, and indeed, much of eastern Tennessee, was pro-Union territory.

Morgan's plan was to stay at the spacious residence of Mrs. Catherine Williams, whom he knew to be pro-Southern herself, even though she had a son serving in each of the two opposing armies, even though the wife of her "Union son" was living with her. Again, Morgan should have known better. On a previous visit, he had had a run-in with Mrs. Joseph Williams, the daughter-in-law whose husband was a Union soldier. At the time, a wounded Yankee had been staying at the Williams' home, and despite being on parole, he tried to send information on Morgan's force to the Federals at Knoxville via a letter in a prayer book carried by the younger Mrs. Williams. Morgan had revoked the man's parole and sent him to Abingdon under guard. The younger Mrs. Williams had been furious.

The old episode did not stop Morgan from now choosing the same overnight abode. He sent a subordinate ahead to clear the way with the elder Mrs. Williams while he, himself, sat astride his horse on a road leading into town as his men filed by on their own mounts. "Much of the glory and prestige of Morgan's old command was gone," wrote biographer Holland, "but Morgan's presence was still inspiring. Cheer after cheer rang out as the wearied troops marched by; unknown to them they were taking farewell of their beloved commander."

To the north, Mattie awaited her husband's return from yet another combat, the seed of a child carried in her womb.

That night rain fell in torrents on Greeneville and the outposts Morgan had established all around the town. With the younger Mrs. Williams absent, ostensibly visiting a family farm not far away, Morgan and members of his staff slept comfortably in the big brick house on Main Street (Andrew Johnson's Homestead also is located on Main Street).

Earlier in the day Morgan had told his staff officer Major A. C. Withers that he didn't expect to be taken alive by the Federals again. That evening, while his compatriots talked or sang songs in the Williams' parlor to pass the time, Morgan was not himself. He was moody and again remarked, "Do you know that they have sworn never to take me prisoner again?"

It was early the next morning, right after daybreak, that the Union troopers struck—slipping into town under cover of the rain and darkness, they had surrounded the Williams' house. Then, rifle fire heard nearby! Mrs. Williams alerted Morgan, who pulled on a few clothes and hastily retreated to the garden with another staff officer.

Trying to slip unseen to the nearby stables, where their horses were quartered, they found Union soldiers blocking the way. They retreated to a space beneath a small adjoining church. The rifle fire was by now heavy, ripping through the air all around. Major Withers joined Morgan and the other staff officer after "creeping through the shrubbery." Withers then momentarily returned to the nearby house and found, by looking through the windows, that the streets all around were infested with the Union troopers. No avenue of escape presented itself.

He returned to the hideyhole beneath the church and told Morgan he ought to surrender. "As he spoke there was a sudden clatter above them as the Federals smashed in the door of the church," wrote biographer Holland.

Morgan said surrender was out of the question. Once more, for a third time in the past 24 hours, he said, "It is useless, they have sworn never to take me prisoner."

He was not far wrong. Seconds later, the three officers crept out of their hiding place and started for the house—Morgan thought they might barricade themselves in it and hold out until his troops deployed around the town could come to the rescue. He and his two officers separated for the short passage.

Then a woman's voice rang out from across Main Street. "That's him—that's Morgan, over there among the grape vines."

Then, by the account Withers later provided, came Morgan's voice. "Don't shoot, I surrender."

A Union soldier was sitting astride a horse outside the yard fence, just 20 feet away. His was the third voice. "Surrender and be God damned, I know you."

He fired his rifle, Morgan gave a stifled "Oh God!" as he fell forward, fatally wounded.

The exultant trooper yelled, "I've killed the dammed horse thief!"

In seconds, a crowd of Union soldiers rushed to the spot, pressed right through the fence and draped Morgan's body on the back of a horse to be paraded through the town. Withers was shocked a while later, after himself being taken prisoner, to have the Yankees show him his chief's body tumbled into a roadside ditch, nude except for underdrawers and besmirched with mud and blood.

After Withers protested to a pair of Union commanders, Morgan's body finally was carried to the Williams' home, "where Withers and Captain James Rogers of Morgan's staff were permitted to wash and dress it."

It was a humiliating and unworthy end for one of the Confederacy's greatest heroes, even if he had fallen a step or two from grace by his own ill-considered decisions. In the inevitable postmortems, incidentally, it was fairly well established that the younger Mrs. Williams, obviously suspect as an informer, really had been out of town and returned late the next morning, unaware that Morgan had been in her mother-in-law's home once again.

In the North, the newspapers were predictably exultant, the Chicago *Tribune* saying, for instance, that the Rebel raider "has suddenly passed unto death, much to the regret of associate horse thieves and peace sneaks." Predictably, too, but a bit too late— the Southern press mourned the passing of a great hero—"one of the noblest Southern soldiers and gentlemen," proclaimed the Richmond *Examiner*.

A week after funeral services in Abingdon, Mattie attending, Morgan's body arrived in Richmond encased in a pine box covered with a Confederate flag. Escorted to the State Capitol, also the Confederate Capitol, it was viewed by thousands shuffling past in attitude of sorrow and respect. Neither Jefferson Davis nor Morgan's old commander Braxton Bragg was among those who attended the last rites before the box was placed in a vault to await re-burial in Morgan's hometown of Lexington, Kentucky, after the war. As for Mattie . . . well, "If Mattie was present," said biographer Holland, "the papers did not mention it." Perhaps a second funeral for her slain husband was just too much for her to bear.

PARALLEL SPIES

The South may have had its alluring female spy Belle Boyd, but the North had a bold beauty of its own whose life story often would parallel that of Belle Boyd. Both were captured and quite correctly accused of their sub rosa activity, but of the two, it was the Union's Pauline Cushman who came closer to the hangman's noose.

"Pauline" in reality was Harriet Wood, native of New Orleans, raised in Michigan and a Union loyalist through and through. She began her espionage career as a Union agent nosing about St. Louis, Missouri, for Confederate spies. "She did this with aplomb," writes Donald E. Markle in his book *Spies & Spymasters of the Civil War*.

She accomplished her missions early in the war in secret, without fanfare. Assigned next to Nashville, again to pinpoint Rebel spies in the Union-held town, she did resort to one safe form of fanfare after all—as an actress, she could appear on stage without creating suspicion. Always, she was careful to maintain her actress "cover."

In the East, Belle Boyd was just the opposite. Arrested several times during the war as a spy for the Confederacy, she was bold and brassy about her activities. She loved the notoriety and left no doubt as to her affiliations. Sent to Baltimore from Virginia after one arrest, she proudly displayed the Confederate flag from her railroad car's window. In Baltimore, she so dazzled the warden that he set her loose.

That was her way . . . known for her activities, she somehow still got her man among Union soldiers—and his information—time and time again. Arrested another time, she sang *Dixie* from her jail cell at the top of her lungs.

In the war's western theater, a much more subtle Pauline Cushman and her spymasters arranged to have her offer a toast to

Jefferson Davis on her stage in Nashville (some accounts say Louisville, Kentucky). As a result, she was "thrown out of town"—exactly the cover she sought. Her spying behind Confederate lines followed—she produced much more vital intelligence than Belle Boyd ever did, says Markle.

In 1863, however, while seeking information on Braxton Bragg's Army of Tennessee, she was captured. Documents on her person proved her true role to the satisfaction of Bragg, who ordered her executed forthwith—hanged. If the sentence had been carried out, notes Markle, "Miss Cushman would have become the only female spy hanged by either side during the entire Civil War."

As events turned out, fortunately, a Union raiding party descended on the area—Shelbyville, Tennessee, and environs—just in time to scatter the Rebels holding the brave actress-spy and she was released.

Her cover was "blown," but a grateful Union Army—some of its officers, anyway—gave her the honorary title of "Major," and as "Major Cushman" she continued with her stage career both during the last years of the war and thereafter.

Belle Boyd, who had even married and conscripted a Union officer during the war, also pursued a postwar stage career. Both women were able to boast of their wartime spying activities as a drawing card for their audiences, but Pauline's fortunes gradually declined, and she died in San Francisco—some say as a suicide—after stints as a dressmaker's assistant and charwoman. Her gravestone, supplied by the Union veterans of the Grand Army of the Republic, gave her simple but appreciative epitaph: "Pauline Cushman," it says, "Federal Spy and Scout of the Cumberland."

Belle Boyd, living until 1900, or six years beyond her Union rival, died on a visit to Kilborn, Wisconsin, for a stage appearance—she by then had written a book on her wartime exploits and married twice more, as well. Her burial in Wisconsin, writes Markle, "was funded by the women's auxiliary of the Grand Army of the Confederacy." In death, each recalled by her own compatriots of the war days, they were parallel again.

ACQUIRING A NEW NAME

Having freedom, surprisingly, was not all joy for the Southern blacks who had been slaves . . . who were used to being slaves . . . according to a black man raised on a Virginia plantation and called "Booker" in slavery days.

One of the first things many newly-freed blacks wanted to do, quickly, was to take on a new name—not the master's name, but almost any name other than the master's. "In some way," wrote Booker later, "a feeling got among the coloured people that it was far from proper for them to bear the surname of their former owners, and a great many of them took other surnames."

Booker, only a boy at the time, recalled the very moment that freedom came—was announced—for the slaves at his plantation in Franklin County, Virginia, where his mother, incidentally was the cook; where their cabin (he slept there on rags on the floor) was the plantation kitchen. His father was unknown, but was thought to be a white man from another farm-plantation nearby, and his stepfather was a slave from a neighboring plantation who came visiting once in a while. His stepfather, in fact, hadn't been seen for a while, because he had run away, escaped slavery, and found sanctuary in West Virginia, where he had a job in the salt mines outside Charleston.

The morning that young Booker and his fellow slaves heard about their freedom they were told to gather at the "big house." "All of our master's family were either standing or seated on the veranda of the house, where they could see what was to take place and hear what was said. There was a feeling of deep interest, or perhaps sadness, on their faces, but not bitterness."

A stranger, probably a Union officer, "made a little speech and then read a rather long paper—the Emancipation Proclamation, I think." Next, "we were told that we were all free, and could go when and where we pleased."

The reaction among the former slaves at first was excitement, joy and more. All to be expected. Young Booker's mother leaned down and kissed her children, "while tears of joy ran down her cheeks." And among the other newly-freed slaves, "for some minutes there was great rejoicing and thanksgiving, and wild scenes of ecstasy." In this case, on this plantation, it seems, "no bitterness," and in fact "there was pity among the slaves for the former owners."

All to be expected? Except that the "wild rejoicing on the part of the emancipated coloured people lasted but for a brief period, for I noticed that by the time they returned to their cabins there was a change in their feelings."

What had happened? "The great responsibility of being free, of having charge of themselves, of having to think and plan for themselves and their children, seemed to take possession of them . . . In a few hours the great questions with which the Anglo-Saxon race had been grappling for centuries had been thrown upon these people to be solved. These were the questions of a home, a living, the rearing of children, education, citizenship, and the establishment and support of churches." Remarkably, in just a few hours, "the wild rejoicing ceased," replaced in the slave quarters by "a feeling of deep gloom."

Being free was a serious thing, many were realizing. The older people, especially, found it frightening. After all, "their best days were gone." They had spent their lifetime as slaves. Where to go, what to do instead?

"Besides, deep down in their hearts there was a strange and peculiar attachment to 'Old Marster' and 'Old Missus', and to their children, which they found it hard to think of breaking off." Was it any wonder then, that "gradually, one by one, stealthily at first, the older slaves began to wander from the slave quarters back to the 'big house' to have a whispered conversation with their former owners as to the future?"

Young Booker and his family did not stay around very long, and it wouldn't be long before he took steps to remedy the fact he had only one name to his name!

First, though, his mother and her children had to journey to West Virginia to join Booker's stepfather. They left their Virginia home and crossed over mountains, streams and valleys on foot—the trip took several weeks, naturally. And one day, Booker would reverse the trek—500 miles on foot—to attend school and work

292

as a janitor at Virginia's Hampton Institute. He then, after other important stops on the way, would go on to operate Tuskegee Institute in Alabama as its widely esteemed president and become a towering leader among American blacks.

First, though, before any of these things could come to pass, he had to attend basic, elementary school classes in West Virginia . . . and then settle the issue of his name. At school, "I noticed that all of the children had at least two names and some of them indulged in what seemed to me the extravagance of having three."

The youngster from Virginia was ready the first time the schoolmaster called the roll and asked for his full name. "I calmly told him 'Booker Washington' as if I had been called by that name all my life; and by that name I have since been known."

Well, not quite—for later in life the black educator found out his mother actually had given him another name soon after he was born in 1858 or 1859, and that was Taliaferro. And so, as he recounted in his autobiography, he became Booker T. Washington, finally and forever more.

CLOSE CONNECTIONS

Relatives and relationships (plus a wee bit of nepotism) among the Civil War's principal figures crop up so frequently you would think we had been a tiny European principality going through an internal shake-up of the royal court, rather than a bloody division of a great nation lying athwart an entire continent.

So it was that briefly visiting in the "King's Palace" in the national capital—the Lincoln White House, that is—was the grieving widow of a recently killed Rebel general. Twice, that is.

Among the generals still living, a leading "Royalist" commander, George McClellan, was married to the former love of a leading Rebel officer, Ambrose Powell "A.P." Hill. For that matter, Thomas J. "Stonewall" Jackson was married to Daniel Harvey "D.H." Hill's sister. Both men were generals . . . but at least *they* fought together, as fellow Confederates.

For that matter again, the South's great and reliable General A.P. Hill was married to the Southern cavalry raider John Hunt Morgan's sister Kitty, more fondly known (to Hill, at any rate) as Dolly. The rending national division was seen again in the familial connections of "Jeb" Stuart, who died at the home of his brother-in-law Brewer, future Surgeon General of the Confederacy. Stuart's wife, the former Flora Cooke, counted a brother as a brigadier in the Confederate Army and a brother-in-law (married to her sister Julia) as a general in the Union Army. Still another close connection was "Mudwall" Jackson, second cousin to "Stonewall."

On the same side, Robert E. Lee was the son of the Revolutionary War hero Henry "Lighthouse Harry" Lee, while Robert E. Lee's wife Mary Custis Lee was the daughter of George Washington Parke Custis, adopted son of George Washington . . . but grandson, actually, of Washington's wife, the Widow Martha Custis.

And then again, Ulysses S. Grant, as commander of the Union armies late in the war, enjoyed the services of his brother-in-law (and West Point roommate), Frederick T. Dent, on his staff—indeed, Army officer Dent later served Grant, *President Grant*, in the White House as Grant's military secretary. At the same time, a White House occupant until his death was Grant's father-in-law, former Mississippi slaveowner Frederick Dent, father to Julia Grant and her brother, young Fred.

On the south side of the Potomac, down in Richmond, that is, not only did Robert E. Lee's eldest son Custis serve as an aide to Confederate President Jefferson Davis, but so did the President's nephew Joseph Robert Davis, like Custis also a Confederate brigadier.

Then too, the son of a former U.S. President fought on the Rebel side—Louisiana's Dick Taylor, son of the late Zachary Taylor (once, too, father-in-law to Jefferson Davis, based on Davis' first marriage to Taylor's daughter Knox, who died of a fever shortly after their wedding).

Robert E. and George Washington Custis Lee, father and son, were not the only members of the same Lee family to take part in the Civil War. It may take a scorecard to keep track, but Robert E. Lee's other son in Confederate service was cavalry officer William Henry Fitzhugh "Rooney" Lee, while General Fitzhugh

Lee was a nephew of Robert. On the other hand, Confederate General Stephen Dill Lee was no relative, but the Confederacy's Admiral Sydney Smith Lee *was* related . . . as Robert's brother. Still another distant relative was Samuel Phillips Lee . . . a *Union* naval officer!

Among the "lesser nobility" of the war, brothers took part on opposite sides—witness Kentucky's two army generals named Crittenden, Thomas and George, one Union, one Confederate, respectively. Friends split along similar lines, especially true of the many West Point professionals found on either side of the battlefield. Confederate General James Longstreet, for instance, had attended future Union General Grant's wedding in 1848 to Julia.

The Jefferson Davises, for that matter, had kept lingering Northern friendships from their *ante-bellum* days in Washington or through other ties. Mrs. Davis, Varina Howell by birth, was the grandchild of a New Jersey governor.

It was the Lincolns, though—and Mary Todd Lincoln, especially—who may have endured the most painful and complex genealogy chart of any principal players of the Civil War. With both born in Kentucky, itself a state of competing loyalties, it was inescapable that a few relatives would land on opposite sides. Consider the complications implicit in the number of Mary Todd Lincoln's Southern-leaning siblings. Born of Robert Smith Todd's first wife, Eliza, she counted five siblings from that marriage, while another eight siblings (half brothers and sisters) were the result of her widowed father's second marriage, to Elizabeth Humphreys.

Not only did Mary Todd, as First Lady of the land, have a half-sister, Elodie, living in Selma, Alabama, and married to a Confederate officer during the war, but her half-sister Emilie was married to a Rebel brigadier general, Benjamin Helm, whom Abraham, Mary's husband, had appointed as a paymaster in the United States Army—that is to say, *Union Army*—shortly *after* Fort Sumter. Helm had turned down the proffered commission, however, and joined the Confederate Army. A graduate of West Point himself, he advanced to the rank of brigadier general and was killed in the battle of Chickamauga in September of 1863. Emilie at the time was living in Selma also, probably with sister Elodie.

Not only was the White House in mourning for the likeable Helm, but President Lincoln was left in a delicate spot. Just as George McClellan once had allowed Robert E. Lee's wife safe passage through Union lines, now Lincoln was asked to allow Confederate General Helm's widow to pass through Federal-held territory after attending her husband's funeral in Atlanta. She wished to go home with her children, to her mother in Lexington, Kentucky.

Even more sensitive for Lincoln, she apparently was halted by Federal officers who wanted her to take the Union oath of allegiance. Lincoln had to intervene and order her forwarded to Washington. In Washington, the Rebel widow, together with daughter Katherine, stayed for a period of time in the White House with the Lincolns.

Emilie also wanted the President's help in safeguarding her investment in supplies of cotton stranded down South. Lincoln, no doubt with misgivings, wrote a note giving her amnesty, also based on her taking the oath, and saying, too, "Mrs. Helm claims to own some cotton at Jackson, Mississippi, and also some in Georgia; and I shall be glad upon either place being brought within our lines, for her to be afforded the proper facilities to show her ownership, and take her property."

Returning home, she kept asking . . . and asking. Now she wanted to provide clothing for Rebels held prisoner at Camp Douglas. She returned to the White House for another visit in the fall of 1864, still desirous of protecting her cotton. Shortly after that visit, upon learning of the death of her half-brother Levi, she turned on Lincoln, calling Levi "another sad victim to the powers of more favored relations." She also charged in a letter to Lincoln, "your *minnie* [sic] *bullets* have made us what we are." She said that fact gave her "additional claim" in seeking Lincoln's favors, and called herself "a woman almost crazy with misfortune."

Lincoln tried to help her with the cotton, but apparently was frustrated when it accidentally burned up. After the Civil War and the assassination of her in-law in the White House, Emilie Todd Helm had to eke out a living as a musician . . . until another Lincoln, Abraham's oldest son, Robert, came to the rescue—he used his influence to obtain her an appointment as postmistress in Elizabethtown, Kentucky.

Meanwhile, Mary Todd Lincoln's half-brothers David, Alexander and Sam, and her brother George all served in the Southern armies. Still another half-sister, Martha, allegedly took advantage of a Lincoln pass to smuggle medicines to her favorite side in the war—once again, the Confederacy.

Lee's Final Order

General Order #9
Hd Quarters
Army of Nor. Va.
10 April 1865

After four years of arduous service marked by unsurpassed courage and fortitude, the Army of Northern Virginia has been compelled to yield to overwhelming numbers and resources.

I need not tell the brave survivors of so many hard fought battles, who have remained steadfast to the last, that I have consented to this result from no distrust of them.

But feeling that valor and devotion could accomplish nothing that could compensate for the loss that would have attended the continuance of the contest, I determined to avoid the useless sacrifice of those whose past services have endeared them to their countrymen.

By the terms of the agreement, officers and men can return to their homes and remain until exchanged. You will take with you the satisfaction that proceeds from the consciousness of duty faithfully performed, and I earnestly pray that a Merciful God will extend to you His blessing and protection.

With an unceasing admiration of your constancy and devotion to your country, and a grateful remembrance of your kind and generous consideration for myself, I bid you an affectionate farewell.

R. E. Lee
Gen'l

Julia Reads A Note

Just a few days after the surrender at Appomattox and Julia Dent Grant thought it all was so very odd. First, the man who came to her hotel room with a message from Mrs. Lincoln. Then, the four "peculiar" men sitting together at lunch. Finally, the angry-looking man, "dark, pale", who galloped past the Grant couple's carriage late that day and "glared in a most disagreeable manner." And last, the mysterious letter.

It was Good Friday, April 14. The Grants—still buoyed by the excitement of great events—had begun their day in a room at Willard's Hotel (today's Willard International Hotel) after returning the day before from City Point on the James River opposite Richmond. Julia Grant was anxious to return to their cottage in Burlington, New Jersey, outside Philadelphia, for a few days of quiet and rest . . . for resumption of a normal life!

Her husband (she called him "Ulys") wasn't sure he could wind up his affairs in Washington quite in time. "I wish I could," he told her, "but I have promised Mr. Lincoln to go up this morning and with him to see what can be done in reference to the reduction of the army."

That appointment was scheduled for nine o'clock in the morning, but before the Union's victorious general could leave his hotel quarters there came a tap at the door. It was a message from Abraham Lincoln—one of his last, ever. It said to please come at eleven o'clock instead of the earlier hour because his son Robert had just returned from his own army duty, "and I want to see something of him before I go to work."

That would make it even more difficult for the Grants to get away in time for the train trip to New Jersey, but the general still promised his wife to do whatever was possible about leaving that day.

After he left their room came another rap at the hotel door, and when Julia Grant innocently said, "Come in," there appeared "a man dressed in light-colored corduroy coat and trousers and with a rather shabby hat of the same color."

When she told the stranger she had expected a bellboy

bringing cards, he "reddened," bowed to her and asked if she indeed were Mrs. Grant.

Assured that she was, the man said he had been sent by Mrs. Lincoln, "to say she will call for you at exactly eight o'clock to go to the theater."

Perhaps this odd messenger didn't know it, but Julia Grant wasn't all that enamored of Mary Todd Lincoln's ways—they had had a couple of run-ins, you might say, while the Lincolns visited the Grant headquarters at the Richmond-Petersburg apex just days before.

But let Julia Grant relate her own reaction: "To this I replied with some feeling (not liking either the looks of the messenger or the message, thinking the former savored of discourtesy and the latter seemed like a command), 'You may return with my compliments to Mrs. Lincoln and say I regret that as General Grant and I intend leaving the city this afternoon, we will not, therefore, be here to accompany the President and Mrs. Lincoln to the theater.'"

You would think that a White House messenger at that point would bow out of the room and hurry on back with the reply—after all, why should he care who went to Ford's Theatre with the Lincolns? But no bowing for this messenger.

No, by Julia Grant's own account (*The Personal Memoirs of Julia Dent Grant*, first published in 1975), he hesitated, then was bold enough to say: "Madam, the papers announce that General Grant will be with the President tonight at the theater."

Julia Grant wasn't going to enter a debate with the man. She simply told him to deliver her reply as given and dismissed him! Oddly, he smiled as he left. Oddly, too, it was only a short time before Julia Dent Grant would see the same strange messenger again—as she had lunch the same day with General John A. Rawlins' wife and two of their respective children.

Four men came into the dining room together. "I thought I recognized in one of them the messenger of the morning, and one, a dark, pale man, played with his soup spoon, sometimes filling it and holding it half-lifted to his mouth, but never tasting it."

The same slow-eater "seemed very intent on what we and the children were saying." He was so disconcerting to Julia Grant that she thought he was "crazy." When Julia Grant asked Mrs. Rawlins to take a furtive look at the four men, she agreed that there was "something peculiar about them." Julia then suggested they might be Southern partisans, "a part of Mosby's guerrillas." She told her friend the suspect men "have been listening to every word we have said."

The incident only added to Julia Grant's unease on this day, this fateful day. In the morning, after dismissing the "messenger" from Mrs. Lincoln, Julia had sent word to her husband "entreating him" to take her home to New Jersey that evening and stressing that she did not wish to go to the theater. "I do not know what possessed me to take such a freak," she wrote later, "but go home I felt I must." And again at lunch, Julia Grant blurted out to her friend Mrs. Rawlins, "I believe there will be an outbreak tonight or soon [of guerrilla or partisan activity, apparently]. I just feel it, and I am glad that I am going away tonight."

By the time of her late lunch, Julia Grant had heard back from her husband—he had been attending a Cabinet meeting, but his message was: Pack the trunks, they indeed would take the late afternoon train for Philadelphia!

So it was that in the late afternoon they were leaving Willard's in a carriage bound for the railroad depot. Just then, "this same dark, pale man rode past us at a sweeping gallop on a dark horse—black, I think." The "same" as at lunch.

The mysterious rider forged 20 yards ahead, turned and swept back, "and as he passed us both going and returning, he thrust his face quite near the General's and glared in a disagreeable manner."

Grant was startled enough to "draw back" as the stranger made his return circuit. In reply to a pleasantry offered by their companion in the carriage, General Daniel Rucker's wife, Grant said, " . . . I do not care for such glances."

Neither of the Grants knew it just then, but they had just brushed up against John Wilkes Booth. As Julia Grant said in her memoirs, her mysterious, corduroy-clad "messenger" was one of the four men at lunch, she was "perfectly sure," and so was Booth, the very same man who had ridden past the Grants' carriage with such glaring countenance.

It was that very night that Booth shot Lincoln at Ford's Theatre, as is well known. But what had the assassin been doing all day? That morning, Booth's crisscross travels around the Federal capital included a stop to visit fellow conspirator Lewis Paine, who later said his assignment from Booth was to assassinate Ulysses S. Grant.

Booth encountered theater owner James Ford, who excitedly told the actor that a large crowd was expected at the theater that night—to see Grant!

Booth made other stops and conducted other errands, but also dropped out the sight of latter-day historians for an hour or two. Could it have been for a late luncheon with three co-conspirators, in view of Julia Grant's nearby table?

Late in the afternoon, publicly in view again, Booth hired a lively horse from Pumphrey's Livery Stable at the Mall and then was seen riding the mare, sometimes at a canter, on nearby streets. He allowed her to race a few blocks up Pennsylvania Avenue.

He made a stop at the theater, spoke to a property man, James Maddox, then raced off again.

He soon was at the corner of 14th Street and Pennsylvania, location of the Willard's hostelry. He encountered a fellow actor, one John Matthews, and asked him to deliver a letter to the editor of the *National Intelligencer*.

While they were talking, they saw across the street a company of Union soldiers marching along as escort for a column of prisoners. "My Great God, Matthews! I have no longer a country," exclaimed Booth.

Just then, wrote Theodore Roscoe in his book *Web of Conspiracy*, Grant's carriage, with a small cavalry escort, was leaving Willard's for the rail depot. "Booth angled the nimble mare over for a closer look at the General." Then, as the carriage continued on its way, he rode back to the Willard—quite likely passing the carriage coming and going, as Julia Grant wrote later.

Booth found out from the "curbstone loungers" that the Grants were off to the Philadelphia train and New Jersey. That meant one less target available at the theater that night . . . but also fewer escorting soldiers and officers to get in the way!

The Grants, apparently safe on their train, had not quite reached their destination of Burlington that night when they heard of the horrifying events at Ford's Theatre. They had passed through Philadelphia and were waiting for the ferry to take them across the Delaware River to their next train in New Jersey. As they ate dinner in a restaurant near the ferry landing, Grant was handed three telegrams, one after the other. "The General looked very pale."

When Julia asked what had happened, Ulysses told her Lincoln had been assassinated (actually, he didn't die until the next morning). Grant then accompanied his wife and their daughter Jesse to the cottage at Burlington, then returned during the night to Washington by special train.

The very next morning, a still stunned Julia Grant found a chilling letter in the flood of telegrams and mail that reached the Grants in the immediate aftermath of the assassination. "General Grant, thank God, as I do," it said, "that you still live. It was your life that fell to my lot, and I followed you on the [railroad] cars. Your car door was locked, and thus you escaped me, thank God!"

Could the letter have been from Lewis Paine?, whose real name was Lewis Thornton Powell? Unlikely, since it was, without a doubt, Paine-Powell who brutally attacked and almost killed Secretary of State William Seward and his son Frederick at their Washington home the night of the Lincoln assassination.

Paine-Powell, along with four others who took part in the Lincoln plot, was hanged for his own bloody deed, and Booth died in a fire marking the end of his escape attempt. But . . . the writer of the mysterious letter to General Grant? No one knows even today.

FREEDOM STILL DENIED

Freedom was at hand, right there, within her grasp, but slave child Armaci Adams didn't know it. Richmond long since had fallen. The slaves were free, and Lincoln, even Lincoln was dead!

And still . . . on a lone farm in Tidewater Virginia, the young black girl *slaved* on. No one had told her. *Slaved* on and . . .

Dey never give me my age. White folks kept hit an' never give it ter me.

She might have been five years old when Richmond fell in 1865; then again, she might have been about 15. It's hard to tell.

Before Emancipation, life as a slave to Isaac Hunter and his "Missus" was sheer hell. In fact, you could call them both "hell cats." The old Marse was a preacher, but just too wicked anyway. *Las' time I seed 'im he was comin' f'om a revival drunk.* Mean and wicked.

That time, before Emancipation, when poor Uncle Toney ran away and was caught. *Ole man Hunter an' his son beat 'im all de morning. Dey took turns. After a while dey got tired an' went in ter dinner and lef him hanging 'dere. He was tied up in de air wid his han's crossed an' his toes jes touchin' de groun'.*

The father and son went back to beating him again . . . until the middle of the afternoon. They then "pickled" him, soaking him with salted water, and let him down. He "mos' nigh" died, but he did live, only to be sold down South upon his recovery.

Meanwhile, most of the Hunter slaves were being sold off. Armaci probably would have been, too, but for an accident. As she told it many years later, the Hunters never provided enough to eat, and she used to sit by the side of a fireplace poaching corn. One day, her dress caught fire and she was badly burned on the neck and legs before a passerby saw her running with her dress blazing, threw his coat around her and smothered the fire. She was on crutches "fur a lon' time."

One day, the slave cook, Aunt Rose, was looking at young Armaci and crying. And she said, "Honey, I don' never 'spect ter see you anymo'." Armaci was too young to understand at first.

The next day, the Marsa took her and a team of pretty claybank ponies to Norfolk—to sell both Armaci and the animals. As they proceeded down Main Street, the girl saw a man up on a block and people "jes a-hollerin' 'roun' him"—bidding. The next thing she knew, her "ole man" took her into the back of a vacant store and took off her clothes. Then he and another man looked her over—"examined me." But the prospective buyer balked *'cause he 'fraid I won' be no good on account o' de burn scars.*

Armaci went back to Huntersville and never was sold. Soon, only two men were left to work the farm, while the young, unsalable girl, not yet into her teen-aged years, was left to do all the housework.

Another job, in time, was minding the turkeys, a thankless task because "dey runs eve'y which-a-way." One day after Richmond had fallen to the Union armies, there were some Union soldiers across a creek at some fairgrounds. She noticed one of the soldiers "patrolin' by" with his rifle on his shoulder, and soon she heard a loud bang. Seconds later, the soldier came into view again, with a turkey slung across his shoulder.

One o' dem turkeys done got 'cross de creek an' dat sojer done shot 'im.

Here was trouble, real trouble, for the slave girl! She was "scared weak" when she realized. She herded the rest of the turkeys together and hustled them back to the farm . . . but too late. The Missus was standing outside and counting the big birds. All at once she yelled, "Isaac! One o' dem yaller turkeys is gone!"

Dat man grabbed me an' strip me naked—after freedom min you—an' whupped me wid a bull whup ontwill I fainted. Atter dat I don' know how long he beat me. When I come 'roun 'dey were washin' me down in pickle.

At the time of that incident, Armaci was "free" in theory. All slaves were free by the end of the Civil War in April 1865, if not earlier, in theory, by Lincoln's Emancipation Proclamation. All but a relative handful, that is, who didn't know, weren't told . . . like Armaci. In an 1930s interview transcript subsequently published in *Weevils In The Wheat, Interviews With Virginia Ex-Slaves* edited by Charles L. Perdue, Jr.; Thomas E. Barden and Robert K. Phillips, she calculated she was about 13 before she escaped the Hunter farm in Huntersville.

"How long I been free, I don' know," she said so many years later. "I wondered why eve'body done gone, but dey kept me so close in de house I couldn' fin' out." The Hunters, by their former slave girl's account, clearly did their best to keep her from learning

she could walk away, free, at any time. She finally did find out
. . . and ran away.

She found refuge with a black family named Foreman at
nearby Norfolk Mission College, found work and never went back
to the Hunter place . . . not ever!

SURPRISINGLY KIND FATE

When, at the tender age of 16 or 17, Dorence Atwater went
off to the American Civil War with the 1st Connecticut Cavalry
Squadron in August of 1861, he surely had no idea that he was
destined to become a prisoner, at one time or another, of both
warring governments . . . and, somewhat later, to wind up a good
friend and literary model for Robert Louis Stevenson in the South
Seas Islands.

Such destiny was not yet clear even after his unit was taken
over by the 2nd New York Cavalry, nor yet when young Dorence
managed to survive the fiercely fought battles of Second Bull Run,
Cedar Mountain, Fredericksburg, Chancellorsville, Brandy Station, Chantilly, even Gettysburg.

Right after Gettysburg, though, he was captured while on
courier duty. He spent eight slow months as a prisoner in Richmond, then was sent to the Confederacy's notorious Andersonville
Prison, where Zurich-born Commandant Henry Wirz, a doctor,
was allowing Union prisoners to die of neglect and/or starvation.
After two months in the stockade at Andersonville, the Connecticut youth became ill and was transferred to the prison hospital.
Upon his recovery, he became clerk to the hospital surgeon.

Dorence now sat at a desk beside Wirz himself, and
Dorence's clerical job was to post the paperwork on the deaths of
his fellow prisoners.

Unknown to Wirz and his cohorts, Dorence Atwater maintained a duplicate list, which he took with him when he was
paroled in March of 1865, less than a month before the Civil War
ended. That list eventually allowed the Federal government to

identify and mark thousands of Union graves in what is now known as Andersonville National Cemetery, but the same Federal government in 1865 fought young Dorence Atwater's attempts to publish his list for the sake of the POW families. Court-martialed and dishonorably discharged, he briefly was sentenced to hard labor in prison!

In the meantime, Clara Barton, future founder of the American Red Cross, took up the fight and the graves were marked after all. Journalist Horace Greeley of the *New York Tribune* published the list in 1866; and, as happy end to the story, young Atwater was vindicated in his efforts.

Well, not quite . . . nor does his story really end there. He managed, for instance, to win appointment in 1871 as U.S. consul in Tahiti. He became a friend of Robert Louis Stevenson and even appears in the Scots-born author's *Ebb Tide*. They were partners in a small steamship business, but Atwater also compiled a personal fortune in pearls and gold. He married into South Seas royalty as well.

It wasn't until 1898, however, that the Federal government finally relented and gave him an honorable discharge from military service. His hometown of Terryville, Connecticut, a few years later dedicated a memorial to its native son. He traveled back to New England from his South Seas island to visit the memorial in 1908 and was on his way back to Tahiti, when, stricken ill, he suddenly died in California.

Burial was in the islands, where another memorial—a monument—was erected in further tribute to Dorence Atwater, the lad from Connecticut. Who at Andersonville in those difficult war years would ever have guessed?

Always A Clear Course

In the view of the Union general who prosecuted his side of the Civil War more successfully than anybody else, there was one reason for the Civil War, and one reason only. "The cause of the great War of the Rebellion against the United States," wrote this ex-general, ex-Union commander and ex-President many years later, "will have to be attributed to slavery."

Ulysses S. Grant, on his deathbed (from throat cancer) as he completed his memoirs, minced no words and held back no feelings. "There were two political parties, it is true, in all the states," he said, but in the South "the slaveowners, even as a minority, governed both parties."

Not only that, wrote Grant as well, "The fact is, the Southern slave-owners believed that in some way, the ownership of slaves conferred a sort of patent of nobility—a right to govern independent of the interest or the wishes of those who did not hold such property." Further, "They convinced themselves, first, of the divine origin of the institution and, next, that that particular institution was not safe in the hands of any body of legislators but themselves."

Grant found it most illogical that supposed states-righters would insist upon reluctant states joining the Confederacy. In some of the states following South Carolina's secession course, wrote Grant, "the Union sentiment was so strong that it had to be suppressed by force." In this vein, Grant listed Maryland, Delaware, Kentucky and Missouri, "all slave states . . . [that] failed to pass ordinances of secession; . . . [and yet] they were all represented in the so-called congress of the so-called Confederate States."

In short, Grant summed up, "The South claimed the sovereignty of States, but [also] claimed the right to coerce into their confederation such States as they wanted, that is, all the States where slavery existed."

Grant was afraid of civil war as early as 1856, when the presidential election of that year gave him his first opportunity to vote even though he already was in his thirties. He voted for a Democrat, despite the Republican Party's reputation as the party of abolition. Throughout the country, he later wrote, "Treason to the Government, was openly advocated and was not rebuked." He feared the election of a Republican as President would mean "the secession of all the Slave States, and rebellion."

Reluctantly, Grant cast his ballot for James Buchanan. "Under these circumstances [the probable secession of Southern states] I preferred the success of a candidate whose election would prevent or postpone secession, to seeing the country plunged into a war the end of which no man could foretell. With a Democrat elected by the unanimous vote of the Slave States, there could be no pretext for secession for four years."

Over that period, Grant hoped, "the passions of the people would subside."

But they didn't, and in 1860 the Republican Abraham Lincoln was voted into office. Grant this time couldn't vote (and would have voted for Lincoln's opponent Stephen Douglas) because he recently had moved to Galena, Illinois, to help operate his father's leather-goods store there. Grant's hopes for declining passions of course were unrequited.

Even so, Grant felt that most people expected the more extreme Southern States only to pass "ordinances" of secession, and stop there. "The common impression was that this step was so plainly suicidal for the South, that the movement would not spread over much of the territory and would not last long," he said.

Even in the South itself, he was convinced many years later, "the prevailing sentiment" was against actual secession.

But the slave-owners and demagogues held sway, and unnecessary tragedy was the result, he clearly felt.

Grant did not directly criticize Buchanan for any of his actions—or *inactions*— in the last months of his presidency Grant merely said that the Buchanan Administration "looked helplessly on and proclaimed that the general government had no power to interfere [with secession]; that the Nation had no power to save its own life."

Grant saved his heat for two key Cabinet members under Buchanan—his Secretaries of War and the Navy. They were "secessionists" who, in Grant's view, acted treasonably!

War Secretary John B. Floyd (former Governor of Virginia and later a Confederate general), for instance, "scattered the army so that much of it could be captured when hostilities should commence." He shifted cannon and small arms from Northern arsenals to supply centers in the South, "so as to be on hand when treason wanted them." The Navy "was scattered in like manner," and Buchanan did nothing to stop his Cabinet members from "preparing for war upon their government, either by destroying its resources or storing them in the South until a *de facto* government was established with Jefferson Davis as its President and Montgomery, Alabama, as the Capital."

By that time, the two Southern sympathizers had left the Cabinet—"Loyal men were put in their place. Treason in the executive branch of the government was estopped."

But . . . "The stable door was locked after the horse had been stolen."

Grant didn't mention that Floyd was found innocent by a Congressional committee on the charge that he dispersed arms to the South in anticipation of the coming hostilities. The Virginian (his middle name Buchanan) later met Grant himself in battle—at Fort Donelson, Tennessee, a famous Grant victory over the Rebels. But Floyd escaped capture at Fort Donelson (as did Nathan Bedford Forrest and Gideon Pillow), and a good thing, too, in Grant's strongly held view. "Well may he have been afraid to fall into the hands of National troops," Grant wrote. "He would no doubt have been tried for misappropriating public property; if not for treason, had he been captured."

As events unwound, Floyd died of natural causes in August 1863, before the charge could be put to the test, before the war itself was over.

Grant in the meantime had achieved at Fort Donelson a major battlefield success for the Union. He had yet to weather the public clamor over casualties incurred at Shiloh (never mind, said Lincoln afterward, "He fights"), but his reputation grew with his victories at Vicksburg, Chattanooga and, finally, his relentless, casualty-strewn campaign wearing down Robert E. Lee's Army of Northern Virginia from spring of 1864 to the surrender at Appomattox in April of 1865.

Whatever the personal resources he drew upon to withstand the now truly staggering losses in men he accepted as the price of his victory, Grant's memoirs leave no doubt as to his motivation—

the South had rebelled, and its rebellion was treason, so far as he was concerned. The Civil War had been "a fearful lesson," he wrote at the end of his memoirs and close to the end of his life, but still, "It is probably well that we had the war when we did . . . "

Just a week after finishing his work, he, himself, was dead, succumbing, finally, to his cancer of the throat. He had fought off even death to finish his memoirs, which raised $450,000—money badly needed by his estate to pay off his debts and provide for his surviving family.

WAR'S STING DELAYED

The Civil War spared Danville, Virginia, any real grief until the very end . . . past the end, if you count Appomattox as the penultimate moment of all.

Oh, it took some Danville boys, yes, to be sure. But *spared* as a community, for there was little fighting here on the Dan River at the borderline of Virginia and North Carolina. To be sure also, Danville was a part of the overall picture. In the Confederate government's last days, it stopped here in its flight from Richmond, and made a third capital out of Danville. But only for a week . . . Richmond fell on April 3, 1865, and Lee surrendered at Appomattox, not 70 miles from Danville, on April 9, and on April 10, Jefferson Davis and his government, what was now left of it, took to the rail lines again and headed farther south . . . into history. (After one more stop, that is, at decidedly *un*welcoming Greensboro, North Carolina.)

All of which left Danville alone again, shaken and still agog at what had passed so suddenly in the last few days, the small city totally unsuspecting that here and now the wartime tragedies that had struck so many communities over the past four years, especially in the South, were about to leave scars on Danville, Virginia, as well.

It may have been children, small boys at play.

The arsenal was located at the low end of Craighead Street,

against the river and below the Richmond and Danville railroad station. Here, carefully stored away and usually well-guarded were gunpowder, cartridges, and various other munitions and explosives. Not the sort of thing, normally, to concern two local women who left home that morning fully expecting to return later to hearth and family. And expected, too.

"No one knows how the powder was ignited," said L. Beatrice W. Hairston in her 1955 book *A Brief History of Danville, Virginia: 1728-1954*, "but suddenly a tongue of flame gushed up and a tremendous explosion shook the town. Crash followed crash as one after another the explosives went off, and the building itself leaped into the air, to fall in pieces."

The shame was that at least 14 persons were killed, including the two local woman—"drowned when they flung themselves into the river to extinguish the flames in their clothing." That is to say 14 bodies, "terribly mangled," were recovered on site and nearby (and still others injured in the explosion died later).

Just the day before, Danville had heard of the war's probable end with Lee's surrender to Grant on April 9 . . . and now this!

Few outside of Danville heard or spoke of the city's terrible loss, so intent was the Nation on the fast-unfolding larger events. In Mobile, Confederates were leaving their fortresses. In North Carolina, Sherman was still advancing northward, but he and Confederate General Joseph Johnston soon would come to terms. In Washington, Abraham Lincoln made a speech at a White House window, stressing reconciliation . . . his last public speech, it so happens.

There were many the night of April 11 in Danville, Virginia, who didn't care for a moment what was going on elsewhere, as everywhere the war was ended or ending . . . for there, in Danville, Virginia, its sting had just been felt.

Pair For Two

A few more "stats" illustrate the extent of Virginia's role in the Civil War before all the shooting died down. As reported by Editor Kenneth H. Phillips in the magazine *Great Battles*, Virginia furnished the site of the first real (albeit, small) battle of the war—at Phillipi, on June 3, 1861. The Old Dominion *provided*, if that is the right word, the war's first major land battle, First Bull Run. It was the scene of the world's first engagement between ironclads, in Hampton Roads. And while Petersburg may have been under siege longer than any other American city in history, is there any place other than Winchester, Virginia, that changed hands more often than the upper Shenandoah Valley city's 72 such change-overs?

As Phillips noted, Virginia led the way in several other wartime departments as well. "Thirty-eight percent of all battalion-size units of the Southern army hailed from Virginia," he wrote. "More men, Northerners and Southerners alike, spilled their blood on Virginia's terra firma than in any other state involved. Of all the railroad lines in the South—a major mode for moving men and supplies—Virginia dominated, with 1,771 miles of track, 20 percent of the total in the Confederacy. Virginia also led the way in producing war products, with a resounding 32 percent of all manufactured goods used to support the war effort."

And . . . one more such "stat": "Virginians, of course, still boast that their 79 generals outnumbered, almost 2-to-1, the number of generals from any other Southern state."

Himself Virginia-born and -raised, Phillips has another sort of "stat" to report, more a tale than a stark fact, but true nonetheless.

Two Virginians served in Stonewall Jackson's fabled "Stonewall Brigade," and in time each was wounded in the leg. And each then lost his injured leg.

They went home, and by the turn of the century, "having become related by marriage," they were living in the same Nelson County home. For one, it was his father's home, for the other it was his father-in-law's home.

"Once a year they traveled by train to Lynchburg to buy supplies they were unable to raise on the farm. The two Rebel veterans would buy *one* pair of shoes—one man wore the left and the other wore the right."

How would Ken Phillips know such intimate (and telling) detail? "They were my great-grandfathers."

FINAL GLIMPSES

Over the "smoke-blackened" streets of Richmond, wrote "Mrs. General Pickett" in *Lippincott's* magazine of May 1906, right up to the front door of "the old Pickett house" in that dramatic April of 1865 came a surprising figure—Abraham Lincoln. He was looking for Confederate General George Pickett's uncle, really—an old friend and law associate. On the same visit to the freshly defeated, desolated city, Lincoln had passed through the White House of the Confederacy and walked the downtown streets, with crowds of happy, shouting, cheering blacks thronging around him and his soldier escort.

"Mrs. General Pickett," was surprised to see the Union President at her doorstep, to be sure. And he did ask for her husband, famous for Pickett's Charge at Gettysburg . . . "perhaps wishing," she wrote 40 years later, "in his generous heart to offer the comfort of a cordial handshake to the soldier he had once known in his ambitious youth, whose hopes had gone down with the pride and glory of Richmond."

When Lincoln was told neither gentleman was in, he asked for Mrs. Pickett. "The inquiry was answered by a lady who came forward with a baby in her arms and saw at the door a tall, strong-visaged stranger, with earnest, careworn features and a kindly look in his tender, melancholy eyes."

She spoke. "I am George Pickett's wife, sir."

He spoke, "And I am Abraham Lincoln."

"The President?"

"No; Abraham Lincoln, George's old friend."

They chatted, and before Lincoln turned to go he held the baby, "Little George" by name, and submitted to "a dewy baby kiss."

Handing the child back, Lincoln spoke again "in that deep and sympathetic voice which was one of his greatest powers over the hearts of men."

Pretending to address "Little George," he said, "Tell your father, the rascal, that I forgive him for the sake of your mother's sweet smile and your bright eyes." And then he was gone.

* * *

A little-known hero of the Lincoln Assassination on April 14, 1865, was Lincoln's guest in the presidential box at Ford's Theatre, Major Henry Riggs Rathbone. He and step-sister Clara Harris, daughter of U.S. Senator Ira Harris of New York, had agreed to join the Lincolns after General and Mrs. Ulysses S. Grant and others had declined the presidential invitations.

When John Wilkes Booth entered the Lincolns' booth and shot the President, Rathbone jumped to his feet trying to stop him. He was stabbed in the arm for his efforts but struggled with Booth anyway—and may have been responsible for Booth losing his balance in the leap to the stage that broke the assassin's leg. The combat veteran (Antietam, Fredericksburg) is credited, in any case, as the man who shouted, "Stop that man!" and thus gave the alarm at Ford's that night.

Rathbone then helped the nearly prostrate Mary Todd Lincoln to the Peterson House across the street, where the dying Lincoln had been taken. Rathbone had lost so much blood by now that he fainted.

Two years later, Rathbone and his step-sister married. Unfortunately, the story doesn't end there, for in 1894, after moving to Germany as a U.S. consul, a now-insane Rathbone, said to be jealous of their children, murdered his wife Clara. He was convicted and committed to an asylum for the rest of his life.

His son Henry, a Congressman from Illinois, later authored the bill that authorized the Federal government's purchase of the

Osborn Hamilton Ingham Oldroyd collection of Lincolnia (for $50,000) that is still the nucleus of the Lincoln museum at the restored Ford's Theatre in Washington today.

Oldroyd, incidentally, was such a dedicated collector of Lincoln memorabilia that he once rented Lincoln's home in Springfield, Illinois, for ten years, married a woman from Springfield, became custodian of the same home when it was acquired as a historical site by the State of Illinois, then somehow arranged to move his collection—and himself—into the Peterson House in Washington where Lincoln died . . . and Rathbone had fainted for loss of blood.

* * *

After slowly riding his horse Traveller home to Richmond, to the house on Franklin Street where Mary Custis Lee awaited him, Robert E. Lee had a few days to think. He then wrote to a friend, "I am looking for some little, quiet home in the woods, where I can procure shelter and my daily bread . . . I wish to get Mrs. Lee out of the city as soon as practicable."

The city, ruined, Federally occupied, was a depressing place. Mrs. Lee herself had made note of the fact. "Gen'l Lee," she wrote to a cousin, Mary Meade, on April 23, "is very busy settling up his army matters & then we shall *all* probably go to some of those empty places in the vicinity of the White House [their son "Rooney's" plantation on the Pamunkey River that had been turned into a Union supply depot early in the war]."

Richmond, she said, "is an utter scene of desolation."

There had been excitement when Lee first appeared—approaching the city on his horse, with an escort of just five companions, a few days after the surrender at Appomattox. He had hoped to slip into town without fanfare, but people spotted the familiar figure. The news flew ahead of the slow-moving party. By the time he reached the borrowed house on Franklin Street, called home for the moment, a crowd had gathered, people cheering and waving handkerchiefs, or pushing forward in hopes of shaking the great man's hand.

He mounted the front steps of the row house, turned to

salute his well-wishers with a tip of the hat, then he went inside to greet his invalid wife and other family members.

The Robert E. Lee who came home to his wife that April day was the same highly principled man she had known before, always calm and supportive, but quieter, even more grave than ever. And worn, both emotionally and physically. Neither one's health was what it once was, she now a real invalid confined to a chair, he with heart problems dating back at least to the weeks before Gettysburg. Then he was 56, now he was only 58.

They couldn't go home to their Arlington House, seized by the government and turned into a cemetery by now. They wouldn't want to stay in Richmond . . . and Lee thought he should set an example for his compatriots in defeat by finding work, beginning a new life.

A saviour now stepped forward—Mrs. Elizabeth Randolph Cocke offered refuge in a small cottage on her Derwent estate in Powhatan County, a short drive today from Richmond. The Lees were glad to accept and escape the torn capital city. They traveled together by slow canal boat in early June. Their packet left one evening and arrived at dawn the next day, putting in at Pemberton Landing on the James River canal system above Richmond.

Their eldest son, Custis, had ridden the faithful Traveller out from the city; he and the son of their patron, Captain Randolph Cocke, were waiting to greet the Lees as they arrived . . . just in time for breakfast at Mrs. Cocke's nearby home, Oakland. They stayed there a full week, then moved into the four-room cottage, accompanied by daughters Agnes and Mildred.

In the wake of her final weeks in war-battered Richmond, Mrs. Lee wrote that she and her family now encountered "a quiet so profound that I could even number the acorns falling from the splendid oaks that overshadowed the cottage."

As Lee rebuilt his strength at Derwent, all kinds of offers came to him, less a defeated general than the general of a defeated South. Said one daughter: "They are offering my Father everything but the thing he will accept; a place to earn honest bread while engaged in some useful work."

One *useful work* that Lee heartily endorsed was education .

. . and it was at Derwent that he received the offer to come to Lexington, Virginia, as president of Washington College, for an annual salary of $1,500 and housing in the President's House on the campus of today's Washington *and Lee* University in Lexington. Lee accepted, arriving to take his place as head of the small school on the afternoon of September 18.

Wrote a student: "I went to the window and saw riding by on his old war-horse Traveller the great soldier . . . Slowly he passed, raising his brown slouch hat to those on the pavement who recognized him, and not appearing conscious that he more than anybody else was the center of attention."

Not only that, he wore a military coat, but with all signs of rank, even the military buttons, removed. "He doubtless would have laid it aside altogether, but it was the only one he had, and he was too poor to buy another."

Mrs. Lee waited until the campus residence was ready later that fall, then made the journey to Lexington by canal boat again . . . a trip taking several days. Lee greeted her while seated on Traveller, and at her new home, their youngest son, Robert, carried the invalided Mary Custis Lee up the stairs to her room—the only room in the house completely furnished . . . the furniture made by a one-armed Confederate veteran of the Civil War.

* * *

Both Robert E. Lee and "Stonewall" Jackson called upon another legendary Confederate general on their respective deathbeds, and that was A.P Hill. Not only did Jackson call for Hill as he died in 1863, so did Lee years later, in 1870, in his home on the campus of Washington College. Fading now, Lee said, "Tell Hill he *must* come up." And then, those famous, final words that Lee uttered as, like so many others before him, he passed . . . "Strike the tent."

VARINA:
FORGOTTEN FIRST LADY

by Ingrid Smyer

Varina:
Forgotten First Lady

Everyone knew her—this feisty, elegant and, as some described her, often regal First Lady of the Confederate States of America. But not everyone loved her.

A true Southern belle and so much more, Varina Howell Davis, wife of Jefferson Davis, President of the Confederacy, was a devoted wife, a conscientious mother, an astute manager of plantation affairs and a keen student of current events. In time, this survivor of most difficult years matured to become writer of a most comprehensive biography of Jefferson Davis.

Her dark beauty and vivacious personality could have propelled her straight from the pages of a romance novel, a captivating, fiction-like heroine always totally committed for or against a person or idea. This trait, coupled with her dynamic ability in so many areas, may explain the devotion she stirred among so many of her contemporaries and the vehement hatred seen in so many others.

A mere girl when she met the distinguished but older Davis (she was 17 and he was 36), she came away with a rather mixed first impression. "I do not know whether this Mr. Jefferson Davis is young or old," she wrote her mother. "He looks both at times." Varina decided, to her dismay, that he must be old since he was only two years younger than her own mother.

Years later, writing her memoirs, she remembered the first

time she and Jefferson went riding together one fateful Christmas holiday when she was a guest at "The Hurricane", the plantation belonging to Joseph Davis, the elder brother who filled the role of father for the younger Jefferson. "He rode with more grace than any man I have ever seen and gave one the impression of being incapable either of being unseated or fatigued," wrote Varina.

What she didn't mention was that she, too, was a polished rider who kept up with the best. That particular day she made a fetching picture in her bonnie blue riding costume with plumed hat.

Born into a prominent family of Natchez, Varina was accustomed to the good things of life. Raised at "The Briers" on the outskirts of town, she had led a sheltered life typical for a plantation girl of her day, but she longed for wider horizons. She once wishfully described the extent of her travels as *autour de ma chambre.*"

Then, in 1843, came the invitation from Joseph Davis, a close family friend, for Varina to spend the Christmas holidays with his family at The Hurricane, 30 miles below Vicksburg. Perhaps the elder Davis hoped that this vibrant young lady would shake his widower brother from his long grief over the death of Sarah Knox Taylor, daughter of future President Zachary Taylor, just months after their marriage. In the eight years since, he certainly had shown no interest in remarriage. With his best years slipping away, he remained in isolation on a Mississippi plantation . . . and his recent interest in the male-dominated politics of the day was not likely to find him a wife, either.

Enter Varina Howell, tall, attractive, full of energy and grace. She had just changed her little-girl curls for a more sophisticated smooth hairdo, with her long tresses parted in the middle and swept up on either side. Her thick dark hair crowned an oval face with soft features and dark eyes. Those eyes—a dominant feature—often danced with fire, at other times they were soft and friendly.

This striking young lady also happened to be brainy—although she had attended a female seminary in Philadelphia for two terms, she later in life gave full credit to her home-bound tutor of 12 years' standing, Judge George Winchester, for "the little learning I have acquired," and more than that, for his "pure, high standard of right." Thanks to the good judge she excelled in Latin and the English classics. Always well informed, she read the *National Intelligencer* regularly, and rarely was loathe to express her thoughts on the issues of the day. A Whig and Episcopalian, as were most of her social set, she held strong opinions. Thus her observation about the younger Davis at their first meeting when she wrote her mother: "Would you believe it, he is refined and cultivated, and yet he is a Democrat!"

Politics aside, theirs was an immediate attraction, followed by a whirlwind romance. Varina fell in love with the stately, serious-minded soldier-turned-planter; he in turn was entranced by her stimulating conversation, her quick wit and her good looks.

In those few weeks at his brother's plantation they spent many happy hours together, but he also took her to "Brierfield," his land adjacent to the vast Hurricane holdings, to show her the fields he had turned into a plantation of his own. Before she returned to Natchez in January, they became engaged. Thus began a lifelong devotion which took them through good times and bad . . . very bad, indeed!

If Varina's new love came from a moneyed family, Varina could boast an impressive pedigree all her own. Grandfather Richard Howell served with distinction under General Washington as both soldier and secret agent. He subsequently became governor of New Jersey. His third son, Varina's father, William Burr Howell by name, left home at an early age to seek his fortune, served in the Navy during the War of 1812 and eventually settled high on a bluff of the Mississippi River at Natchez. Here he was befriended by Joseph Davis, who later served as groomsman at his wedding to one of the belles of Natchez, Margaret Louisa Kempe. She was the daughter of Colonel James Kempe, from Dublin, Ireland, who fought alongside Andrew Jackson in Alabama and New Orleans, then settled in Mississippi, amassed a fortune and married a Virginia girl, Margaret Graham. Grandmother Kempe was to be a role model for young Varina—both had fiery tempers, matched with worldly charm and strong convictions.

Jefferson and Varina were married in a simple ceremony at her home, with little time spent on formal arrangements. The wedding had been put on hold for many months due to a lingering fever that weakened the bride-to-be. Still recovering, she was determined that they should wed at once. For the wedding (on February 26, 1845), she wore a white embroidered Indian muslin trimmed in lace and set off by a pink rose from the garden in her hair. A breakfast followed in a drawing room filled with white hyacinth.

Then came a wedding trip by river boat to visit his sister's house in Louisiana, the very place Knox had died. The sojourn also included a stop at the unfortunate woman's grave. This may have been done at Varina's suggestion, since throughout her life she always honored the memory of her husband's first love. After a visit to husband Jefferson's mother at the family home in Woodville, it was on to New Orleans before settling into their potentially pleasant life on the plantation. Here, at her husband's Brierfield, Varina made a gracious transition from teenager to capable wife.

But politics had entered their peaceful picture. Davis, who had taken part in a political meeting for the first time in his life the same week that he and Varina met, soon acquired a seat in Congress. But now war intervened, too—the West Point graduate marched off to the Mexican War, where he would earn a hero's spurs and become reunited with his former father-in-law, General Zachary Taylor.

With Mexico soon defeated, it wasn't long before Taylor rode his own military coattails straight into the White House. Joining the Taylors in Washington just as quickly were *Senator* and Mrs. Jefferson Davis of Mississippi. (First appointed to the Senate to complete a deceased member's unexpired term, Davis had then won the same seat in his own right in the election of 1848, coincident with Taylor's election.)

This move to Washington was to tap Varina's social skills as never before. But she was unintimidated in the least by capital society, and she soon was a familiar figure in the most prestigious salons of Washington. Her political astuteness won her many friends—and some obviously jealous enemies. Her powers of observation would serve her well as she made mental notes of the famous and not-so-famous, passing along her insights to her idealistic husband, still a neophyte in the political game . . . and somewhat unbending in manner. Her vivacious personality made up for his native aloofness. And it certainly did not hurt their social standing to be embraced as intimates of the First Family in the White House, the Zachary Taylors. In fact, Senator Davis and his wife would be with the family when the President was dying from a stomach ailment in July of 1850.

It wasn't long, again, before the Mississippi couple would be seen as close friends with still another White House occupant, Franklin Pierce, a bona fide Yankee by virtue of his New England background—in sharp contrast to the late President Taylor's Virginia heritage. Indeed, Davis would serve in Pierce's Cabinet as Secretary of War, 1853-57.

Returning to their Mississippi plantation whenever possible, Varina and Jefferson tended to their flower gardens and improved their land. They took daily rides on fast racing horses, and "enjoyed the exercise exceedingly," she wrote. "Nothing could be more pleasant than the dense shade through which we could ride for miles in air redolent of the perfume of the moss, flowers, wild crabapple and plum blossoms." But the specter of politics continually intruded and she "began to know the bitterness of being a politicians's wife," she wrote many years later. Her situation "meant long absences, pecuniary depletion from ruinous absenteeism, illness from exposure, misconceptions, defamation of character; everything which darkens the sunlight and contracts the happy sphere of home."

Even so, Varina blossomed in motherhood with the birth of a son named Samuel, in 1852. She still missed her husband, who was off campaigning for his "Yankee" friend Franklin Pierce. In a very human, surprisingly candid letter for her day, she wrote him that "your wife's courage is giving out about your staying away for such a time. I feel the want of you every hour, though I try not to be so selfish."

But the elections of 1852 soon were past, the Davises had returned to the Nation's capital as Jefferson joined Pierce's Cabinet. These days in Washington were happy ones for the

Mississippi couple, he enjoying his work in the War Department, she participating in social and political affairs even while developing a satisfying role as serious helpmate to her husband.

Varina often would wait up for Jefferson, then they would burn the midnight oil working on a project together, she doing double duty as researcher and secretary. And it was in these Washington days, working alongside her husband, that Varina came to idealize him—perhaps too much. At least one historian, Clifford Dowdey, has written that she was helpmate in the true sense of the word but where she "failed him" was in "never turning her analytical gaze on the man she regarded as perfect, virtually godlike."

And . . . quite true, Varina's historic, 1890 memoir of their days together glorified her husband and offered justification for all he had accomplished . . . or tried. Her *Jefferson Davis: A Memoir by His Wife* also was her repudiation of detractors from both North and South. And if her writing is often valued for the sketches peppered throughout of the leading figures of her times, it provides insights, some unintended, into Varina's own make-up.

Her husband lost his Cabinet post with the arrival of the James Buchanan administration in 1857—but no great matter, since Jefferson Davis was back again as a Senator from Mississippi. And Varina, for her part, already had been one of the newly-installed President's favorite Washington ladies. For Varina the social swim merely continued . . . except that soon, too soon, the inevitable was upon them all.

The long debate was over, it was now a fait accompli . . . South Carolina, soon followed by five more Southern states, Mississippi among them, had seceded, had left the Union.

The Southern legislators of course would be taking their leave very shortly. Like his fellow solons, Jefferson Davis delivered a final speech in the Senate of the United States, his address stressing a plea for peace. "There was scarcely a dry eye in the multitude as he took his seat," noted Varina.

These were dramatic times, and nowhere was it more obvious in the next few days than in Washington, where the streets were crowded with teary-eyed friends bidding good-byes. "As the planter's coaches went rumbling off to the South, laden with the fine trappings of their luxurious existence," wrote Varina biographer Ishbel Ross in her book *First Lady of the South*, "the Davises made a quiet and unostentatious departure but were greeted at many stops as they traveled South." They were returning to their beloved land to prepare for what he predicted would be "a long and severe struggle."

That was in January 1861, and in February, Varina and Jefferson, at home once again, were tending their roses at Brierfield, when they received the historic message that was to change their lives forever. Indeed, the rocky road ahead would never lead them back to their cherished rose garden as they knew it at that moment.

As Jefferson Davis read the message saying that he had been selected for the presidency of the newly-formed Confederate States of America, "he looked so grieved," said Varina, "that I feared some evil had befallen our family." He left the next day for Montgomery, Alabama. Varina was to follow later with the children—Margaret, 6, (oldest child Samuel had died in 1854), little Jeff, 4, and Joseph, 2, plus Varina's sister Maggie, now a permanent member of the family. Varina put her house in order and left by boat to join her husband in the capital of the new Confederacy.

A seven-gun salute announced Varina's arrival as she sailed up the Alabama River on the *King*. While she was warmly greeted by old friends from Washington days, the general public now showed a great deal of curiosity about this stately woman of 35, elegantly dressed and coiffured, her dark hair in Grecian braids.

These were heady days. Her husband and his associates were inventing a new nation. Varina, with much expected of her on the social scene, set a pace that quickly established the same tradition of hospitality she had enjoyed in the national capital. She entertained in a formal and sophisticated way, her receptions and dinners impressing the Confederates who crowded into Montgomery. But there would be critics to decry her fancy soirees and eventually to dub her "Queen Varina"

For all her own new responsibilities, she was more sensitive than ever to the towering problems her husband had been called to shoulder. Diarist Mary Chesnut, a good friend throughout the war and ever after, made an entry in her diary at this time that is revealing: "Mrs. Davis does not like her husband being made President." Apparently, Varina also told Mary Chesnut, "General of the Armies would have suited his temperament better." For one thing, Varina was afraid her husband was not yet apt in the art of politics.

Varina, herself by now quite polished in the political realm, won the respect of the men who surrounded the President, especially Confederate Cabinet member Judah Benjamin, with whom she developed a lasting friendship. As Varina became known for her sparkling wit and quick mind, critics of her President-husband suggested he leaned too much on his wife in matters of state. But she, better than anyone, understood the need to smooth the way for her Jefferson, who still struck some associates as inordinately stiff, even cold.

The move from Montgomery to Richmond, new capital of the Confederacy, presented a hurdle of a different kind for Varina. Accustomed to the warm, open manners of the Deep South, she found a sometimes chilly reception from the established social leaders of the very traditional Richmond. But her natural resilience still stood her in good stead as she pursued a social agenda in support of Jefferson Davis, despite the grim backdrop of a horrifying war.

Indeed, a darkness was descending upon Varina's beloved South. Forts Henry and Donelson fell, then came the disaster at Shiloh. New Bern, North Carolina, and New Orleans soon were in the hands of the Union. The naval yards of Virginia were lost. Gettysburg and Vicksburg became twin benchmarks in the sad litany for the struggling nation.

Personal tragedy struck, too. In April of 1864, five-year-old Joe Davis, playing on an open porch at the White House of the Confederacy in Richmond, climbed a railing and fell to his death on the brick walk below. Varina wandered around in a daze while Jefferson Davis, besieged by the South's troubles on every front, had no time for personal grief . . . except for what pain was in his heart of hearts.

The loss seemed to soften the antagonism some still held for Varina. "People do not snub me any longer," she wrote to Mary Chesnut, "for it was only while the lion was dying that he was kicked; dead, he was beneath contempt." And an afterthought: "Not to say I am worthy to be called a lion, nor are the people here asses."

Varina was underestimating herself, for if not a lion, she had the heart and courage of one. She continued to give her strong shoulder to Jefferson as disaster begat disaster on the war front— the siege of Petersburg, the fall of Atlanta, Sherman's march to the sea.

One ray of sunshine did lighten the grim days—a baby girl was born to Varina on June 27, 1864. Named Varina Anne, she was called "Winnie" (a pet name Jefferson had used for his wife) and would soon be known as the "Daughter of the Confederacy."

"She looks like a little rosebud," wrote the proud mother.

Meanwhile, after the fall of Atlanta, the President had gone to visit his troops and was making speeches around the South to shore up confidence. Along the way he stopped off in Columbia, South Carolina, to visit the Chesnuts, who were renting a small cottage there. Mary Chesnut had to scrimp and save to put together a decent repast in the face of ever-worsening shortages—and her family's reduced financial fortunes. As she did her best to provide fitting hospitality, she told the visiting Jefferson Davis, "It is the wind-up, the Cassandra in me says: and the old life means to die royally."

In Richmond, Varina, too, was trying to make ends meet, no longer able to indulge in her sometimes regal ways. As she sold off some of her elegant clothing, she gave up the most colorful dresses— especially painful to part with was a favorite green silk. But she didn't expect to wear it again anytime soon, since she was always in mourning. Indeed, Varina for the rest of her life was rarely seen in any color but black.

In those final days in Richmond, Varina coped as best she could with her limited largess and the mounting pressures created by the South's looming defeat. She won over many more of her critics, while strengthening the respect that others already accorded her. Robert E. Lee, for instance, remained loyal to both Davises until the very end; he always did treat Varina with unusual respect, even admiration. He quite obviously understood the burdens she carried along with the "menfolk"; he saw the constant attention she gave her husband, along with her readiness to help her friends. She often caught Lee's ear with some special plea on behalf of friends concerned for a son, brother or husband. Lee was aware, too, that Varina sometimes sat in on meetings her husband held with various delegations come to discuss serious matters, such as the exchange of prisoners.

As calamity now followed calamity, the very heart of the South was bleeding. "Darkness seemed now to close swiftly over the Confederacy, and about a week before the evacuation of Richmond," Varina wrote later, "Mr. Davis came to me and announced the necessity for our departure." She begged to stay and be near him, but he was adamant that she must seek safety, saying, "I have confidence in your capacity to take care of our babies." In the end, Varina packed away a few things, while much of their household goods (which Davis called "trumpery") were sold to a dealer, who wrote a large draft on a Richmond bank for the items. Never cashed, the check remained among Varina's personal effects after her death.

The First Lady of the Confederacy now gathered her teenage sister and the four Davis children—Margaret, 9; Little Jeff, 8; Little Billie, 3; and Winnie, still an infant—"to go forth into the unknown."

The huddled, despairing group of Davises, escorted by Presidential secretary Burton Harrison and three daughters of close friends, left Richmond on a train pulled by a "worn-out engine." Twelve hours later—with no arrangements for sleeping quarters—they reached Danville, Virginia, then it was on to Charlotte, North Carolina. After a brief reprieve in a rented house that had been arranged in advance, their flight continued, across South Carolina at Chester and Abbeville, to another Abbeville via tiny Washington, Georgia. And at last to Irwinville in south Georgia. All hectic and harried, uncomfortable and uncertain. But throughout their separate flights—Jefferson Davis was now on the run also—

the two fugitives kept in touch by courier, their letters stating and re-stating their abiding love for one another. Theirs perhaps was one of history's greatest love stories.

Jefferson Davis had just missed his wife when he arrived in Charlotte with his Cabinet. At the "dreadful" news of Lee's surrender on April 9, Varina had continued on her southward journey. After a harrowing train ride as far as Chester and a five-mile walk in the darkness through mud while carrying a "cheerful little baby in my arms," Varina and her entourage had arrived in Abbeville, South Carolina. Here, her gloom momentarily was dispelled when a courier delivered a long letter from her husband dated April 23. "Dear Wife," it began, "this is not the fate to which I invited [you] when the future was rose colored to us both; but I know you will bear it even better than myself and that of us two I alone will ever look back reproachfully on my past career . . . Farewell, my dear, there may be better things in store for us than are now in view, but my love is all I have to offer and that has the value of a thing long possessed and sure not to be lost . . . "

Varina at once responded: "It is surely not the fate to which you invited me in brighter days, but you must remember that you did not invite me to a great Hero's home, but to that of a plain farmer. I have shared all your triumphs, been the only beneficiary of them, now I am but claiming the privilege for the first time of being all to you now these pleasures have past [sic] for me."

Before they would meet again, Varina of course heard about the Lincoln assassination, which had come like a thunderclap just days after Lee's surrender at Appomattox. Her response to this news had been immediate: "I burst into tears," she later wrote, tears "which flowed from the mingling of sorrow for the family of Mr. Lincoln and a thorough realization of the inevitable results to the Confederates, now that they were at the mercy of the Federals."

This prescience was to prove true over and over again for Varina and her beloved South. But for now the dark clouds over the separately fleeing Davises lifted ever so slightly—suddenly they were reunited. In the vicinity of Milledgeville, Georgia, Varina's party had paused and was under guard because of the constant danger of marauders . . . when up rode her worn but still stately horseman. Jefferson and Varina were together again.

But not for long. Exhausted, the two had little time to talk . . . talk over so much. While the children danced around in joy, husband and wife, historic figures now, made plans for her to escape to Nassau and to join him wherever, whenever, possible. But the moment couldn't last . . . Davis had to leave her briefly, then returned one night. Encamped by a stream, Jefferson and Varina were aroused next morning by the sound of horses' hoofs—Union cavalrymen. And then gunfire—by mistake they were firing at each other, and two troopers were killed. Jefferson stepped out of the tent, hesitated a moment. Then, disguised by a shawl Varina threw over him, he attempted to walk quietly away. But no such good fortune—he was seized, captured. Thus, on May 10, 1865, began the long, dreadful months of imprisonment for the President and Varina's long struggle to free him.

Transported over rutted roads in broken-down carriages, and then by train to Macon, Georgia, next hustled onto a rusted river tug, and finally placed aboard the ocean steamer *William P. Clyde* at Savannah, the weary and bedraggled captives arrived in a few days at Hampton Roads, Virginia. Here, without so much as a moment's warning, Jefferson Davis was removed from his loving wife. Varina wrote that he had only time to approach her and say, "It is true, I must go at once." But he also was able to whisper quickly, "Try not to weep, they will gloat over your grief." His body trembled as he embraced her—then he was gone, to be incarcerated at Fortress (Fort) Monroe on May 22, 1865.

Jefferson Davis was treated harshly. He was placed in a cold damp cell, and for a few days was held in leg irons. Not even Varina's words can quite convey the deprivation and humiliation he suffered: "Worn down by privation, over-exertion, and exposure, my husband was in no condition, when thrown into prison, to resist exciting causes of disease." Said she also: "The damp walls, the food too coarse and bad to be eaten, the deprivation of sleep caused by the tramping of sentinels around the iron cot, the light of the lamp which shone full upon it, the loud calling of the roll when another relief was turned out, the noise of unlocking the doors . . . [all] produced fever, and rapidly wasted his strength." Davis was refused his mail—even a trunk containing a change of clothes.

Varina and the children were taken back to Savannah, where she had no family connections or friends. Here, without funds, she momentarily was held under house arrest at the Hotel Pulaski. Many citizens of the grand old Georgia city welcomed her, but any attempt to help her husband fell on deaf ears. For months, the only news she received of him came from newspapers. As Mrs. Robert E. Lee wrote to a friend, "She [Varina] writes very sadly, as well she may, for I know of no one so to be pitied."

Finally, with no really meaningful response to the pleas she directed in letters to government officials of all kinds, friends or even remote acquaintances in Washington and elsewhere, she contacted Horace Greeley, famous as a New York newspaper editor . . . and also known to champion lost causes. Even though he had reviled Jefferson Davis in his newspaper, he also had called for the due process of law in dealing with the Southern leader, whose very life hung in the balance in the hysteria still lingering from the Lincoln assassination. Varina now hoped that a public outcry over her husband's treatment would prompt even greater support from Greeley. She wrote to him: "How can the honest men and gentlemen of your country stand idly by to see a gentleman maligned, insulted, tortured and denied the right of trial by the usual forms of law?" And, indeed, Greeley did take up the cause to the extent that he engaged legal counsel on behalf of the imprisoned Jefferson Davis. In time, the Federal government's prosecutors found no evidence of complicity in the Lincoln plot and would even back off the charges of treason based on secession. Still, he was kept confined.

Varina would stop at nothing until she could win her husband's freedom. Now she went to the top. She wrote President Andrew Johnson, who himself faced legal problems in the form of impeachment proceedings.

Her efforts having positive effect at last, she soon was on her way to Washington. It was in late May of 1866 that Varina returned to the capital where once she had been sought after and admired as the wife of the young Senator from Mississippi. This time appearing as the wife of the world's most famous prisoner, she created a sensation. Her friends of old, though, were quick to notice the changes wrought by the years of suffering. Her eyes, once so sparkling, were now deep set and sad—yet those who studied her could sense a new dimension about Varina, a depth that seemed to sustain her in all her anguish.

The President received her cordially—she even felt sorry for such a political innocent now being demeaned by his own party. Gratifyingly, too, the immediate result of the meeting was that Davis was allowed more freedom within his prison walls. Soon, Varina was allowed to move in with him.

Many months would pass, however, before Jefferson Davis was granted his freedom. After the better part of two years he finally was released on bail in Richmond, and "strangely enough," wrote Hugh MacCulloch, in his book *Men and Measures of Half a Century*, "Horace Greeley and Gerrit Smith, the distinguished abolitionists, were among the signers of his bond."

All of Richmond, meanwhile, had taken to the streets to greet the reunited couple the day of his bond hearing in the city that had played such an important role in their lives. They were given the very same suite at the Spotswood Hotel that they had shared in happier (if uncertain) days here so long ago. And after the bond hearing . . . free at last! But more tests yet lay ahead as Varina set out to find a place in the sun—both figuratively and literally—for herself and her weary, woefully wounded husband, now a man without a country.

As pleased as the Davises were, Richmond was a city of painful memories, and they were anxious to rejoin their children in Lennoxville, Canada.

After a stopover in New York, the Davis couple at last had a joyful family reunion in Canada. Staying to enjoy the company of family, friends and a few Southern compatriots, Varina and Jefferson found solace in the simple pleasures. But for Varina, soothing her husband's proud soul was demanding. The long cold Canadian winter of 1867 left her restless. She was not content to sit out the rest of their lives on the sidelines. She persuaded her husband to join her in a search for new horizons. The "king and queen in exile" would move on.

First it was to Cuba for a brief sojourn, then to New Orleans, with a rousing welcome there from old friends and Confederate diehards. Finally came the heart-breaking return to Brierfield—the buildings burned, the fields overgrown, the roses covered in bramble. Since it no longer could be home to them, they returned to Lennoxville, where they had established residence in a pension. The next summer, at Varina's urging, they sailed for England.

Here the old conviviality and flair of her earlier days had to be in held in abeyance, since Varina found it hard to accept invitations from wealthy lords and ladies while she could not reciprocate in expensive Victorian style. Traveling on the Continent, Varina and Jefferson soon found their financial resources low, and he reluctantly accepted a position as president of an insurance company in Memphis.

And so this Southern city on the Mississippi River became home for a while. Varina again made many new friends, but much of the stimulating social scene, once so much a part of her life, eluded her now. Things did not go so well for Jefferson, either. Deciding there was no future for him in the business world, he once again took his wife off to England.

As fate would have it, a wealthy plantation owner whose husband had recently died was traveling in England. Sarah Dorsey, another vivacious, ambitious woman—and an old Mississippi acquaintance—heard about Jefferson's wish to write his own memoir. She had recently bought Beauvoir, a beautiful estate on the Mississippi coast. She offered the wandering former President of the Confederacy a place to come home to.

Bidding Varina good-bye—a chronic heart condition, more and more troublesome these days, prevented her from attempting the ocean voyage at this time—Jefferson returned alone to his native Mississippi. And there, in the fresh air and ocean breezes of an idyllic setting, Jefferson began to unwind. A pavilion set off from the main house became his haven, and the book he had already lived began to unfold on paper. Thus began his two-volume tome, *The Rise and Fall of the Confederate Government*.

Many months would pass before Varina was strong enough to leave England. When she did return to America, for once she did not rush into the arms of her husband—she went to Memphis to be with her daughter Margaret, who had lost her first baby.

But more than concern for her daughter then kept her away from Jefferson. Sarah Dorsey, whom Varina had known when they were both young girls in Natchez, now posed an intrusive threat. By midsummer, Varina, hoping to squelch gossip about her husband and Mrs. Dorsey, moved to Beauvoir and achieved a truce with Sarah. Never doubting the unabiding love of her husband, nor her enduring devotion for him, Varina made her peace with Jefferson, too. But her resentment toward Sarah she would carry to the grave.

And Jefferson, who had been none too happy over their separation, needed her more than ever. She stepped naturally again into the role she had filled so often as his assistant and collaborator.

Most of the Confederate government papers had been lost or destroyed, making it difficult to set forth the history of the fallen nation. For three long years they interviewed principal players, taxed their own memories and worked side by side. Finally, the book was finished. It was four o'clock in the morning, and Varina had been taking dictation since eight in the evening.

Though never a financial success, the memoir accomplished the end for which they so long had labored: "setting the righteous motives of the South before the world," Varina wrote later.

During these years Mrs. Dorsey had died in New Orleans, where she had moved to receive medical attention. Before she left, she sold Beauvoir to Jefferson and made him the executor of her estate.

Beauvoir now proved to be the haven the Davises needed in their golden years. Son Jefferson had died and daughter Winnie, also settled at Beauvoir, was a constant companion to her father. Jefferson Davis never took his Federal oath of allegiance and never attempted to have his American citizenship restored. But during Jimmy Carter's presidency he was at last restored as a citizen of the United States of America.

After Jefferson died in 1889, Varina lived on into the 20th century. She wrote her two-volume memoir, which was widely acclaimed. Ironically, she moved to New York and, predictably, soon became a grande dame in the social, cultural and literary world. On October 16, 1906, she died there, far from the river country of Mississippi, where she and a handsome, graceful rider twice her age once had met, so many years before . . . to begin a life together more dramatic than any fiction.

THE CIVIL WAR—
A SHORT CHRONOLOGY

1861

First year: Confederate States of America formed, February. Inauguration of Lincoln, March 4. Firing on Fort Sumter, April 12. Philippi, in western Virginia, first real battle, June 3. Rich Mountain, also in western Virginia, July 11. First Battle of Bull Run (First Manassas), July 21. Confederates enter Kentucky, September 3-4. Battle of Ball's Bluff, Virginia, October 21. Jefferson Davis now elected regular President of the Confederacy, November 6.

***

1862

Second year: Fort Donelson falls to U.S. Grant, February 16. Battle of Valverde, future New Mexico, February 21. Jefferson Davis inaugurated in Richmond, no longer "Provisional President," February 22. Ironclads *Monitor* vs. *Virginia* battle in Virginia's Hampton Roads, March 9. Shiloh, April 6-7. Virginia's Peninsula campaign, April-July. Stonewall Jackson's Shenandoah Valley campaign, April-June. Second Bull Run, August 28-30. South Mountain and Antietam, Maryland, September 14-17. Lincoln issues his Emancipation Proclamation, September 22 (to be effective January 1, 1863). Fredericksburg, December 13. Battle of Murfreesboro, Tennessee, begins December 31.

***

1863

Third year: Chancellorsville, May 1-4, Stonewall Jackson mortally wounded by his own men. Vicksburg campaign underway. Cavalry battle of Brandy Station, Virginia, June 9. Gettysburg, July 1-3. Vicksburg falls to U.S. Grant, July 4. Draft riots in

New York City, July 13-15. John Hunt Morgan captured in Ohio, July 26. Chickamauga, September 19-20. Chattanooga, November 23-25.

***

1864

Fourth year: The Wilderness, May 5-6, begins U.S. Grant's sledgehammer campaign to wear down Robert E. Lee's Army of Northern Virginia. Spotsylvania, May 8-21. Jeb Stuart mortally wounded at Yellow Tavern, Virginia, May 11. Battle of New Market (with VMI Cadets), May 15. Cold Harbor, June 1, as Grant approaches Richmond. Petersburg, battle and siege, begin June 9. Battle of Atlanta opens, July 22. Petersburg's Crater explosion, July 30. Battle of Mobile Bay, August 5. Winchester and Cedar Creek mark continuing struggle in Virginia's Shenandoah Valley, September and October. Lincoln re-elected November 8. Sherman's March to the Sea, November 16-December 21. Battles of Franklin and Nashville, Tennessee, November 30 and December 15-16, respectively.

***

1865

Fifth and last year: Second Union amphibious assault takes Fort Fisher, North Carolina, January 13-15. Lincoln re-inaugurated, March 4. Siege of Mobile, March 25-April 12. Lee abandons Petersburg, Richmond falls, Lee surrenders to Grant at Appomattox, Virginia, April 3-9. Lincoln assassinated, April 14. Confederates under Joseph Johnston surrender to William Tecumseh Sherman in North Carolina, April 26. More surrenders, May 4-26. Jefferson Davis captured, May 10. The Civil War is over.

Acknowledgements and
A Select Bibliography

On a personally-known level, the authors wish to acknowledge the contribution to this volume of several invaluable advisers, fact-checkers and other helpers, without whom we never would have been able to bring forth the foregoing by time of the 130th anniversary of Appomattox, April, 1995. And so, our heartfelt thanks to Shirley Burke Cunningham, production manager par excellence, editor, too (and husband Jack, not only for enduring many interruptions to a once-tranquil home life, but also as our "Murfreesboro Connection"); to our production assistant Ruth Estep for faithful, often "hurry-up" service; and to fact-checkers, proofers, design-and-production mentors, etc., Champ Clark; the Cowles History gang (Jon Guttman, Ken Phillips, Greg Lalire, Gregg Oehler, Lori Flemming); the Special Collections staff, Alderman Library, University of Virginia, Charlottesville, Virginia; and, last, but far from least, at Papercraft Printing and Design, also in Charlottesville, Lani Boaz and John Conover.

On equally important level, but in most cases a faceless crowd not known to us except through their works, we thank and acknowledge with due humility all those whose careful, painstaking efforts before ours have produced the great body of literature available on the American Civil War. Since we make *no* claim to present brand-new material unearthed from unknown primary sources, but instead rely upon the narrative nuggets to be mined from previously published material, we hasten to commend to our readers all those who have gone before us as authors in this field, whether as historians, participants who told their stories in print, or historical-journalists like ourselves. And so, our sources for this work were:

Albert, Don E., ed., *Rebels on the Rio Grande, The Civil War Journal of A.B. Peticolas* (University of New Mexico Press, Albuquerque, 1984)

Alexander, E. Porter, *Military Memoirs of a Confederate: A Critical Narrative*, with introduction by Gary Gallagher (Da Capo Press, New York, 1993)

Ballard, Michael B., *A Long Shadow: Jefferson Davis and the Final Days of the Confederacy* (University Press of Mississippi, Jackson, 1986)

Bergeron, Arthur W., *Confederate Mobile* (University Press of Mississippi, Jackson, 1991)

Blaisdell, Albert F. (adapted) *Stories of the Civil War* (Lothrop, Lee & Shepard Co., Boston, 1890)

Boykin, Edward, ed., *The Wit and Wisdom of Congress* (Funk & Wagnall's Company, New York, 1961)

Browning, Robert M. Jr., *From Cape Charles to Cape Fear: The North Atlantic Blockading Squadron during the Civil War* (University of Alabama Press, Tuscaloosa, 1993)

Butters, Pat, *From the Fields of Battle to the Oval Office* (Washington Times, February 19, 1994)

Catton, Bruce, *The Coming Fury; Terrible Swift Sword; Never Call Retreat*, The Centennial History of the Civil War, Vols. I-III (Doubleday & Company, Garden City, N.Y., 1961)

Clark, Champ and the Editors of Time-Life Books, *Decoying the Yanks: Jackson's Valley Campaign* (Time-Life Books, Alexandria, Va., 1984)

Coco, Gregory A., *War Stories: A Collection of 150 Little Known Human Interest Accounts of the Campaign and Battle of Gettysburg* (Thomas Publications, Gettysburg, 1992)

Connell, Evan S., *Son of the Morning Star: Custer and the Little Big Horn* (North Point Press, San Francisco, 1984)

Coulling, Mary P., *The Lee Girls* (John F. Blair, Winston-Salem, N.C., 1987)

Dabney, Virginius, *Virginia: The New Dominion* (University Press of Virginia, Charlottesville, 1971)

Davis, Varina, *Jefferson Davis, Ex-president of the Confederate States of America: A Memoir by His Wife*, 2 vols., Nautical & Aviation Publishing, Baltimore, 1990 reprint, with introduction by Craig L. Symonds)

Davis, William C., *The Orphan Brigade: The Kentucky Confederates Who Couldn't Go Home* (Stackpole Books, Mechanicsburg, Penna., 1980)

Dedmondt, Glenn, *Southern Bronze* (Palmetto Bookworks, Columbia, S.C., 1993)

Douglass, Frederick, *Narrative of the Life of Frederick Douglass, An American Slave, Written by Himself* (New American Library, Inc., New York, 1968)

Dowdey, Clifford, *Lee Takes Command* (Barnes & Noble, New York, 1993)

Dufour, Charles L., *Nine Men in Grey*, with introduction by Gary W. Gallagher (University of Nebraska Press, Lincoln, 1993)

Duke, Duer, *Alabama Tales* (Vision Press, Northport, Ala., 1994)

Eisenschiml, Otto, and Newman, Ralph (*The Civil War, The American Iliad as Told by Those Who Lived It*, with introduction by Bruce Catton (Grosset & Dunlap, New York, 1956)

Freeman, Douglas Southall, *Lee*, abridgement by Richard Harwell of *R.E. Lee* (Scribner's, New York, 1961)

Fretwell, Jacqueline K., ed., *Civil War Times in St. Augustine* (St. Augustine Historical Society, St. Augustine, Fla., 1986)

Gallagher, Gary, ed., *Two Witnesses at Gettysburg* (Brandywine Press, St. James, N.Y., 1994)

Grant, Ulysses S., *Personal Memoirs of U.S. Grant*, with introduction by William S. McFeely (Da Capo Press, New York, 1962)

Grimm, Herbert L., Roy, Paul L., Rose, George, *Human Interest Stories of the Three Days Battle of Gettysburg* (Gem Inc., Gettysburg, 1983)

Hay, Peter, *All the Presidents' Ladies: Anecdotes of the Women Behind the Men in the White House* (Viking, New York, 1988)

Hendrick, Burton J., *Statesmen of the Lost Cause: Jefferson Davis and His Cabinet* (Little, Brown and Company, Boston, 1939)

Hennessey, Joseph, ed., *The Portable Woolcott* (Viking, New York, 1946)

Holland, Cecil Fletcher, *Morgan and His Raiders* (Macmillan, New York, 1943)

Hood, John Bell, *Advance and Retreat*, with introduction by Richard M. McMurray (Da Capo Press, New York, 1993)

Johnson, Robert Underwood and Buel, Clarence Clough, eds., *Battles and Leaders of the Civil War*, Vols I-IV (The Century Co., New York, 1884-1888)

Jones, Katharine M., ed., *Heroines of Dixie: Spring of High Hopes;* and *Heroines of Dixie: The Winter of Our Discontent* (Ballantine Books, New York, 1974)

Kelly, C. Brian, *Warren Akin's Christmas in Richmond* (Washington Times, December 25, 1993)

———— and Smyer, Ingrid, *Best Little Stories from the White House* (Montpelier Publishing, Charlottesville, Virginia, 1992)

————, et al., *Military History* magazine (Cowles History Group, Leesburg, Va., 1984-1994)

Lawliss, Chuck, *The Civil War Sourcebook, A Traveler's Guide*, (Harmony Books, New York, 1991)

Lewis, Lloyd, *Sherman: Fighting Prophet* (Harcourt Brace, New York, 1932)

Long, E.B. and Barbara, *The Civil War Day by Day: An Almanac 1861-1865* (Doubleday, Garden City, N.Y., 1971)

Luvaas, Jay; Cullen, J.P. (Photos by Bake, W.A.), *Appomattox Court House* (National Park Service, Washington, D.C., 1980)

MacArthur, Douglas, *Reminiscences* (McGraw-Hill, New York, 1964)

MacDonald, Rose Ellzey, *Mrs. Robert E. Lee* (Robert B. Poisel, Pikesville, Md., 1973; Ginn & Co., Boston, 1939)

Mallinson, David, *Drummer Boys*, America's Civil War magazine (Cowles History Group, Leesburg, Va., November 1992)

Manarin, Louis H., and Dowdey, Clifford, *The History of Henrico County* (University Press of Virginia, Charlottesville, 1985)

Markle, Donald E., *Spies & Spymasters of the Civil War* (Hippocrene Books, New York, 1994)

McHenry, Robert, ed., *Webster's American Military Biographies* (Dover Publications, New York, 1984)

Mitchell, Patricia B., *Cooking for the Cause* (Sims-Mitchell House Bed & Breakfast, 242 Whittle Street, SW, Chatham, Va., 24531, 1988)

Mobley, Joe A., *James City: A Black Community in North Carolina, 1863-1900* (North Carolina Division of Archives and History, Raleigh, 1981)

Morris, Roy, Jr. *Sheridan: The Life and Wars of General Phil Sheridan* (Crown Publishers, New York, 1992)

Neely, Jr., Mark E., *The Abraham Lincoln Encyclopedia* (Da Capo Press, Inc., New York, 1984)

Perdue, Charles L., Barden, Thomas E. and Philips, Robert K., eds., *Weevils in the Wheat, Interviews with Virginia Ex-slaves* (University Press of Virginia, Charlottesville, 1976)

Phillips, Kenneth, *Great Battles* magazine (Cowles History Group, Leesburg, Va.)

Randall, Ruth Painter, *Mary Lincoln, Biography of a Marriage* (Little, Brown and Company, Boston, 1953)

Riddle, Albert G., *Recollection of War Times* (G.P. Putnam's Sons, New York, 1895)

Roberts, Nancy, *Civil War Ghost Stories and Legends* (University of South Carolina Press, Columbia, 1992)

Robertson, James I., Jr., *The Stonewall Brigade* (Louisiana State University Press, Baton Rouge, 1963)

—*General A.P. Hill: The Story of a Confederate Warrior* (Random House, New York, 1987)

Roscoe, Theodore, *The Web of Conspiracy* (Prentice Hall, Englewood Cliffs, N.J., 1959)

Ross, Ishbel, *First Lady of the South: The Life of Mrs. Jefferson Davis* (Harper & Brothers, New York, 1958)

Ryan, D. David, *Four Days in 1865: The Fall of Richmond.* (Cadmis Marketing, Richmond, Va., 1993)

Sifakis, Stewart, *Who Was Who in the Civil War* (Facts on File, New York, 1988)

Simon, John Y., ed., *The Personal Memoirs of Julia Dent Grant*, with introduction by Bruce Catton, including *First Lady As An Author*, by Ralph Newman (Southern Illinois Press, Carbondale, Illinois, 1975)

Snyder, Louis L., and Morris, Richard B., eds., *A Treasury of Great Reporting* (Simon & Schuster, New York, 1962)

Sterkx, H.E., *Partners in Rebellion, Alabama Women in the Civil War* (Fairleigh Dickinson University Press, Rutherford, N.J., 1970)

Taylor, L.B. Jr., *The Ghosts of Fredericksburg . . . and Nearby Environs* (Copyright 1991 by L.B. Taylor, Jr.)

————, *The Ghosts of Charlottesville and Lynchburg . . . and Nearby Environs* (Copyright 1992 by L.B. Taylor, Jr.)

Taylor, Richard, *Destruction and Reconstruction* with introduction by Edwin C. Bears (Bantam Books, New York, 1992)

Vaughan, Mary C. and Brocker, L.P., *Women at War: Civil War Heroines* (reprint of 1867 edition by Longmeadow Press, Stamford, Conn., with Platinum Press, Woodbury, N.Y., 1993)

Washington, Booker T., *Up from Slavery: An Autobiography* (First published by Doubleday, New York, 1901)

Wamsley, James S., with Cooper, Anne M., *Idols, Victims, Pioneers: Virginia's Women from 1607* (Virginia State Chamber of Commerce, Richmond, 1976)

Waugh, John C., *The Class of 1846: From West Point to Appomattox: Stonewall, McClellan and Their Brothers*, with foreword by James M. McPherson (Warner Books, New York, 1994)

Wert, Jeffrey, *General James Longstreet, The Confederacy's Most Controversial General* (Simon & Schuster, New York, 1994)

Wheeler, Richard, *Lee's Terrible Swift Sword* (Harper/Collins, New York, 1952)

Wiley, Bell Irvin, ed., *Letters of Warren Akin, Confederate Congressman* (University of Georgia, Athens, Ga., 1959)

Williams, Frederick D., ed., *The Wild Life of the Army: Civil War Letters of James A. Garfield* (Michigan State University Press, 1964)

Wills, Brian Steel, *A Battle from the Start: The Life of Nathan Bedford Forrest* (Harper/Collins, New York, 1992)

Woodward, C. Vann, ed., *Mary Chesnut's Civil War* (Yale University Press, New Haven, Conn., 1981)

Zeitlin, Richard, *Old Abe the War Eagle* (State Historical Society of Wisconsin, Madison, 1986)

Special Mention

Bruce, Philip Alexander, *History of the University of Virginia, 1819-1919*, Centennial Edition, Vol. III (Macmillan Company, New York 1921)

About The Authors

C. Brian Kelly, previously a prize-winning journalist, is editor of *Military History* magazine of Leesburg, Va., and a lecturer in news writing at the University of Virginia in Charlottesville. As a reporter for *The Washington Star*, he was named 1976 Conservation Communicator of the Year by the National Wildlife Federation; was cited for his political reporting by the American Political Science Association and for local reporting by the Washington-Baltimore Newspaper Guild. Ingrid Smyer has been a freelance writer and editor, ballet teacher, civic and political activitist. She and her husband Brian Kelly own and operate Montpelier Publishing, P.O. Box 3384, University Station, Charlottesville, VA 22903.

Also Available From Montpelier

—*Best Little Stories from World War II* by C. Brian Kelly (215 pages, $10.95, ISBN 0-9624875-0-3)

—*Best Little Stories From The White House* by C. Brian Kelly, with *First Ladies in Review* by Ingrid Smyer (255 pages, $12.95, ISBN 0-9624875-4-6)

Inside illustrations: Edwin Forbes relief etchings, *Thirty Years After;* and J. Serz, Universtiy of Virginia 1856, steel engraving, all courtesy Special Collections, University of Virginia. Also, Civil War scenes from *Stories of The Civil War,* Albert Blaisdell, 1890 book. Other art from *Patriotic Cuts,* Dover Books, Mineola, New York.